Paddling
South Carolina

A Guide to the State's Greatest Paddling Adventures

Johnny Molloy

FALCONGUIDES

GUILFORD, CONNECTICUT
HELENA, MONTANA

This book is for Keri Anne Molloy.

An imprint of Rowman & Littlefield
Falcon, FalconGuides, and Outfit Your Mind are registered trademarks of Rowman & Littlefield.

Distributed by NATIONAL BOOK NETWORK

Copyright © 2015 by Rowman & Littlefield
Photos: Johnny Molloy
Maps: Trailhead Graphics, Inc. © Rowman & Littlefield

British Library Cataloguing-in-Publication Information available

Library of Congress Cataloging-in-Publication Data

Molloy, Johnny, 1961-
  Paddling South Carolina : a guide to the state's greatest paddling adventures / Johnny Molloy. – First Edition.
      pages cm
  "Distributed by NATIONAL BOOK NETWORK"–T.p. verso.
  Includes index.
  ISBN 978-0-7627-8505-6 (paperback : alk. paper) – ISBN 978-1-4930-1447-7 (e-book) 1. Canoes and canoeing–South Carolina–Guidebooks. 2. Kayaking–South Carolina–Guidebooks. 3. South Carolina-Guidebooks. I. Title.
  GV776.S62M65 2015
  797.12209757–dc23
                    2015012946

∞™ The paper used in this publication meets the minimum requirements of American National Standard for Information Sciences—Permanence of Paper for Printed Library Materials, ANSI/NISO Z39.48-1992.

Devil Hole Falls tumbles loudly into a cove of Lake Jocassee (paddle 3).

Contents

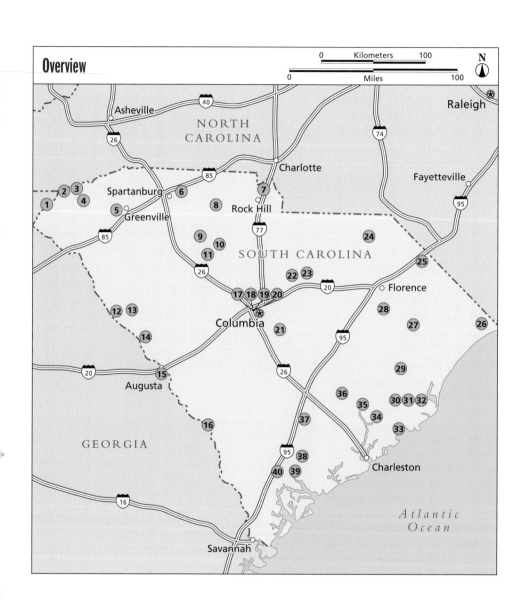

Acknowledgments

Thanks to my wife, Keri Anne, for paddling many a river with me; thanks also to Tom Janzen, Betty Beamguard, and Clare Ryan. A big thanks to Doug Hartley for his advice and direction. Thanks also to Archie down in Moncks Corner for promoting paddling throughout the Palmetto State.

Thanks to Wenonah for their Spirit II ultralight canoe and to Old Town for the Old Town Penobscot. Thanks to Sierra Designs for the great tents, sleeping bags, and clothes used on and between paddling adventures in the Palmetto State.

Paddler prepares for departure (paddle 6).

Introduction

Enjoying the natural aquatic abundance of South Carolina was an extension of my camping, hiking, and paddling obsession that began in the Smoky Mountains of Tennessee more than two decades ago. Starting out as a hiker, I soon moved to paddling, then moved on to writing about the outdoors. After becoming an outdoor writer, I had the opportunity to write a tent camping guide and a hiking guide for the Palmetto State. These books, coupled with other adventures in South Carolina, opened my eyes to the rich paddling opportunities there.

The opportunity came my way to pen a paddling guide to South Carolina, an aquatic jewel of the South. I jumped on it excitedly and began systematically exploring the waterways of Carolina landscape for great paddling destinations. I sought to include paddling destinations that would not only be rewarding but also would be exemplary paddles of the varied landscapes offered. In the Upstate, paddling destinations can be found in lakes and rivers. Paddle the still waters of mountain-rimmed Lake Jocassee to visit waterfalls. Shoot the rapids of the famed Chattooga (yes, there is a not-too-rough section most folks can paddle) or the milder rapids of the upper Saluda just outside Greenville, or make a fun float down the upper Pacolet.

And what good is a South Carolina paddling guidebook without including South Carolina's contribution to great rivers of the world—the Congaree. This river flows through the botanically rich heart of the Palmetto State. On the Congaree, you can run rapids in downtown Columbia, then enter a remote stretch bordered by broad sandbars backed by wondrous, ancient hardwood forests with a high canopy unseen elsewhere in the world. Goodale State Park offers the Big Pine Tree Creek Canoe Trail, where you twist and turn among the cypresses rising in an old mill pond. The Edisto River makes a serpentine course through the back of beyond. Explore the old rice-field canals along Wadboo Creek. Wambaw Creek courses through a coastal wilderness in the Francis Marion National Forest. It is something you must experience for yourself—with the help of this guidebook, of course. Then, when you cobble the paddling destinations together, this book presents a mosaic of Palmetto State beauty and biodiversity that is hard to beat!

As you may guess, the hardest part of writing this book may have been picking out the paddling destinations. With each of these waterways, I sought out a combination of scenery, paddling experiences, ease of access—including shuttling, when necessary, and a reasonable length for day tripping. Now it is your turn—get out there and paddle South Carolina!

South Carolina Weather

Each of the four distinct seasons lays its hands on South Carolina. Elevation factors into weather patterns in the Upstate. Summer can get hot, but it is generally cooler there. The mountains also receive the most precipitation, some of the heaviest in the

East, though it arrives with slow-moving frontal systems in winter, including snow, and with thunderstorms in summer. Fall offers warm days followed by cool, crisp evenings. Spring varies with elevation, too, and climbs its way from the Lowcountry to the Upstate. Upstate paddlers must be prepared for cool to cold conditions on the water in winter and early spring, the time when the foothill waters will be running at their fullest—and their coldest. However, most streams included in this guidebook can be paddled well into the summer, most year-round.

The Midlands generally has hot summers and moderate winters. Early spring is the most variable, with periodic warm-ups, broken by cold fronts bringing rain and then chilly temperatures. Later, temperatures stay warm and become hot by June. Typically, mornings start clear, then clouds build, and hit-or-miss thunderstorms occur by afternoon. The first cool fronts hit around mid-September. Fall sees warm, clear days and cool nights with the least amount of rain. Precipitation picks up in November, and temperatures generally stay cool, broken by occasional mild spells. Most Midlands streams can be paddled year-round, though, as with the Upstate, they'll be running their boldest during winter and early spring. Summertime paddlers should consider beginning their trips in the morning to avoid the heat of the day and afternoon thunderstorms.

The Lowcountry offers the warmest climate, yet it has four distinct seasons. During the long summer, highs regularly reach the 90s, and a thunderstorm will come most any afternoon. Warm nights stay up in the 70s. Fall brings cooler nights and warm days with less precipitation than summer. Winter is variable: Highs push 60 degrees. Expect lows in the 30s, with temperatures in the 20s during cold snaps. There are usually several mild days during each winter month. Precipitation comes in strong continental fronts, with persistent rains followed by sunny, cold days. Snow is uncommon, though not unheard of. The longer days of spring begin the warm-up process, becoming even hot, but temperatures can vary wildly. The Lowcountry has a longer paddling season, but you must also be prepared for the variety of conditions on the water here. Mild winter days can offer decent paddling in this region, as the insects will be absent and the sun will be much less intense.

Flora and Fauna

The landscape of South Carolina offers everything from crystalline mountain streams flanked with rhododendron and yellow birch to dense swamp forests bordering remote waterways to tidal waterways bordered by palmetto-studded isles. A wide variety of wildlife calls these dissimilar landscapes home.

Deer will be the land animal you most likely will see while paddling South Carolina's waterways. They can be found throughout the state. A quiet paddler may also witness turkeys, raccoons, or even a coyote. Don't be surprised if you observe beaver, muskrat, or a playful otter in the water.

Overhead, many raptors, including eagles, falcons, and owls, will be plying the waterways for food. Of special interest is the osprey. Watch for this bird flying overhead with a freshly caught fish in its claws! Depending upon where you are, other

The author pulls his canoe over a fallen tree on Long Cane Creek (paddle 14).

birds you may spot include kingfishers and woodpeckers. Shorebirds will be found along the coast.

The flora offers just as much variety. Along the waterways of the Upstate, regal hardwoods reign over rhododendron and mountain laurel that bloom in late spring and early summer. Still other shorelines will harbor river birch, sycamore, and willow. Massive cypress trees are a common sight along slower, warmer waterways in the Midlands and coastal plain. Wildflowers will grace shorelines throughout the state well into fall.

South Carolina River Regions

The South Carolina Department of Natural Resources (DNR) divides the state into eight major watersheds. They flow from northwest to southeast. Most of them first drain the Upstate, then flow through the Midlands, and empty in the Lowcountry. These drainages cut across this triangular-shaped state. Starting in the west, the Savannah drains the northwestern mountains and flows all the way to the ocean, forming the state line with Georgia. The Salkehatchie watershed drains the streams flowing into the Lowcountry lands around Beaufort and up toward Aiken. It is the smallest watershed in the state. The Saluda, Broad, and Catawba watersheds drain the heart of South Carolina. The three start in the mountains, meet, and flow into the Santee River, and are essentially part of the Santee watershed. The Edisto River flows from lands south of Columbia and is the main component of the ACE Basin, which also includes the Combahee and the Ashepoo Rivers, both large tidal streams. The last watershed is the Pee Dee, covering a large swath of the northeastern South Carolina. It includes the Great Pee Dee, the Little Pee Dee, the Lynches River, and other waterways from Florence to Myrtle Beach.

Your Rights on the River

In South Carolina, landowners along a river or lake own the land but they do not own the water flowing through the land, though they have a right to use it, as long it is not a detriment to others up- or downstream. They do not own the riverbed itself. According to state law on navigability, paddlers and boaters can use the stream "if the natural watercourse is deemed navigable it is subject to the State's navigational servitude to the mean or ordinary high-water lines." A *navigational servitude* means that the state of South Carolina holds the watercourse up to the mean high-water mark in public trust as a recreational resource and mode of travel for members of the public. The riparian owner adjacent to a navigable watercourse is not deprived of access or other riparian rights. The South Carolina Constitution declares that "all navigable waters within the limits of the State shall be common highways and forever free, as well to the inhabitants of this State as to the citizens of the United States, without any tax or impost therefor, unless the same be expressly provided for by the General Assembly." Further, a state statute defines navigability as "all streams which have been rendered or can be rendered capable of being navigated by rafts of lumber or timber by the removal of accidental obstructions and all navigable watercourses and cuts." Later law has determined canals linking two navigable waterways are considered navigable and can be used not only for commercial activities but also for boating, hunting, and fishing. In other words, if you can float down a waterway, then you can use it. This does not mean, however, you can put in anywhere you want in order to use a navigable waterway.

Beyond theoretical law—while you are on the water—what does this mean for the South Carolina paddler? The vast majority of landowners do not mind passage through waters along their property. While paddling, be considerate—don't litter, bother livestock, climb on a dock, or traipse through someone's backyard. Honor posted land signs. If encountered or confronted, be friendly and approachable. However, if you are stopped or you are asked to get off riverside property, then I suggest you paddle on. Adhere to the landowner's request and live to paddle another day. Be apprised that you could be considered trespassing when you portage, camp, or even stop for a lunch break on streamside lands if not on public property. At that point, it is not a great time for debate on South Carolina waterway law.

How to Use This Guide

This guidebook offers trips covering every corner of the Palmetto State. The paddles are divided into the three primary regions—Upstate, Midlands, and Lowcountry. Each paddle included in the book is chosen as a day trip, though overnight camping can be done where noted. The following is a sample of what you will find in the information box at the beginning of each paddling destination:

Enoree River

Explore this intimate waterway that courses through the Sumter National Forest.

County: Union, Newberry
Start: FR 339 ramp
  N34° 30.85' / W81° 36.82'
End: Brazzlemans Bridge
  N34° 25.31' / W81° 31.08'
Distance: 11.8 miles
Float time: About 5 hours
Difficulty rating: Moderate
Rapids: Class I
River type: Sandy Piedmont woods-bound waterway
Current: Fast
River gradient: 2.4 feet per mile
River gauge: Enoree River at Whitmire, SC, minimum runnable level: 300 cfs, maximum: 1,800 cfs
Season: Winter, spring, early summer

Land status: Public—national forest
Fees or permits: No fees or permits required
Nearest city/town: Whitmire
Maps: Sumter National Forest Enoree Ranger District; USGS Quadrangle Maps: Whitmire North, Whitmire South; *Delorme: South Carolina Atlas & Gazetteer*, P.26 1-F
Boats used: Canoes, kayaks, occasional johnboat
Organizations: Sumter National Forest, Enoree Ranger District, 20 Work Center Rd., Whitmire, SC 29178, (803) 276-4810, www.fs.usda.gov/main/scnfs/
Contacts/outfitters: South Carolina Department of Health and Environmental Control, 2600 Bull St., Columbia, SC 29201, (803) 898-4300, scdhec.gov/environment/water

From the information box we can see that the paddle is in Union and Newberry Counties. It starts at the FR 339 ramp in the Sumter National Forest. (By the way, we use these highway abbreviations: FR for a Forest Road; I for Interstate; US means US Highway; and SC stands for South Carolina State highway.) The GPS coordinates for the put-in are given using NAD 27 datum, which you can plug into your GPS for direction finding. The paddle ends at Brazzlemans Bridge.

This example paddle is 11.8 miles long, according to my GPS. The paddle should last around 5 hours, but this is just an average. The time you will spend on the water depends upon whether you fish, picnic, swim, paddle hard, or simply relax. Use the float time as a gauge to help you determine how long you need/want to spend on your particular trip.

The **difficulty rating** is moderate due to shallows created by a shifting streambed and also tree strainers.

The river has no **rapids** per se, but the swift water rates as Class I. This river difficulty rating system goes from Class I to Class VI. Class I has easy waves requiring little maneuvering and few obstructions. Class II rapids may have more obstructions and require more maneuvering, and the rapids may be flowing faster. Most paddles in this guidebook are Class I–II. Class III rapids can be difficult with numerous waves and no clearly defined passage and require precise maneuvering. Class IV–VI increases in difficulty, with Class VI being unrunnable, except by the best of experts.

The **river type** classification reflects its geographical placement within the state and what type of river it is, in this case a sandy Piedmont river bordered in thick forest. The **current** is fast. The **river gradient** reflects the rate at which the river descends during the paddle.

The **river gauge** listed will be near the destination and will help you determine the paddleability of the river. Some rivers, such as this one, have minimum flow rates listed, so you will get on the river only when it has enough water—or stay off when the water is too high. Others that don't have a minimum runnable level can be paddled year-round. Concerning water gauges, the key variable is the height of the river at a fixed point. Gauge houses, situated on most rivers, consist of a well at the river's edge with a float attached to a recording clock. The gauge reads in hundredths of feet. Rating tables are constructed for each gauge to get a cubic feet per second (cfs) reading for each level. Other gauges are measured in height and given in feet. This gauge information can be obtained quickly, often along with recent rainfall measurements! US Geological Survey (USGS) Current Water Data for the United States can be found on the web at waterdata.usgs.gov/nwis/rt. This in-depth website has hundreds of gauges for the entire country updated continually, and graphs showing recent flow trends, along with historic trends for any given day of the year, are available at the touch of a mouse. Consult these gauges before you start your trip!

The best paddling **season** is given to help you get the most enjoyment out of your paddle.

The **land status** of the property bordering Enoree River is public. However, many paddling destinations included in this guidebook border private lands. See Your Rights on the River above. No **fees or permits** are required to paddle. Whitmire is the **nearest city/town**, which will help orient you to the paddle destination area while looking at a map or looking up map information on the Internet. However, quality maps and driving directions are included with each paddle. The **maps** section lists pertinent maps you can use for your paddle, in this case the Enoree District map of the Sumter National Forest, and includes the USGS 7.5-minute quadrangle maps. These "quad maps" cover every parcel of land in this country. They are divided into detailed rectangular maps. Each quad has a name, usually based on a physical feature located within the quad. In this case, the paddle traverses one quad map named "Whitmire." Quad maps can be obtained online at usgs.gov.

Boats used describes what other river users will be floating. The **organizations** section lists groups that are involved with the particular waterway included in the paddle. If you are interested in learning more about the river's health and other water-quality issues, as well as simply getting involved in preserving South Carolina's waterways, consult these groups. Their contact information is listed. The **contacts/outfitters** listing will give you information about any outfitter that operates on a segment of river given, which can help with shuttles.

More important information follows the above listing. Next comes **put-in/takeout** information. This gives you directions from the nearest interstate or largest community first to the takeout, where you can leave a shuttle vehicle, then from the takeout to the put-in. By the way, look before you leap! Some of the put-ins and takeouts use dirt or sand roads just before reaching the waterways. After periods of extreme weather, such as heavy rains or long dry periods, the roads can become troublesome. If you are at all unsure about the road ahead of you, stop, get out, and examine it on foot before you drive into a deep mudhole or get stuck in the sand.

A **paddle summary** follows driving directions. This does what it sounds like it should do—it gives an overview of the paddle trip and an idea of what to expect that will help you determine whether or not you want to experience this waterway. A river summary follows. This gives an overview of the entire river, not just the section paddled. This way you can determine whether you want to paddle other sections of the river being detailed. It also gives you a better understanding of the entire watershed rather than just a section of the river in space and time. Next comes **The Paddle**, which is the meat-and-potatoes narrative with detailed information about your river trip, including flora, fauna, and interesting not-to-be-missed natural features. It also details important information needed to execute the paddle, including forthcoming rapids, portages, bridges, and stops along the way, and the mileages at which you will come across them.

Finally, many paddles have a sidebar. This is simply interesting or helpful information about the waterway that doesn't necessarily pertain to the specific paddle but gives you some human or natural tidbit that may pique your interest to explore beyond the simple mechanics of the paddle. In the case of the Enoree River, the sidebar is about the Brick House Campground, an excellent paddler's basecamp for those plying the streams of the Sumter National Forest.

Equipment

Which Boat Do I Use?

This book covers waterways from crashing mountain rivers to massive waterways and lakes to still and silent swamp streams to narrow creeks barely wide enough for a boat. So, with such variety, what boat do you use? The answer—just like the diversity of paddling destinations in South Carolina—is multiple choices. Canoes and kayaks offer different venues for plying the waters of South Carolina.

The first consideration in choosing a kayak is deciding between a sit-on-top model and a sit-in model, also known as a touring kayak or recreational kayak. Sit-on-tops are what their name implies—paddlers sit on top of the boat, whereas a recreational or touring kayak requires you to put your body into the boat, leaving your upper half above an enclosed cockpit. Ask yourself, what type of waters are you going to paddle? Are you going to paddle near shore, on calm flat waters, or are you going to paddle bigger waters, such as oceanic estuaries? If paddling bigger water, you will need a cockpit. Sit-on-top kayaks are generally more comfortable and allow for more freedom of movement. They also take on water more readily and are used almost exclusively in warmer-water destinations. Sit-in touring kayaks are inherently more stable, since the user sits on the bottom of the boat, rather than on top of the boat. Sit-on-top kayaks make up for this stability shortcoming by being wider, which makes them slower. Base your decision primarily on what types of waters you will be paddling and whether you will be going overnight in your kayak. Sit-on-top kayaks are a poor choice when it comes to overnight camping. However, sit-on-tops, especially recreational models, do have their place and are the most popular paddling boat these days. Smaller waters—such as ponds and gentle streams—are good for sit-on-top kayaks.

Sit-in kayaks are the traditional kayaks, based on models used by Arctic aboriginals. Some factors to consider when choosing a touring sit-in-kayak are length, volume, and steering. The longer touring kayaks are built to cover water and track better. Look for a boat anywhere from 14 to 18 feet in length if overnighting. Recreational models generally stretch from 12 to 16 feet and are lighter, which is good when loading and unloading your vehicle. Sit-on-top kayaks will range generally from 8 to 15 feet. Narrow touring kayaks have less "initial stability"; that is, they feel tippier when you get into them, although their very narrowness prevents waves from flipping the boat over. Wider recreational sit-in kayaks have better initial stability. Recreational kayaks are a very popular choice for paddlers these days.

Kayak materials vary from the traditional skin-and-wood of the Inuits to plastic and fiberglass composites like Kevlar and the waterproof cover of folding kayaks. (Folding kayaks have a collapsible frame that is covered by a skin, thus becoming a kayak.) For recreational kayaks I recommend a tough composite model, simply because they can withstand running up on sandbars, scratching over oyster bars, or being accidentally dropped at the boat launch. I look for durability in a boat and don't want something that needs babying.

For touring kayaks, consider storage capacity. Gear is usually stored in waterproof compartments with hatches. Look for watertight patches that close safely and securely. The larger the boat, the more room you will have. This is a matter of personal preference. Today, there are not only single kayaks but also double kayaks and even triple kayaks. Most touring kayaks come with a foot-pedal-based steering system using a rudder. Overall, kayakers need to be fussier when choosing their boats than do canoeists, as kayaks are more situation specific. Surf the Internet and read reviews

The Black is deservedly a state scenic river (paddle 29).

thoroughly to get an idea of what you want, then go to a store that sells kayaks and try them out. Look for "demo days" at these outdoor stores. Borrow a friend's kayak. A well-informed, careful choice will result in many positive kayaking experiences. What about a whitewater kayak? These are used for many of South Carolina's wild whitewater streams, most of which are not included in the guidebook; this volume is designed for a larger audience of recreational paddlers.

When looking for a canoe, consider the type of water through which you will be paddling. Will it be still bodies of water or moving rivers? Will you be on big lakes and maybe the ocean, mild whitewater, or sluggish streams? Canoes come in a wide array of oil-based materials, and they are molded for weight, performance, and durability. Don't waste your time or money with an aluminum canoe. They are extremely noisy and are more likely to get hung up on underwater obstacles rather than slide over them. Consider material and design. Canoe materials can range from wood to fiberglass to composites such as Polylink 3, Royalex, Kevlar, and even graphite. I prefer more durable canoes and thus seek out the tougher composites, such as Royalex.

Canoe design comprises the following factors: length, width, depth, keel, and bottom curve, as well as flare and tumblehome.

- **Length.** A canoe should be at least 16 feet long for carrying loads and better tracking. Be apprised that shorter canoes are available and are often used in ponds, small lakes, and smaller streams for shorter trips.
- **Width.** Wider canoes are more stable and can carry more loads but are slower. Go toward the middle, neither too narrow and tippy nor wide and slow.
- **Depth.** Deeper canoes can carry more weight and shed water but they can get heavy. Again, go for the middle ground.
- **Keel.** A keel helps for tracking in lakes but decreases maneuverability in moving water.
- **Bottom curve.** The more curved the canoe bottom, the less stable the boat. Seek a shallowly arched boat, as it is more efficient than a flat-bottom boat but not as tippy as a deeply curved boat.
- **Flare.** The outward curve of the sides of the boat, flare sheds water from the craft. How much flare you want depends upon how much whitewater you expect to encounter.
- **Tumblehome.** Tumblehome is the inward slope of the upper body of the canoe. A more curved tumblehome makes it easier to get the paddle into the water.
- **Rocker.** The curve of the keel line from bow to stern, rocker is important. More rocker increases maneuverability at the expense of stability. Again, go for the middle ground.

And then there are situation-specific canoes, such as whitewater or portaging canoes. Whitewater boats will have heavy rocker and deeper flare, but will be a zigzagging tub on flat water. Portaging canoes are built with extremely light materials and will have a padded portage yoke for toting the boat on your shoulders. I recommend multipurpose touring/tripping tandem canoes, those with adequate maneuverability so you will be able to adjust and react while shooting rapids. You want a boat that can navigate moderate whitewater, can handle loads, and can track decently through flat water. If you are solo paddling a tandem canoe, weight the front with gear to make it run true. However, if you have a solo boat, you can't change it to a two-person boat.

Consider the Old Town Penobscot 16' RX, long a favorite of mine. It is a great all-around boat that I have used on varied trips, from day paddles on rivers to multinight adventures, over years and years. Ultralightweight canoes, such as those built by Wenonah, are designed to be carried from lake to lake via portages, but they have their place throughout South Carolina's waterways. I highly recommend the 17-foot Wenonah Spirit II. At 42 pounds, this ultralight Kevlar boat can perform well in the water and not break your back between your vehicle and the shore. I used it often while writing this book. Other times you may be going down rivers with significant stretches of whitewater, where you will want a boat that can take bone-jarring hits from rocks in the mountains and Upstate. Finally, choose muted colors that blend with the land and water.

Which Paddle Do I Use?

Wood is still holding on strong as a material for paddlers, though plastics dominate the market, especially lower-end paddles, such as those used by outfitters, and also ultralight high-end paddles. Some cheap varieties combine a plastic blade with an aluminum handle. Bent-shaft paddles are popular as well, though I don't recommend them myself. They are efficient as far as trying to get from point A to point B, but while floating you are often drifting and turning, making constant small adjustments, turning the boat around and doing all sorts of maneuvers other than straightforward paddling in a line. Bent-shaft paddles are poor when it comes to precision steering moves. How about a square versus rounded blade? I prefer a rounded blade for precision strokes, whereas a power paddler, maybe the bow paddler, will desire a square blade. Paddles can vary in length as well, generally from 48 to 60 inches. I recommend a shorter paddle for the stern paddler, because that is the person who makes the small adjustments in boat direction. A shorter paddle is easier to maneuver when making all these small adjustments, not only in the water, but also when shifting the paddle from one side of the boat to the next.

Kayak paddles are double bladed; that is, they have a blade on both sides, resulting in more efficient stroking. Kayakers seem more willing to part with a lot of money to use an ultralight paddle. Almost all kayak paddles are two piece, snapping in the middle. This makes them easier to haul around, but more importantly, it allows paddlers to offset the blades for more efficient stroking. Four-piece blades are not unusual, though. Kayak blades are generally 6 inches by 18 inches, with paddles averaging between 7 and 8 feet in length. Weightwise, expensive paddles can be 24 ounces or less, while average paddles are 30 to 40 ounces. Like anything, you get what you pay for. A paddle leash is a wise investment to prevent losing your paddle.

Whether in a canoe or a kayak, an extra paddle is a smart idea. It's easy to stow an extra paddle in the canoe, but it can be more troublesome in a kayak. A four-piece paddle is easier for a kayaker to stow.

Paddling Accessories

Life Vest

In the bad old days, I would use anything that would meet Coast Guard standards just to get by. But now I use a quality life vest, not only for safety, but also for comfort. The better kinds, especially those designed for sea kayaking, allow for more freedom of arm movement.

Chair Backs

These hook on to the canoe seat to provide support for your back. I recommend the plastic models that cover most of your back, providing extra lower lumbar support. The more elaborate metal and canvas chair backs get in the way of paddling. However, having no chair back on multiday trips can lead to "canoer's back"! Recreational kayakers can enhance their seats with pads for their behind and back.

Dry Bags

Waterproof dry bags are one of those inventions that give modern paddlers an advantage by leaps and bounds over those of yesteryear. These dry bags, primarily made of rubber and/or plastic, have various means of closing themselves down that result in a watertight seal, keeping your gear dry as you travel waterways, whether they are oceanic or riverine. Today's choices of dry bags, which can range from tiny personal-size, clear dry bags in which you might throw things such as sunscreen, keys, insect repellant, and a hat, to massive rubber "black holes" with built-in shoulder straps and waist belts designed not only to keep your stuff dry but to be carried on portages. Dry bags come in various sizes and different shapes, designed to fit in the tiny corners of a kayak or an open canoe. They can be long and thin to hold a tent, or wide, which will fit most anything. Kayakers should consider deck bags, which are attached to the top of the kayak just in front of the paddler. Store your day-use items in them.

Kayakers prepare at the put-in (paddle 22).

Plastic Boxes

Plastic storage boxes, found at any mega retailer, come in a variety of sizes and shapes. They are cheap, sit easily in the bottom of the canoe, and can double as a table. Store items in here that you don't want smashed, such as bread. However, they are not nearly as waterproof as a rubber dry bag. Consider using these if you are on flat water.

Paddler's Checklist

- ❑ Canoe/kayak
- ❑ Paddles
- ❑ Spare paddle
- ❑ Personal floatation device
- ❑ Dry bags for gear storage
- ❑ Whistle
- ❑ Towline
- ❑ Bilge pump for kayak
- ❑ Spray skirt for kayak
- ❑ Paddle float/lanyard for kayak
- ❑ Maps
- ❑ Throw lines
- ❑ Boat sponge

Other items you may want to consider depend upon your personal interests as a paddler, for example, fishing gear, sunglasses, trash bag, GPS, weather radio, camera, watch, sunscreen, lip balm, extra batteries, binoculars, wildlife identification books.

Traveling with Your Boat

Boats, whether they are canoes or kayaks, need to be carried atop your vehicle en route to the water. How you load your boat not only depends upon whether it is a canoe or kayak, but it also depends upon what type of vehicle you use and whether you have an aftermarket roof rack. No matter how you carry your boat, tie it down securely, not only for the sake of your boat but also for that of your fellow drivers, who will be endangered if your boat comes loose. I have seen a canoe fly off the car in front of me, and I know what a boat will do to a car after sliding off the side of said car while it's still tied on! After cinching your boat down, drive a short distance, then pull over and recheck your tie job. I recommend using the flat straps with buckles, which are sold at any outdoor retailer and also big box stores.

A quality aftermarket roof rack installed atop your vehicle makes for a much safer way to transport boats. Invest in one of these if you're paddling frequently. I have one made by Yakima. Roof racks can be customized to different types and numbers of boats as well. And don't skimp on tie-down straps either; this is what holds the boat to the rack.

Parking

In writing this book, among other South Carolina guidebooks and over fifty outdoor guides, I have parked all over the country, often for days and weeks at a time. Use your intuition when leaving your vehicle somewhere. It is always best to arrange for someone to look after your car, and a small fee is worth the peace of mind. National, state, and county parks with on-site rangers are good choices for leaving your vehicle overnight. Also, check with fish camps and liveries, as many provide shuttle service and a safe place to park. Private businesses sometimes allow over-nighters to park in their lots; be sure to ask permission and offer to pay. When parking for day trips, it is better to leave the vehicle near the road rather than back in the woods, out of sight.

Shuttles

River trips require a shuttle. Setting up these shuttles can be a pain, but the payoff is getting to explore continually new waters in an ever-changing outdoor panorama. The closer you are to home, the more likely you are to be self-shuttling. Always remember to go to the takeout point first, leaving a car there, with the put-in-point car following. Leave no valuables in your car. Take your keys with you and store them securely while you are floating!

Outfitters can save you the hassle of shuttling and allow you to leave your car in a safe, secure setting. Of course, you will pay for this service. This especially helps on river trips that are far from home. Don't be afraid to ask about prices, distances, and reservations. Also ask about camping and potential crowds, especially during weekends. If outfitters are available, they are listed with each paddle in this book.

Paddling clubs gather in groups to go on trips together. Not only can paddlers ride together to said river, but they also can work out shuttles. Also, multiple cars parked together reduce the possibility of a break-in.

Paddling Safety

A safe paddler is a smart paddler. Be prepared before you get on the water and you will minimize the possibility of accidents on the water. And if they do happen, you will be better prepared to deal with them.

Lightning

Lightning can strike a paddler. Play it smart. When you sense a storm coming, have a plan as to what you will do when it hits. Most plans will involve getting the hell off the water. Seek shelter in a low area or in a grove of trees, not against a single tree, and then wait it out.

Poisonous plants

Yep, poisonous plants are growing out there. You know the adage: Leaves of three leave it be. If you are highly allergic to poisonous plants, check ahead for the area in which you will be paddling, then take the appropriate action, such as having antihistamine creams.

Bugs

Sometimes when paddling we consider the possibility of death by blood loss from mosquitoes, but actually your chances of dying from a bug bite in the wild are less than your chances of dying on the car ride to the river. Watch out for black widow spiders and ticks with Lyme disease (though you can't tell the ones with Lyme disease until you get it). A real danger is bee stings to those who are allergic to them.

Snakes

Paddlers will see snakes along rivers, especially on sunny streamside rocks, a preferred area for copperheads. Water moccasins will be found around slower-moving Lowcountry streams. I have seen other snakes swimming while I float by in a boat. Give them a wide berth, and they'll do the same for you.

Sun

When paddling South Carolina, the sun can be your enemy and your friend. You welcome its light and warmth. Then it tries to burn your skin, penetrate your eyes, and kick up gusty winds. Finally you lament its departure every night as darkness falls. Sun can be a real threat no matter where you are. While boating, you will be on the water, and thus open to the prowess of old Sol. Be prepared for sun. Have sunscreen, a hat, bandanna, and long pants and long-sleeve shirt. Clothes are your best defense. Put on the sunscreen before you get in the sun. Consider covering your hands. I have personally seen several cases of sun poisoning on paddler's hands.

Heat

Whether the sun is shining brightly or the day is overcast, high temperatures can cause heat stroke or heat exhaustion. While paddling, take shade breaks and swim to cool off in the heat of summer.

Cold

In our eagerness to hit the river, especially after a string of nice March days, we take off for the nearest stream, disregarding the fact that twenty-one days of March are classified as winter, and the waterways can be really cold then. The possibility of hypothermia is very real if you take a tumble into the water. Try to stay dry if at all possible—it is easier to stay dry and warm, or even dry and not so warm, than to get wet and cold, and then warm up.

Medical Kit

Today's medical kits have come a long way. Now you can find activity-specific medical kits that also come in different sizes for each activity, including paddling. Medical kits designed for water sports come in waterproof pouches. I recommend Adventure Medical Kits, adventuremedicalkits.com. They have a good variety of kits and also divide their kits into group-size units as well, so whether you are a solo paddler or on a multiple-boat, multiple-day river trip, you will have not only the right kit but the right-size one.

Camping

Overnight camping can add to the South Carolina paddling experience. Where camping is a possibility, I have noted it in the paddling narratives. Other places may have strict private-property situations or other elements that prohibit camping. However, you may want to consider camping either before or after your paddle. Check out the plethora of South Carolina state parks, national parks, national forests, and other public lands.

Final Note

Just remember, paddling South Carolina is about having a good time, whether you are sea kayaking on Lake Jocassee, winding along a remote Piedmont stream, or stroking a blackwater Lowcountry waterway. Now, get out there and make some memories!

Map Legend

Transportation

- - - - - - Paddling Route
=(95)= Interstate Highway
=(15)= US Highway
=(651)= State Highway
=[101]= Forest Road
- - - - - - Trail
+——+——+ Railroad

Water Features

Body of Water
River or Creek
Waterfall/Rapid

Land Management

National Forest
Wilderness Area
State Park/Wildlife Refuge

Symbols

◤ Put-in/Takeout
🅿 Parking
🌳 Picnic Area
❓ Visitor Center
╱ Dam
⌣ Bridge
⛺ Campground
24 Mileage Marker
■ Structure/Point of Interest
🎫 Ranger Station
🚤 Boat Launch
▲ Mountain/Hill
✪ Capital
○ Towns and Cities

The Upstate

A paddler shoots a rapid right through the hole (paddle 6).

1 Chattooga River

County: Oconee
Start: SC 28 River Access
    N34° 54' 11.9" / W83° 10' 54.0"
End: Earls Ford
    N34° 52' 32.9" / W83° 13' 43.7"
Distance: 7.0 miles
Float time: 4 hours
Difficulty rating: Moderate to difficult
Rapids: Class I-II, III (Big Shoals)
River type: Mountain whitewater river worthy of its designation as a Wild and Scenic River
Current: Moderate to swift
River gradient: 11.2 feet per mile
River gauge: Chattooga River near Clayton—1.2 feet minimum runnable level, 3.0 maximum runnable level

Season: Apr through Nov
Land status: Public, Sumter National Forest, Chattahoochee National Forest
Fees or permits: A free river float plan must be filed
Nearest city/town: Walhalla
Maps: Chattooga Wild and Scenic River; USGS Quadrangle Map: Satolah
Boats used: Decked kayaks, canoes, rafts
Organizations: Chattooga Conservancy, 2368 Pinnacle Dr. Clayton, GA 30525, (706) 782-6097, chattoogariver.org
Contacts/outfitters: Wildwater Rafting, Ltd., PO Box 309, Long Creek, SC 29658, (800) 451-9972, wildwaterrafting.com

Put-in/Takeout Information

To takeout: From the intersection of SC 28 and SC 107 north of Walhalla, take SC 28 west for 2.5 miles to Chattooga Ridge Road in Mountain Rest. Turn left on Chattooga Ridge Road. Follow Chattooga Ridge Road for 3.5 miles and turn right onto Earls Ford Road. Follow Earls Ford Road for 3.9 miles to dead-end at the parking area. **To put-in from takeout:** Backtrack on Earls Ford Road for 3.9 miles, then take a left on Chattooga Ridge Road and follow it for 3.5 miles. Turn left on SC 28 West and follow it 4.4 miles to the Highway 28 River Access.

Paddle Summary

This float traverses the most doable section of the wild and scenic Chattooga River, which forms the boundary between Georgia and South Carolina. The protected river corridor offers unspoiled mountain scenery at its finest. The trip is challenging for the novice paddler, though it's much tamer than other sections of the Chattooga downstream. That being said, it does have several solid Class II rapids with one Class III rapid, Big Shoals. Be apprised that the takeout from the river at Earls Ford requires a 0.25-mile uphill carry to the parking area.

River Overview

The Chattooga River deserves its wild and scenic designation, and then some. Culled

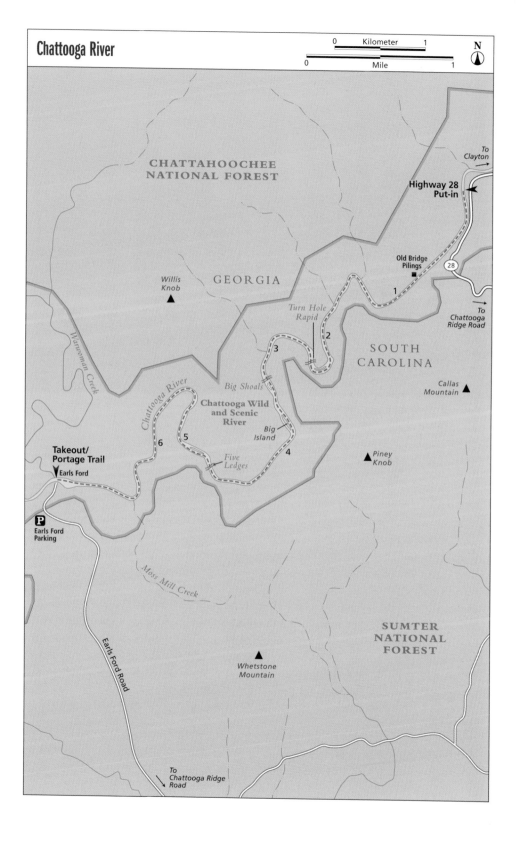

Chattooga River

0 Kilometer 1

0 Mile 1

N

To
Clayton

**Highway 28
Put-in**

CHATTAHOOCHEE
NATIONAL FOREST

Old Bridge
Pilings

*Willis
Knob*

GEORGIA

28

To
Chattooga
Ridge Road

*Turn Hole
Rapid*

1

2

3

SOUTH
CAROLINA

*Callas
Mountain*

Big Shoals

Chattooga River

**Chattooga Wild
and Scenic
River**

*Big
Island*

*Piney
Knob*

6   5

4

Hammon Creek

*Five
Ledges*

**Takeout/
Portage Trail**

▼ Earls Ford

P

**Earls Ford
Parking**

Moss Mill Creek

SUMTER
NATIONAL
FOREST

Earls Ford Road

*Whetstone
Mountain*

To
Chattooga Ridge
Road

Looking downstream on a calm stretch of the mountain-rimmed Chattooga

from the Sumter National Forest of South Carolina, the Nantahala National Forest of North Carolina, and Georgia's Chattahoochee National Forest, this river corridor protects one of the most significant free-flowing streams in the Southeast. The river itself is 50 miles long, starting in North Carolina, then heading southwest for 40 miles, forming the Georgia–South Carolina border before meeting the Tallulah River and forming the Tugaloo River. The Chattooga is perhaps best known for being the backdrop of the Burt Reynolds's movie *Deliverance*. It was around that time, in 1974, that the Chattooga was designated a wild and scenic river, a place where rafters, canoers, kayakers, and anglers enjoy this valley of massive boulders, clear trout- and bass-filled waters, and deep forests. The following section of river is the mildest in terms of rapids. Downstream, the following 20 miles of waterway—known as Section 3 and Section 4—have rapids up to Class V and are known for both their challenging nature and extraordinary scenery. Additionally the wild and scenic river corridor offers 36 miles of river hiking, and more in adjacent national forest lands, which include the Ellicott Rock Wilderness.

The Paddle

You can lengthen your trip by putting in at the Highway 28 Bridge that crosses the Chattooga at South Carolina–Georgia state line. This adds a little less than 2 miles to

THE RUSSELL FARMSTEAD

Near the site of the Highway 28 Bridge was once the Cherokee village of Chatuga Old Town. This settlement took advantage of the flats among the steep mountains that rise from the Chattooga. This Cherokee living place consisted of a small village of no more than ten to fifteen homes with less than one hundred people living here. By the 1750s, this Cherokee town had been abandoned, likely due to smallpox. The same flats beside the Chattooga proved alluring to white settlers who came after them. Today, you can visit the Russell farmstead, located on the South Carolina side of the Chattooga between the Highway 28 Bridge and the put-in for this paddle. It is signed.

The Russell farmstead was a hub of activity—farm, stagecoach stop, and inn in the late nineteenth and early twentieth centuries. The historic site contains the foundations and remains of the Russell house and nine outbuildings, including barns, corncrib, springhouse, and pig farrow. The Russell farm site was first settled in the 1820s by Ira Nicholson, but the Union destroyed his house in 1864. William Russell purchased the property in 1867 and built most of the buildings, including the main house. The large house was gradually expanded and provided rooms for travelers. It was a two-story frame building dating from the 1880s with a projecting rear two-story ell added around 1890. A two-story front porch was also added later. William Russell performed the function of a local doctor and dentist. A blacksmith shop was located at the farm. William Russell died in 1921, and his wife died in 1935, but the family continued to operate the establishment into the 1950s. In 1970, the federal government purchased the property. A fire destroyed the main house in 1988.

your paddle. The put-in is on the southwest side of the bridge. A trail leads down to the river. Be apprised that many anglers will be in the river around the bridge on nice days.

Make sure to file a float plan before you get on the river. You can file your float plan at either the put-in or the takeout. The Highway 28 put-in, where this trip begins, has a steep concrete ramp that leads down to the rocky river. Here, the Chattooga is about 50 to 60 feet wide, completely wooded with species such as mountain laurel, maple, and hemlock, the latter unfortunately dying from hemlock woolly adelgid. A few houses line the South Carolina side for a bit. The clear water has a brownish tint, and pyrite—fool's gold—shimmers in the sandy shallows. The Bartram Trail, a footpath, runs along the Georgia bank, which is to your right as you travel downstream. The paddling is easy at first, with just a few minor shoals. At 0.8 mile, pass the remnants of an old wooden bridge in a long slack pool. As you make a curve to the right, you can look downstream directly at Oakey Top Mountain.

Islands border the river that widens to over 100 feet in places. Occasional logjams and sandbars accumulate on the river's edge. White pines and shortleaf pines tower high on the forested hills. The rapids remaining Class I as you cruise downriver amid large boulders, especially at low water. At 2.4 miles, the Chattooga goes over a small shoal then makes a nearly 180-degree turn to the right before reaching the first named shoal—Turn Hole Rapid. A nice high beach, suitable for camping, collects at the base of the rapid on river right. It will also collect unwary paddlers. This rapid has several routes that change as the waters rise and fall, so stop and scout it.

The river narrows, and several small smaller rapids lie between Turn Hole Rapid and Big Shoals, which you reach at 3.3 miles. Look for a pine island in the middle of the river, combined with a roar suitable for a Class III rapid. Large boulders line the river. You can paddle up to the boulders, then scout your route over the fairly short rapid. Most paddlers go far right or far left, and at higher water, down the middle. Novices, don't be afraid to portage.

Once beyond Big Shoals don't forget to look upstream for another view of Oakey Top. Below Big Shoals, the river continues to divide into islands, and the scenery remains magnificent. The longest island is appropriately called Big Island. Just below Big Island, look for the old Big Island ford crossing the shallows here with roadbeds extending away from the Chattooga. A long pool ensues. Doghobble and mountain laurel grow in thickets along the river, while white pines tower above the rest of the forest.

At 4.5 miles, reach the Five Ledges rapid. This Class II rapid has multiple ledges and multiple routes. Two islands split the river amid the Five Ledges. Most paddlers stay to the right of the islands. Moderate shoals and superlative scenery continue. The Chattooga makes a hard curve to the right, west, at 6.4 miles, as Moss Mill Creek flows in from your left. Pass a few more islands downstream. You will recognize Earls Ford, as Warwoman Creek comes in on the right, just downstream of a large gravel bar on river left. Now the real fun begins as a portage trail leads 0.25 mile to the takeout.

2 Waterfalls of Western Lake Jocassee Paddle

Explore the Thompson River arm of mountain-rimmed Lake Jocassee, visiting three waterfalls during your still-water paddle.

County: Oconee
Start: Devils Fork State Park
  N34° 58.029' / W82° 57.227'
End: Devils Fork State Park
  N34° 58.029' / W82° 57.227'
Distance: 10.5 miles
Float time: 6 hours
Difficulty rating: Moderate
Rapids: None
River type: Lake
Current: None
River gradient: None
River gauge: Lake level can be found at duke-energy.com/lakes/; full pool is 1,100 feet
Season: Year-round

Land status: Mostly public
Fees or permits: Entrance fee required to launch at Devils Fork State Park
Nearest city/town: Salem
Maps: South Carolina DNR Lake Jocassee; USGS Quadrangle Maps: Salem, Reid
Boats used: Kayaks, canoes, motorboats
Organizations: South Carolina Department of Natural Resources, Rembert C. Dennis Building, 1000 Assembly St., Columbia, SC 29201, (803) 734-9100, dnr.sc.gov
Contacts/outfitters: Devils Fork State Park, 161 Holcombe Circle, Salem, SC 29676, (864) 944-2639, southcarolinaparks.com

Put-in/Takeout Information

To takeout: From Pickens, drive on US 178 north for 9 miles to SC 11. Turn left on SC 11 and follow it 12.5 miles to reach Jocassee Lake Road. Turn right on Jocassee Lake Road and follow it 3.5 miles to enter the park. Veer left at the first split, away from park headquarters. Pass the campground on your right and continue to the next split. Head left to the motorized and nonmotorized boat ramp. The right fork goes to a nonmotorized boat ramp, but do not start there, despite the name.
To put-in from takeout: Put-in and takeout are the same.

Paddle Summary

This lake paddle is set against a backdrop of mountains rising over 2,000 feet above what is arguably South Carolina's most scenic lake. Here, you will leave Devils Fork State Park, with the lake's only public boat ramps, and head northwest under a mantle of Southern Appalachian splendor. Make your way into the Thompson River arm of the lake, where Thompson River flows into Lake Jocassee. Discover a whitewater cascade on the main river and a steep unnamed waterfall of a tributary. Next, make your way back toward Devils Fork State Park, stopping by impressive Wrights Creek Falls, with its three-tiered cataract behind, which you can paddle. Your final lakeside waterfall flows off Double Spring Mountain, as an unnamed tributary makes a long,

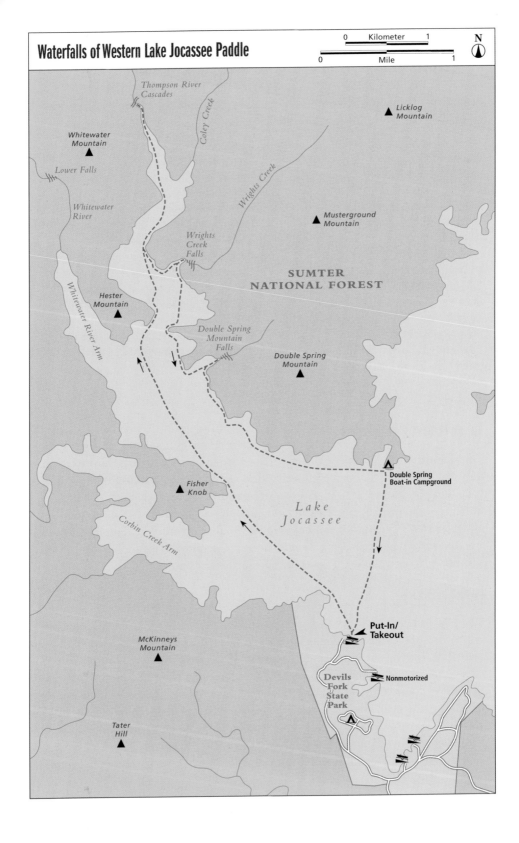

Waterfalls of Western Lake Jocassee Paddle

Thompson River Cascades

Coley Creek

Licklog Mountain ▲

Whitewater Mountain ▲

Lower Falls

Whitewater River

Wrights Creek

Musterground Mountain ▲

Wrights Creek Falls

SUMTER NATIONAL FOREST

Whitewater River Arm

Hester Mountain ▲

Double Spring Mountain Falls

Double Spring Mountain ▲

Fisher Knob ▲

Corbin Creek Arm

Lake Jocassee

Double Spring Boat-in Campground

McKinneys Mountain ▲

Put-In/ Takeout

Devils Fork State Park

Nonmotorized

Tater Hill ▲

0   Kilometer   1
0   Mile   1

N

narrow drop followed by a shorter, wider fall at its end. Return on the widening lake to visit Double Spring campground, the only boat-in camping allowed here. From there, dash south across open water, returning to the boat ramp. Spring and fall are favorable times to undertake this endeavor—power boaters can be numerous on the lake in summer. I like spring best because the waterfalls are bold and the lake is normally at full pool.

River Overview

Lake Jocassee is fed by four major tributaries flowing from the North Carolina highlands—Whitewater River, Thompson River, Horsepasture River, and the Toxaway River—plus a few other streams and creeks. The 7,500-acre impoundment was dammed in 1973 as a power-generation project of Duke Power. The dam stretches nearly 400 feet high and 1,750 feet long. Most of the 75 miles of shoreline is public property under the auspices of the Sumter National Forest and the South Carolina Department of Natural Resources. This makes for a scenic shore; however, there are some houses along the lake. The area is known as the Jocassee Gorges, for the deeply incised valleys that drop over 2,000 feet from the adjoining mountains. After the lake's damming, most of the gorges were intact and drop directly into the water, resulting in the numerous waterfalls accessible by boat.

The Paddle

From the boat ramp, head northwest through extremely clear waters, transparent enough for the lake to be a diving destination. Double Spring Mountain and Musterground Mountain rise across the lake. The Toxaway River arm stretches north. The lake dam stretches to your right. However, our paddle enters the Whitewater River/Thompson River arm of the lake. Cruise a wooded shoreline, passing around a point at 0.3 mile. Bluffs rise from the crystalline water; trees and the soil holding them occasional slough into the water. Keep northwest, crossing the Corbin Creek arm of the lake to your left. Magnificent mountain scenery rises as a backdrop. Montane vistas of the Jocassee Gorges are continuous.

Come along the slaty edge of Fisher Knob at 1.5 miles. Keep northwest, aiming for Hester Mountain, the ridge that separates Whitewater River arm from Thompson River arm. Some houses are visible to the west. Reach Hester Mountain and the Thompson River arm at 3.0 miles. The embayment narrows. Wild shoreline rises. You may hear Wrights Creek Falls, but save it for later and keep north on the narrowing embayment.

The embayment splits again. Enter the Thompson River arm at 3.9 miles, separated from Coley Creek arm by Gallbuster Mountain, an all-time great Southern Appalachian name. In spring, noisy tributaries will be dropping into the slender arm. Angle left, away from Coley Creek. At 4.7 miles, reach the meeting place of Thompson River and Lake Jocassee. Here, a wet bluff trickles to your right. Dead ahead,

Mountains rise from the shores of Lake Jocassee.

Thompson River makes a noisy 25-foot double drop along big boulders and outcroppings—suitable for sitting upon—only to be silenced as it enters the impoundment. Just upstream, to your left as you face Thompson River, an unnamed tributary creates a 100-foot wall of white froth. Don't miss it!

After lingering, backtrack down the Thompson River arm. Join the left shoreline at 5.6 miles, stay with it, then curve into the Wrights Creek embayment. Reach the waterfall at 6.2 miles, screened by vegetation until you get close. Here, 110-foot Wrights Creek Falls dives from a cliff in stages, first as a narrow drop, then it widens, drops again, and makes a final descent into the lake. You can actually paddle under this lowermost fall when the lake is at full pool. There is also a cave-like overhang here.

From this point, continue along the north shore at the base of Double Spring Mountain. Cross a U-shaped bay, then shoot past a couple of islands at 6.9 miles. These will be connected to the mainland at lower water levels. Turn into a deep embayment at 7.2 miles. Reach Double Spring Mountain Falls at 7.4 miles. This cataract is best seen when the leaves are off, for it is very high. The uppermost portion spills over a naked rock face, then the unnamed stream dances through a boulder field before making a final triangular-shaped spillover near the lake's edge.

Keep southeasterly on the north shore. At 8.0 miles, pass a sheer cliff dropping into the water. Work around a couple of points. The dam comes back into view. Reach the sign indicating Double Spring boat-in campground at 9.3 miles. This fourteen-site overnighting place is accessed via a small bay to the west of the campground sign. From here, head due south across Lake Jocassee. Enjoy more mountain views on this open-water paddle. Return to the boat ramp at 10.5 miles, completing the paddle.

DEVILS FORK STATE PARK

Devils Fork State Park occupies some of Lake Jocassee's awesome shoreline, abutted by walk-in tent sites affording instant water access, and provides a camping alternative for lake visitors. The main tent-camping area spurs onto a wooded peninsula extending into the lake, with a paved trail leading down to the campsites. The mountain slope has been leveled at each site, and views of the mountains are available at many of them.

The drive-up campground has two loops. Trees shade the sites, and ample vegetation screens them from one another. Most have tent pads. Any of these sites will suffice, but the tent sites are far more desirable. And because all sites are reservable, why not go for the ones you like? Reservations are strongly recommended, as the campground fills nearly every weekend from Easter through fall.

This park has two hiking trails. The 1.5-mile Oconee Bells Nature Trail takes you by places where the rare Oconee Bell wildflower grows. The Bear Cove Trail makes a 3.5-mile loop and starts at the day-use area. Most recreation centers on this beautiful lake. There is no supervised swim area, so you'll see campers swimming near their sites. Watercraft access to the lake is made easy at the four park boat ramps.

Jocassee Outdoor Center is just outside the park. They have fishing gear and bait, rent boats, and offer shuttles and guided sightseeing and fishing tours on Lake Jocassee. Visit jocasseeoutdoorcenter.com for more information. Lake Jocassee is worth seeing. And the Jocassee Gorges are worth exploring via the Foothills Trail, which runs along the north shore of Lake Jocassee. Make a reservation to tent camp at Devils Fork and explore to your hearts content, and see if you agree this is one of the best outdoor experiences in the Palmetto State.

3 Waterfalls of Northern Lake Jocassee Paddle

See 80-foot-tall Laurel Fork Falls as well as another cataract on this long paddle in a mountain-rimmed impoundment.

County: Oconee
Start: Devils Fork State Park
    N34° 58.029' / W82° 57.227'
End: Devils Fork State Park
    N34° 58.029' / W82° 57.227'
Distance: 14.2 miles
Float time: 8 hours
Difficulty rating: Difficult due to distance
Rapids: None
River type: Lake
Current: None
River gradient: None
River gauge: Lake level can be found at duke -energy.com/lakes/; full pool is 1,100 feet
Season: Year-round

Land status: Mostly public
Fees or permits: Entrance fee required to launch at Devils Fork State Park
Nearest city/town: Salem
Maps: South Carolina DNR Lake Jocassee; USGS Quadrangle Maps: Salem, Reid
Boats used: Kayaks, canoes, motorboats
Organizations: South Carolina Department of Natural Resources, Rembert C. Dennis Building, 1000 Assembly St., Columbia, SC 29201, (803) 734-9100, dnr.sc.gov/
Contacts/outfitters: Devils Fork State Park, 161 Holcombe Circle, Salem, SC 29676, (864) 944-2639, southcarolinaparks.com

Put-in/Takeout Information

To takeout: From Pickens, drive on US 178 north for 9 miles to SC 11. Turn left on SC 11 and follow it 12.5 miles to reach Jocassee Lake Road. Turn right on Jocassee Lake Road and follow it 3.5 miles to enter the park. Veer left at the first split, away from park headquarters. Pass the campground on your right and continue to the next split. Head left to the motorized and nonmotorized boat ramp. The right fork is to the nonmotorized boat ramp but do not start there, despite the name.

To put-in from takeout: Put-in and takeout are the same.

Paddle Summary

This paddle will take you to one of South Carolina's premier waterfalls via the state's most beautiful impoundment—Lake Jocassee. Be apprised this is a long paddle, and you have a couple of open water crossings that could prove troublesome in windy or stormy conditions. Start this paddle at Devils Fork State Park, then charge north, crossing open water near Double Springs boat-in campground. Next, head up the Toxaway River arm of the lake before turning east to face the cliffs of Bully Mountain. Penetrate farther north before turning into the Laurel Fork Creek embayment. You will pass an access to the Foothills Trail, then hear the roar of Laurel Fork Falls. Enter a misty rock chamber with mossy wet walls into which the falls pours. Return

You can paddle right up to Laurel Fork Falls.

out to the main lake and work south, stopping to visit boat-accessible Devil Hole Falls, an evergreen-enshrouded wall of white pouring into Lake Jocassee. By this point, call on your reserves to skirt the eastern lakeshore, passing islands before making a final open-water paddle to reach the takeout.

River Overview

Lake Jocassee is fed by four major tributaries flowing from the North Carolina highlands—Whitewater River, Thompson River, Horsepasture River, and the Toxaway River—plus a few other streams and creeks. The 7,500-acre impoundment was dammed in 1973 as a power-generation project of Duke Power. The dam stretches nearly 400 feet high and 1,750 feet long. Most of the 75 miles of shoreline is public property, under the auspices of the Sumter National Forest and the South Carolina Department of Natural Resources. This makes for a scenic shore; however, there are some houses along the lake. The area is known as the Jocassee Gorges because of the deeply incised valleys that drop over 2,000 feet from the adjoining mountains. After the lake's damming, most of the gorges were intact. Their waters spill directly into the lake, resulting in the numerous waterfalls accessible by boat.

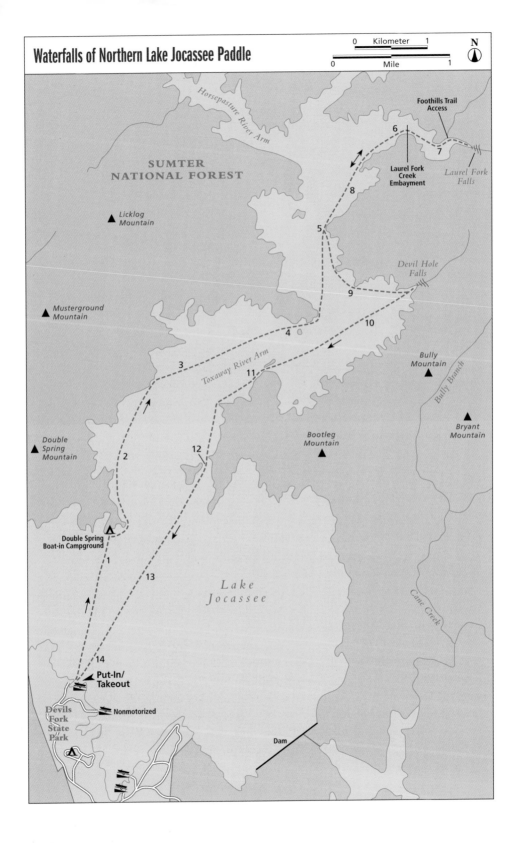

Waterfalls of Northern Lake Jocassee Paddle

0 Kilometer 1

0 Mile 1

N

Horsepasture River Arm

Foothills Trail Access

6

7

Laurel Fork Creek Embayment

Laurel Fork Falls

SUMTER NATIONAL FOREST

8

▲ Licklog Mountain

5

Devil Hole Falls

9

▲ Musterground Mountain

4

10

Toxaway River Arm

3

Bully Mountain ▲

Bully Branch

11

Bootleg Mountain ▲

Bryant Mountain ▲

▲ Double Spring Mountain

2

12

⛺ Double Spring Boat-in Campground

1

13

Lake Jocassee

Cane Creek

14

Put-In/ Takeout

Devils Fork State Park

⛴ Nonmotorized

Dam

⛺

Leave directly north from the Devils Fork State Park boat ramp. The expanse of Lake Jocassee stretches out before you. The Whitewater River arm leaves west, but you keep north for the Toxaway River arm. It is a full mile across the lake to the Double Spring boat-in campground; a campground sign will appear when you get close. From there the paddle keeps north, actually entering the Toxaway River arm, passing a small slender island. Cruise the wooded western shore of the arm. Musterground Mountain rises to your left, as do a host of mountains to the north. This is bona fide Carolina highlands!

The shore curves in coves and points, where trickling branches spill into Lake Jocassee. Underwater rocks reveal the astounding water clarity. Reach a point at 2.8 miles. Here the embayment opens easterly. Islands are visible in the distance. Curve easterly. The stone bluffs of Bully Mountain tower above. Interestingly, loons winter at Lake Jocassee into spring, when you can hear the unique call of this sizable black-and-white bird as it plies the lake.

The Toxaway River arm is wide here. It is helpful to know the wind forecast before departing. During the warm season, there is often a southeasterly afternoon wind, which you may be fighting on your return route. Luckily, as this paddle continues, the lake arm narrows. Occasional buoys in the water indicate shallow areas where rocks could impair motorboat propellers. Pass a piney island at 4.1 miles, then turn north. Devil Hole Falls is across the lake, but save it for later. Instead keep north, joining the right-hand shore, and pass a couple of small islands. You are coming to the Horsepasture River, Toxaway River, and Laurel Fork Creek confluence. At this point, it is 2.0 miles one way to Mill Creek Falls on the Horsepasture River arm, but this paddle angles northeasterly toward Laurel Fork Creek. Enter the Laurel Fork Creek embayment at 5.8 miles. Paddle under a big ol' transmission line ahead, then curve southeast. A small waterslide spills into the lake to your south. Reach the signed Foothills Trail access at 6.6 miles. This gives you the option of walking 0.5 mile to the falls before or after your paddle to it. The roar of 80-foot Laurel Fork Falls is audible from here. Continue traveling into the narrowing embayment to find the upper falls and a big rock. Paddle to the right of the rock, then enter a misty stone cathedral into which lowermost Laurel Fork Falls crashes. What a sight!

From here, backtrack down the clean, clear lake. At 8.4 miles, diverge from your previous route, sticking to the left shore and curving into the shadow of Bully Mountain. Sharp coves cut by streamlets are divided by wooded points. The roar of Devil Hole Creek, pouring from the highlands, resounds across the impoundment. The falls are to the left of the cliffs of Bully Mountain as you paddle toward the peak. Turn into a little cove and reach Devil Hole Falls at 9.5 miles. The visible part drops over a cliff line about 25 feet into the lake. On a summer day, it could be a good 10°F cooler around the falls.

Now it is paddling time. Break southwest across the water, slicing between an island and the shore at 10.9 miles. Curve southwest, passing another island at 11.5 miles. The lake widens as you turn south, working around Bootleg Mountain. Reach the lake's biggest island at 12.0 miles. Paddle along its east shore and it points you south–southwest to the boat ramp. Now you have a 2.0-mile open-water paddle across Lake Jocassee. Hope for north winds or no winds. The lake dam comes into view. Ahead, the concrete boat ramp evolves from myth to mirage to reality. End the adventure at 14.2 miles.

WALKING SOUTH CAROLINA'S ROOFTOP

The 77-mile Foothills Trail runs beside Lake Jocassee and is accessible from this paddle. It traverses the Cherokee Foothills of the Southern Appalachians in South Carolina (and a little bit of North Carolina). In these lands are high ridgelines, wild and scenic rivers, deep rock gorges, wilderness areas, mountain lakes, clear trout streams, towering forests, and a number of incredible waterfalls stretching from one end of the path to the other, including the section that visits Lake Jocassee and the Jocassee Gorges.

The Foothills Trail is well marked and well maintained. The footpath extends from Oconee State Park to Table Rock State Park. No doubt, you will notice the carefully built wood steps, water bars, and bridges allowing hikers to traverse rugged areas through which the path passes.

From within 0.5 mile of Laurel Fork Falls on Lake Jocassee, hikers can use a boat shuttle to access the trail. Beyond Laurel Fork Falls, the Foothills Trail then makes its way up the once-settled valley of Laurel Fork to a second falls, Double Falls, before the big climb up to Sassafras Mountain, at 3,560 feet, the highest point in South Carolina. It continues to its southern terminus at Oconee State Park.

The Foothills Trail is a year-round proposition, though summer can be very hot. Spring offers an abundance of wildflowers in the many lush valleys. Fall presents vibrant colors and cooler temperatures. Winter can be variable, with snow in the high country and entire days below freezing a very real possibility, though milder days occur with regularity. Whether you come by boat or foot, the Jocassee Gorges and the Foothills Trail are real Carolina gems. For more information visit foothillstrail.org.

4 Lake Keowee Paddle

This paddle starts at Keowee-Toxaway State Park and wanders past an island, bluffs, and streams to finally explore wild and serpentine Eastatoe Creek arm of Lake Keowee.

County: Pickens
Start: Keowee-Toxaway State Park
    N34° 56.252' / W82° 53.447'
End: Keowee-Toxaway State Park
    N34° 56.252' / W82° 53.447'
Distance: 6.0 miles
Float time: 3.5 hours
Difficulty rating: Easy to moderate
Rapids: None
River type: Lake
Current: A little in Eastatoe Creek embayment
River gradient: None
River gauge: Lake level can be found at duke
-energy.com/lakes/; full pool is 797 feet
Season: Year-round

Land status: Public, private
Fees or permits: No fees or permits required
Nearest city/town: Salem
Maps: South Carolina DNR Lake Keowee, Keowee-Toxaway State Park; USGS Quadrangle Maps: Salem, Sunset
Boats used: Kayaks, canoes, motorboats
Organizations: South Carolina Department of Natural Resources, Rembert C. Dennis Building, 1000 Assembly St., Columbia, SC 29201, (803) 734-9100, dnr.sc.gov
Contacts/outfitters: Keowee-Toxaway State Park, 108 Residence Dr., Sunset, SC 29685, (864) 868-2605, southcarolinaparks.com

Put-in/Takeout Information

To takeout: From Pickens, drive north on US 178 West for 9 miles to SC 11. Turn left on SC 11 and continue for 7.9 miles to Keowee-Toxaway State Park. Turn right into the part of the state park with the campground, on the north side of SC 11. Follow the main road, Cabin Road, to dead-end at the nonmotorized boat ramp at 0.6 mile.
To put-in from takeout: Put-in and takeout are the same.

Paddle Summary

This fun little paddle finds a slice of nature on a busy lake. Start your adventure at a canoe and kayak launch at Keowee-Toxaway State Park, a jewel of a preserve with a fine campground, trails, and paddling. Head northeast up the narrow Eastatoe arm of Lake Keowee. Discover a little island bejeweled with a little beach. From there investigate a small waterfall. Turn up the Poe Creek embayment, finding the mouth of this little stream. Paddle past rock bluffs before reaching the park lakeside campsite, accessible by foot or boat. Work your way along the southeast shoreline, before turning into the narrow gorge of Eastatoe Creek. This South Carolina scenic waterway forms a slender mountain gorge. As you paddle up the embayment, depending upon water level, the current will begin working against you. About 3 miles in makes for a good place to turn around and then backtrack your way to the state park. The trip is best enjoyed when Lake Keowee is at or near full pool.

River Overview

Lake Keowee is a large reservoir in the northwestern corner of South Carolina, draining the highlands of the Carolinas north of the lake. Interestingly, both the Keowee River and Little River are dammed on this single impoundment, generating electricity for Duke Power. The reservoir is quite big, extending 26 miles long and averaging 3 miles wide, with over 300 miles of shoreline. The lake has numerous other small tributaries in addition to the Keowee and Little Rivers, and these tributaries form numerous bays and coves. Much of the shoreline is covered in housing developments, golf courses, and the like; in fact, there is a housing development across from this paddle. Fortunately for us there are also a few parks, namely Keowee-Toxaway State Park, where this aquatic adventure takes place. The outflow of Lake Keowee pours into Lake Hartwell and the Savannah River.

The Paddle

From the state park paddler launch, curve east around rock revetment. A golf course and housing development stand just across the narrow bay. After turning the corner, you will see an island managed by Duke Power. These islands of Lake Keowee are not open to camping, but you can land on them. Visit the small beach on the south side of the island.

From the island, head southeast to visit a low-flow 30-foot waterfall spilling over a stone face into the reservoir. The blue-green water of Lake Keowee reflects forested hillsides as you paddle along the state park shores. Reach the mouth of Poe Creek and keep along the east shore. Rock bluffs interrupt the forested lake corridor. Curve into a small sandy cove, then reach the state park primitive campsite just before 1 mile. Here, a tiny peninsula harbors four pine-shaded camps. I have camped here, accessing the camp by canoe, and found it fun, despite the proximity of houses nearby.

Curve northeasterly along the shore beyond the camping area. Mountain views open to your north and east. Houses are stretched along the opposite shoreline. McKinney Mountain rises from the shoreline to your right and is within the state park bounds. The shore is mostly forested to the waterline and other times there will be rock and/or soil bluffs. Elsewhere small beaches are exposed, especially when the lake is below full pool.

Paddle past a few little embayments before leaving the bounds of the state park at 1.7 miles. Reach the narrow Eastatoe Creek embayment at 1.9 miles. Here, you turn southeasterly, entering a clearly defined snakelike channel. Wooded hills rise steeply on both sides of the water.

At 2.0 miles, a pair of low-flow waterfalls tumbles into the lake. Heading deeper into the gorge, you will see an extensive sandbar, the first of several deposited by the fast-flowing waters of Eastatoe Creek. The air cools. The section of Eastatoe Creek immediately above the lake has a relatively low gradient and doesn't really form

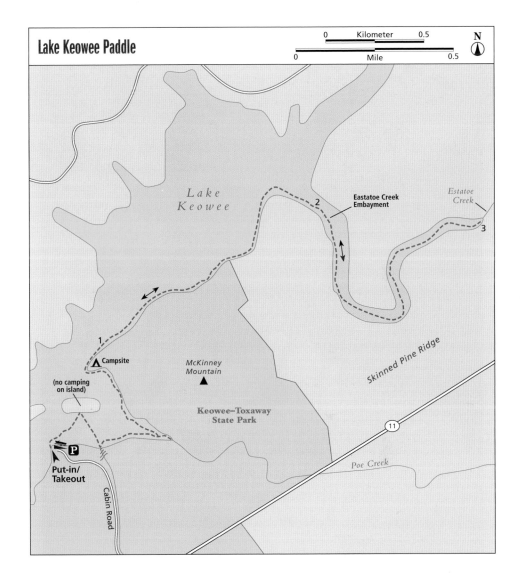

0   Kilometer   0.5

N

0   Mile   0.5

Lake Keowee

2

Eastatoe Creek Embayment

Estatoe Creek

3

1

△ Campsite

(no camping on island)

McKinney Mountain ▲

Skinned Pine Ridge

Keowee–Toxaway State Park

11

🅿

Put-in/ Takeout

Cabin Road

Poe Creek

whitewater, but it certainly does deposit a lot of sand into Lake Keowee. Farther upstream is a different story, for Eastatoe Creek drains the high mountains of South Carolina, including part of Sassafras Mountain, the highest point in the Palmetto State at 3,560 feet. Part of the creek upstream of here is a South Carolina heritage preserve.

Noisy rivulets spill into the embayment as you continue twisting up the vegetation-walled vale. The sandy stream shallows. Stay close to the inside of the bends to minimize current effect. Look for signs of beaver, such as cut sticks and chewed vegetation along the shore. You will find critter tracks in the sandbars. The stream bends enough to where you think it is making a circle but it isn't. At 2.7 miles, Eastatoe Creek curves

Wild azaleas grace the shore of Lake Keowee.

right. Pass some low bluffs along the shoreline. By 3 miles, even at full pool, the current can be strong and rocks rise in midstream. This is a good place to turn around. The first part of the 6-mile return trip should be easy, with the current at your back.

HIKING AT KEOWEE-TOXAWAY STATE PARK

This park trail system, consisting of two interconnected loops, offers a natural bridge over which to walk, rocky views, a primitive campsite, and lake views. The first path, Natural Bridge Trail, takes you through thick forest to Poe Creek, where the creek crossing is a natural bridge. The path then winds through an interesting boulder field before rising to Raven Rock and great views. From here, the trail takes a rugged up-and-down track along McKinney Mountain before diving to meet Lake Keowee. Pass another outcrop and view while leaving the lake. The trail then winds through lower Poe Creek, a classic mountain stream, before climbing again to return to the trailhead after a total of 5 miles.

It is about 0.5 mile from the Meeting House parking area (park ranger station) on the Natural Bridge Trail to reach the wide stone slab of the Natural Bridge. It is so well integrated into the land (after all, it is perfectly natural) that it is not discernable. You cross Poe Creek atop it. To get another view, just after crossing Poe Creek, head left, downstream, then work your way up several feet and you can peer under the Natural Bridge, hearing the stream's babblings echo off the rock slab.

The Natural Bridge Trail climbs to meet the Raven Rock Trail, a world of rock and boulder. Keep uphill, reentering full-fledged woodland before opening onto a wide rock slab. This is Raven Rock. Here, views open to the west amid the pines. This is a partially vegetated rock slab, and the thin soils that accumulate here support pines, lichens, and moss, among other limited species.

The trail drops from the slab rock hill and begins circling McKinney Mountain. Reach the first of four primitive campsites stretched out on a peninsula. These lake-view camps have a metal fire ring and are mostly shaded by pines. You paddle past these; they are accessible by boat. Leave the lake and pass another outcrop where you can look down on Lake Keowee and westward toward Georgia.

Eventually make cool and dark Poe Creek valley, where beech and tulip trees, rhododendron, and ferns thrive. Poe Creek falls in noisy stair-step cascades over mossy rock ramparts. Ahead, cross Poe Creek, later joining the Natural Bridge Trail and looping back to the trailhead, experiencing the land and the water magnificence of Keowee-Toxaway State Park.

5 Saluda River near Greenville

Fun rapids enhance this surprisingly scenic suburban paddle.

County: Greenville, Pickens, Anderson
Start: Saluda Dam Bridge
  N34° 51.1101' / W82° 29.097'
End: Dolly Cooper Park
  N34° 48.217' / W82° 28.233'
Distance: 6.7 miles
Float time: 3 hours
Difficulty rating: Moderate
Rapids: Class I
River type: Suburban stream with mountain characteristics
Current: Moderate
River gradient: 4.9 feet per mile
River gauge: Saluda River near Greenville, SC; minimum 200 cfs, maximum 1200 cfs

Season: Year-round
Land status: Private
Fees or permits: No fees or permits required
Nearest city/town: Greenville
Maps: USGS Quadrangle Maps: Greenville
Boats used: Kayaks, canoes, tubes
Organizations: South Carolina Department of Natural Resources, Rembert C. Dennis Building, 1000 Assembly St., Columbia, SC 29201, (803) 734-9100, dnr.sc.gov
Contacts/outfitters: Saluda River Rafting, 570 N. Fishtrap Rd., Easley, SC 29640, saluda riverrafting.com

Put-in/Takeout Information

To takeout: From exit 40 on I-85, southwest of Greenville, take SC 153 north for 1.5 miles to a traffic light and SC 81 (Anderson Road). Turn right on SC 81 for 0.2 mile, then veer left onto Old Anderson Highway. Stay with Old Anderson Highway for 0.7 mile, then turn left into Dolly Cooper Park. Follow the park road past fields, then drop to a boat ramp at 0.2 mile. Official address: 170 Spearman Circle Rd.

To put-in from takeout: Backtrack from Dolly Cooper Park on Old Anderson Highway, then turn left on Anderson Road (SC 81). Follow it for 2.7 miles to US 25 (White Horse Road). Turn left on US 25 north and follow it for 3.2 miles to a traffic light; turn left on Saluda Dam Road (US 25 bears right at this point). Follow Saluda Dam Road for 1.6 miles. Bridge the Saluda River and turn right into a small parking area just after the bridge. There is limited parking here, so be prudent.

Paddle Summary

This is a perfect weekend paddle in the suburban environs of Greenville. For starters, the takeout and put-in are easily accessed, eliminating long drives and long shuttles. This section of the Saluda River gets pushed out below the Saluda Lake Dam and spills southward in a relatively narrow corridor interspersed with fun, easy-to-read rapids. The waterway exhibits mountain characteristics with its shoals, rocks aplenty, and hilly shores full of evergreens. However, do not be deceived. This is a suburban float, and houses are lined up along much of the waterway. You're never far from the sound of a road. The trip itself passes under three road bridges. Nonetheless, it is a fun and worthwhile adventure.

Start by dancing among bridge abutments old and new, then proceed along, curving through a series of bends broken by Class I rapids. Mark your progress by passing under the aforementioned three bridges, then meet Little Georges Creek. From here, the Saluda makes a quiet journey to reach the takeout at Dolly Cooper Park.

River Overview

The Saluda River drains the highest reaches of Greenville County below the North Carolina state line. There are three prongs of the upper Saluda, all gorgeous mountain tributaries, especially the Middle Saluda, the aquatic pulse of Jones Gap State Park.

PARIS MOUNTAIN STATE PARK

If you live outside the area, consider making a base camp at Paris Mountain State Park, just outside of Greenville. It offers camping, hiking, and mountain biking. Whether on bike or foot, you can climb Paris Mountain via the 3.8-mile Sulphur Springs Loop Trail. The path traces a stream to reach Mountain Lake, a small impoundment. From this quiet body of water it resumes a 700-foot climb past slide cascades. Though views are limited on the peak, you can see the fire-tower keeper's cabin site before working your way back down through piney woods.

The dual-use trails at Paris Mountain State Park are open to hiking and biking Sunday through Friday, but are hiking only on Saturday. After making the climb, you reach the foundation of the old fire-tower keeper's residence, marked by two brick-stone chimneys and steps surrounded by woods. The tower foundation is nearby. In the old days, towers such as these were manned by full-time residents who lived on-site, often using cisterns from roof runoff for water. Nowadays, fire watching is done by planes in times of high fire danger. Save for winter, views are limited up here by the tree cover. The high point of the hike is nearly 1,800 feet. The actual peak of Paris Mountain is to the west and is over 2,000 feet in elevation.

Paris Mountain State Park was developed by the Civilian Conservation Corps in the 1930s and is one of South Carolina's oldest state parks. The many wood-and-stone structures, such as the picnic shelters at the trailhead, offer a rustic man-made beauty that complements the natural scenery, and the park is increasingly seen as an urban getaway for greater Greeneville. The park trail system is growing in popularity, too, with hikers and mountain bikers both plying the numerous paths. A camping area with water and electric sites caters primarily to RVs, but tents are welcome, and trailside camping is available, too.

A paddler shoots for the V in a Saluda River rapid.

The Middle flows to meet the South Saluda and together they join with the North Saluda a few miles above Saluda Lake, below which this paddle begins. After leaving the foothills, the 200-mile-long waterway keeps southeasterly, forming county boundaries and slowing at remnant textile milldams. A big dam forms Lake Greenwood, then the Saluda flows, only to slow again at popular Lake Murray. From there it makes its way into Columbia, culminating in rocky shoals before the Saluda meets the Broad River. Together they form the Congaree River.

The Paddle

The small put-in parking area will likely have bank fishermen parked there as well. It is a steep 50-yard carry down from the parking area to a gravel beach just below Saluda Lake Dam. Saluda Dam Road is overhead. The outflow of Saluda Lake Dam flows strongly just above the put-in. Be careful when you set out, for there are pilings and abutments not only of the road bridge above you but also of old bridges and the abutments of the Southern Railway line. It seems a mini slalom course. The green waters flow quickly.

The river is about 80 feet wide and bordered with hardwoods. At 0.3 mile, pass under a power line. A few streamside houses have appeared, but they don't impair the

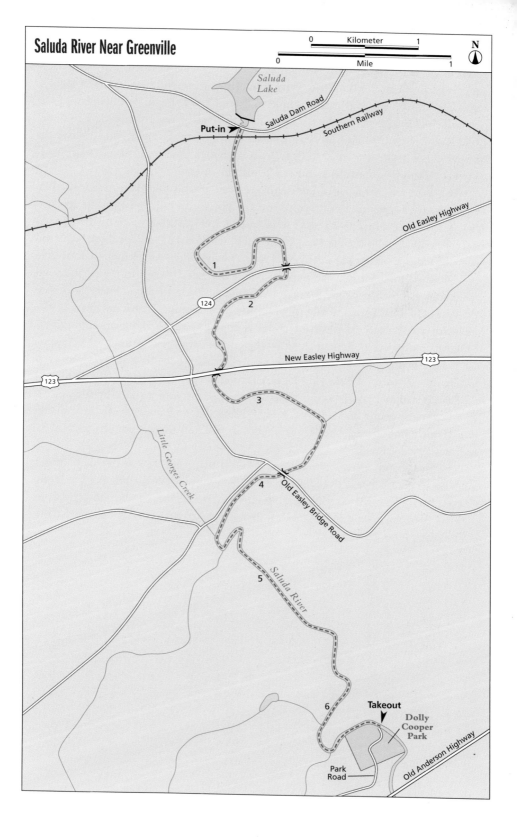

Saluda River Near Greenville

0 | Kilometer | 1
0 | Mile | 1

N

Saluda
Lake

Put-in

Saluda Dam Road

Southern Railway

Old Easley Highway

1

124

2

New Easley Highway

123

123

3

Little Georges Creek

4

Old Easley Bridge Road

5

Saluda River

6

Takeout

Dolly
Cooper
Park

Park
Road

Old Anderson Highway

scenery. The river gradient keeps the water flowing. Small, unnamed tributaries feed the Saluda. Pass a small shoal at 0.5 mile, then the Saluda bends to the right. More shoals lie ahead. At 0.9 mile, pass a riverside drinking establishment on river right as you bend to the left. Navigate a couple of more Class I shoals. At 1.1 miles, paddle by some old bridge pilings. At 1.7 miles, float through another shoal, then go under Old Easley Highway (SC 124) Bridge. Ahead, the river bends right, and you have the biggest rapid of the trip, still a Class I. Pass a large rock shelf on river left. This makes for a good stopping spot. An outfitter is across the water.

The waterway has made a near complete bend around Old Easley Highway. Fun rapids resume as you drift by occasional riverside houses, decks, and the like. Be apprised that much of the shoreline is posted, so be watchful where you stop along the river. At 2.6 miles, glide under the big New Easley Highway (US 123) Bridge. Low bluffs and occasional outcroppings add a geological touch to the paddle. At 3.5 miles, a noticeable but unnamed tributary flows in on your left, as the Saluda bends to the right. At 3.8 miles, look left for a tributary making a little slide cascade, then go under Old Easley Bridge Road. That makes three bridges in just over 2 miles! That is an element of a suburban paddle. Note the old stone bridge abutments just below the current bridge.

Drift southwesterly, pushed along by the current, with fewer rapids. At 4.5 miles, the Saluda bends left, and large Little Georges Creek adds its flow. You can even paddle up the stream a little ways here. A second stream comes in on the right, and the Saluda makes a couple of quick bends, then settles into a southeasterly course. The floating is gentle and relaxing. Keep passing different incarnations of riverside houses, including some newer, fancy abodes in addition to riverside shacks, trailers, and ordinary dwellings.

The river bends resume at 5.6 miles. Make a last major 180-degree bend at 6.3 miles. From here, keep on river right to reach the unmistakable floating dock at Dolly Cooper Park. The dock has a kayak ramp into which a paddler can float directly from the river onto the dock using rollers. It is designed for paddling access by wheelchair-bound water enthusiasts as well.

6 Pacolet River near Spartanburg

Start at sandy Clifton Beach, then punch through simple and fun Class I–II rapids before a relaxed second half of the paddle.

County: Spartanburg
Start: Clifton Beach
N34° 58.701' / W81° 48.916'
End: Pacolet Mills
N34° 55.261' / W81° 44.867'
Distance: 8.1 miles, includes short paddle up Lawsons Fork
Float time: 4 hours
Difficulty rating: Moderate
Rapids: Class I–II
River type: Foothills waterway with rocky rapids
Current: Moderate
River gradient: 5.4 feet per mile
River gauge: Pacolet River below Lake Blalock near Cowpens, SC, minimum 220 cfs, maximum 850 cfs

Season: Year-round
Land status: Private
Fees or permits: No fees or permits required
Nearest city/town: Spartanburg
Maps: Pacolet & Lawsons Fork Blueway; USGS Quadrangle Maps: Pacolet, Pacolet Mills
Boats used: Kayaks, canoes
Organizations: South Carolina Department of Natural Resources, Rembert C. Dennis Building, 1000 Assembly St., Columbia, SC 29201, (803) 734-9100, dnr.sc.gov
Contacts/outfitters: Town of Pacolet, 180 Montgomery Ave., Pacolet, SC 29372, (864) 474.9504, townofpacolet.com

Put-in/Takeout Information

To takeout: From the intersection of US 176 and SC 150 southeast of Spartanburg, take SC 150 east. Wind through the town of Pacolet on SC 150 to reach the bridge over the Pacolet River. Do not cross the river. From here, turn left on Limestone/Sunny Acres Road. then after 0.2 mile turn right into the old Pacolet Mills site and follow the road through a large parking lot to reach the takeout, above Pacolet Mills Dam. Official address: 1461 Sunny Acres Rd.

To put-in from takeout: Leave the old Pacolet Mills site, then turn right on Sunny Acres Road. Climb out of the town of Pacolet and drive 2.1 miles to reach West Main Street. Turn right on West Main Street and follow it for 1.1 miles, then turn right on Goldmine Road. There is a sign here indicating Pacolet River Heritage Preserve. Follow Goldmine Road for a total of 5.9 miles to reach Clifton Beach, just below the Clifton II Dam. The parking is on the west side of the road, and the sandy access is on the right. Official address: 239 Goldmine Rd.

Paddle Summary

This paddle starts at a big beach below the Clifton milldam. The first half of the paddle is exciting, with several Class I and a few Class II rapids. It is an excellent trip for those who want a taste of whitewater without getting in too deep. The first 4 miles of the paddle drop at a gradient nearing 10 feet per mile. You will pass over several rocky drops with mostly straightforward river reads. The Pacolet makes several bends as it passes through foothills. The longest rapid is just before it meets Lawsons Fork. Take the time to paddle up a stream that also offers more difficult whitewater paddling than the Pacolet. Below the confluence with Lawsons Fork, the Pacolet River calms down. Shoals appear but infrequently. Interestingly, you will pass the Pacolet River Heritage Preserve on river right. This locale harbors a natural ecosystem that occurs in this valley. Leave the preserve area beyond Richland Creek, a tributary of the Pacolet. The river slows here, influenced by the downstream Pacolet Mills Dam. Relax during this last segment and take out on river right before the dam.

River Overview

The Pacolet River originates in two branches, one in Polk County, North Carolina, near the community of Tryon, the other in South Carolina. In North Carolina, several tributaries form the North Pacolet River, and it flows southeasterly, entering the Palmetto State near Landrum. The North Pacolet continues its southeasterly journey through the Spartanburg County, where it meets the South Pacolet River just as the South Pacolet is released from Lake Bowen. The South Pacolet River begins on the southeastern slopes of Hogback Mountain in Greenville County. It pushes easterly and slows in Lake Bowen, then meets the North Fork to slow again in Lake Blalock. The main Pacolet subsequently wanders through foothills and slows down a few more times with old mill- and hydro dams, such as the two near this paddle. This area and Lawsons Fork, a major tributary, compose the Pacolet & Lawsons Fork Blueway, and is where this paddle takes place. The 50-mile Pacolet eventually flows free below the town of Pacolet, then works its way to meet the Broad River 5 miles above the town of Lockhart.

The Paddle

After carrying your boat across Goldmine Road, put in at Clifton Beach. The milldam is just above you and is noteworthy since it is angled. The Pacolet immediately splits around an island; take the wider right channel. Note the concrete relic at the end of the island, indicating that the left, narrow channel was likely a dug sluice. Immediately paddle through a few light warm-up shoals interspersed with rocks. You will see a few dwellings and camps along the river, as well as fields and woods among the hills. Sands and mussel shells color the waterway bottom.

At 0.8 mile, the Pacolet makes a big bend to the right. The waterway splits and narrows around a couple of islands. Stay right around both islands and enjoy a couple of good drops. Note a rock wall along the lowermost island. Pass Quinn Branch on your left at 1.6 miles. Work through another rapid at 1.8 miles, then head under a transmission line at 1.9 miles, in the middle of another rapid. At 2.0 miles, jump over

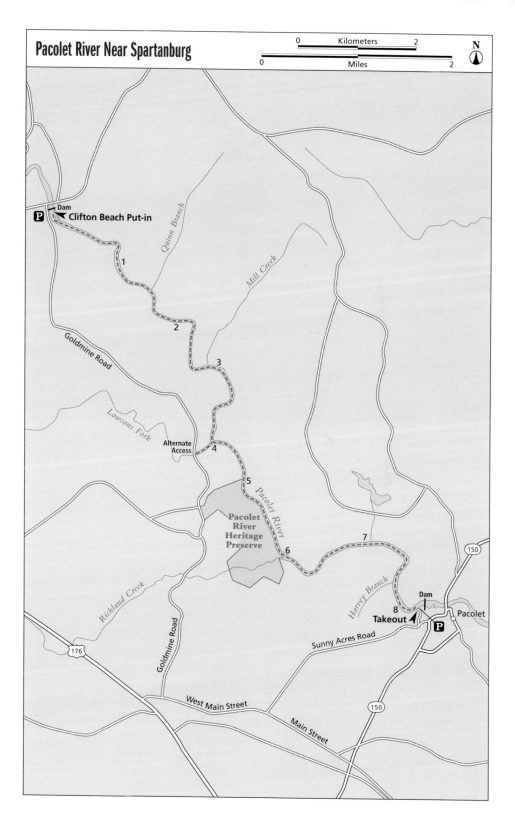

Kilometers

0   2

Miles

0   2

N

Dam
P Clifton Beach Put-in

Quinn Branch

Mill Creek

1

Goldmine Road

2

3

Lawsons Fork

Alternate
Access   4

5

Pacolet
River
Heritage
Preserve

Pacolet River

6

7

150

Richland Creek

Goldmine Road

Harvey Branch

Dam

8
Takeout ▲

P

Pacolet

176

Sunny Acres Road

West Main Street

Main Street

150

Sparkling water, wooded shores, and occasional sandbars await Pacolet River paddlers.

a short, quick Class II drop. Bend left at 2.3 miles, and negotiate another Class II rapid. This one has some large standing rocks in the rapid. Like most rapids on the river, it is a simple straightforward drop; this one is down the middle.

Float beyond a couple of gas-line clearings just ahead. The banks become more heavily forested. At 2.7 miles, make a sharp bend to the left against a wooded bluff. Mill Creek enters on your left at 2.9 miles. Quickly curve to the right. At 3.4 miles, resume a section of shoals that is scattered with rocks. At 3.7 miles, skirt past an island, stay right, and begin the long shoals just above the confluence with Lawsons Fork. This is fun water here.

At 4.0 miles, the Pacolet makes a sharp left bend. A big rock rampart stands on river right just below the confluence; however, stay right and paddle up Lawsons Fork. This section of intimate little stream belies its upstream, challenging rapids. Make your way up 0.25 mile to the bridge at Goldmine Road. This is also an alternate access if you want to avoid the rapids upstream or perhaps only paddle the rapids upstream. Check out the old bridge pilings across Lawsons Fork before backtracking downstream to the Pacolet.

Ahead, pass a sand-dredging operation that may or may not be in operation. The river has widened and the banks lowered. The Pacolet River Heritage Preserve land is on your right. At 5.1 miles, a river-wide rock bar stretches across the river for a Class I rapid. At 6.0 miles, Richland Creek comes in on your right, and this marks the end of the heritage preserve. At 6.2 miles, the river curves left and forms a half-wooded sandbar overlooking a rock outcrop. This is a quiet stretch of blueway. An unnamed stream comes in on river left at 7.1 miles. The Pacolet slows and curves right against a bluff at 7.5 miles. Ahead, signs advise paddlers to avoid the upcoming dam and get on river right. Do such. Make a last bend to the left, passing Harvey Branch. The takeout is ahead on the right. A gravel trail leads to the old Pacolet Mills parking lot, now a paddler's lot.

DEATH ON THE PACOLET

During early June 1903, a warm rain spread over the Pacolet River valley. Farmers welcomed the rains for their crops, because a surefire steamy South Carolina summer was coming. The mills along the Pacolet longed for water, too, for the moving waters of the Pacolet powered their textile mills, where fabrics were spun and then shipped to markets beyond the Palmetto State. The employees of the mills stretched along the river from Converse to Gainesville to Clifton, and on to Pacolet Mills, and for them to work, the mill needed power. The water delivered the power.

Problem was, the rains kept on: one day, two days, three days, four days, and on to five days. But things really got bad on the sixth day. June 6, it was, and somewhere between 7 and 10 inches of rain poured into the Pacolet River valley, overwhelming an already swollen river. A brown torrent of death swept down the valley under cover of darkness, taking people from their homes, sweeping them into the river, bobbing terror-filled citizens screaming for help in their nightclothes. At midnight, the Pacolet was 8 feet above its banks. Four hours later, the river was 20 feet above its banks, an aquatic wall of devastation, crushing the communities built around the riverside mills and the mills themselves. When the waters receded, over eighty people had perished, the worst flood in South Carolina's history.

The Midlands

Cypress trees reflect on the still waters of Lake Cheraw (paddle 24).

7 Catawba River

This tailwater run below Lake Wylie Dam is a fun and regular paddle for Rock Hill and Charlotte residents.

County: York
Start: Fort Mill Access below Wylie Dam
 N35° 1.282' / W81° 0.213'
End: River Park
 N34° 57.358' / W80° 56.969'
Distance: 6.6 miles
Float time: 3.5 hours
Difficulty rating: Easy
Rapids: Class I
River type: Dam-controlled tailwater river
Current: Fast when generating
River gradient: 1.9 feet per mile
River gauge: Duke Energy Water Release Schedule: duke-energy.com/lakes/scheduled-flow-releases.asp. Scroll to find Wylie. Schedules posted 72 hours in advance. USGS gauge:

Catawba River Near Rock Hill, SC; minimum 650 cfs, maximum 6000 cfs
Season: Year-round
Land status: Private/public
Fees or permits: No fees or permits required
Nearest city/town: Rock Hill
Maps: Catawba River Canoe & Kayak Trail Map; Catawba River Canoe Trail; USGS Quadrangle Maps: Lake Wylie, Fort Mill, Rock Hill East
Boats used: Canoes, kayaks, johnboats
Organizations: Catawba River Keepers, catawba riverkeeper.org
Contacts/outfitters: Catawba River Expeditions, (803) 327-9335, catawba-river-expeditions.com

Put-in/Takeout Information

To takeout: From exit 79 on I-77 in Rock Hill, take Dave Lyle Boulevard east through a shopping area and travel 0.7 mile to Red River Road and a traffic light. Turn left on Red River Road and follow it for 0.8 mile to turn right onto Quality Circle. Follow Quality Circle into River Park and dead-end at the takeout and parking area.

To put-in from takeout: Back out of River Park to Red River Road. Turn right (north) on Red River Road and follow it for 2.2 miles to a traffic light and US 21 Business, Cherry Road. Turn right on Cherry Road and follow it 1.3 miles to Sutton Road, crossing the Catawba River en route. Turn left at a traffic light and Sutton Road and follow it 2.0 miles to turn left on New Gray Rock Road. Follow New Gray Rock Road for 1.4 miles to turn left into the Fort Mill Access. Follow the access road a short distance to the put-in address: 2541 New Gray Rock Rd.

Paddle Summary

This is the bread-and-butter float for local residents of Rock Hill, South Carolina, and Charlotte, North Carolina. It is easy to see why: The shuttle is a breeze, the put-in and takeout are easy, and the river makes for a fun float. Of course, the run is better

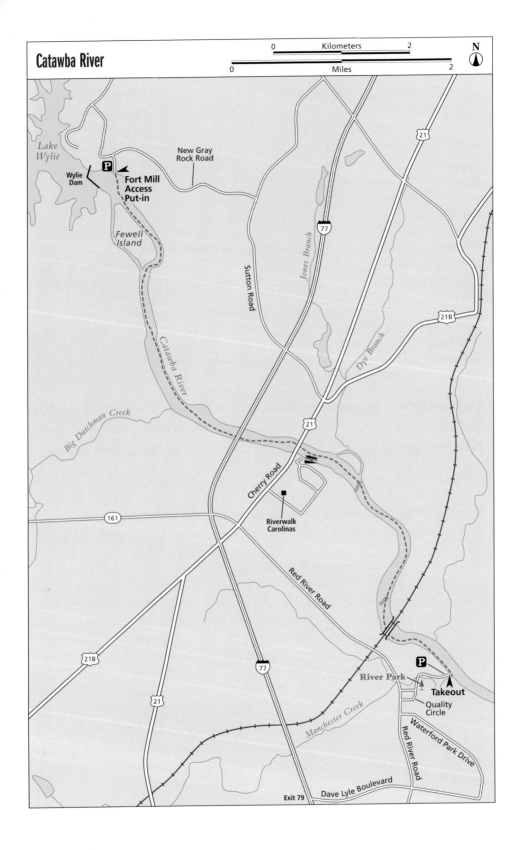

when Duke Energy is generating at the Lake Wylie Dam. You can check the Duke Energy website (listed above) for discharge times, but the power company can and sometimes will change their generation schedule without notice. However, you can check the USGS Catawba River gauge (listed above) to see what the actual flow rate is. It takes about 1.5 hours for the flow to reach the gauge at the US 21 bridge from Wylie Dam. At the lowest flows, the river will be a little rocky and shallow. Anywhere from 2000 to 3600 cfs is good paddling. The river will push you down without the rapids turning crazy. From 3600 to 6000 is considered high water, and the current can be very fast. Above 6,000 cfs, river waves are washed out and paddling is not recommended; it can be quite dangerous if you flip. At normal flows, the few rapids are Class I and pose no hazard.

Start at the large landing below Wylie Dam. The river is quite wide here and has a slough. Just downstream is Fewell Island, home of a Camp Canaan. Either side of the island is passable, though the left side is much wider. Make a southerly cruise and enjoy surprisingly uncivilized banks. The normally hasty current will push you downstream as you pass Big Dutchman Creek, and then under the I-77 and US 21 bridges. Below here on your right is the old Celanese site, where a former mill has

THE SPIDER LILY

The Catawba River is home to one of the most interesting riverside flowers, not only in South Carolina but also in the entire United States. Botanically known as *Hymenocallis coronaria*, it is commonly called the spider lily. It grows along shoals of this river near Landsford Canal State Park, downstream of this paddle, in purportedly the largest numbers anywhere. You can launch from the park and paddle to the flowers, or take the 1.5-mile (round-trip) Canal Trail to an overlook of the flowers. Peak blooming time is May and June. Check the park for bloom times. It does grow elsewhere in the Southeast, in a few select river locations. In Georgia, the spider lily grows on the Broad River, the Savannah River near Augusta, and along the lower Chattahoochee and Flint Rivers. In Alabama, you can find spider lilies along the Cahaba River south of Birmingham, where they are known as Cahaba lilies. With a limited number of plant colonies in the Southeast, the spider lily is susceptible to water pollution, especially siltation and sediment runoff.

Spider lilies are found in open, well-lit rocky shoals of streams and rivers, such as can be found on the Catawba River. The waters must be clean, swift moving, and well oxygenated. America's famous early naturalist William Bartram is credited with first describing the spider lily in 1773, along the Savannah River. "Nothing in vegetable nature is more pleasing than the odoriferous *Pancratium fluitans* (spider lily), which alone possesses the little rocky islets which just appear above the water." Bartram's scientific name was changed, partly due to the sphinx moth, which pollinates the lily on nocturnal flights across the shoals.

Looking out as the swift Catawba bustles downstream below Wylie Dam

been turned into a business and housing park; it includes a boat launch and a greenway. You will then curve with the river, soaking in the scenery. The chilly water coming from the base of Lake Wylie is great for a cold dip on a steamy day, though river stopping spots are limited by the steep banks. The final leg of the trip passes under a railroad bridge, then you reach the takeout on river right, where Manchester Creek joins the Catawba River at River Park. Note that River Park also has a fine set of hiking trails that travel along the river.

River Overview

The 320-mile Catawba River is born high on the Blue Ridge of North Carolina. Some of its mountain tributaries include the famed Linville River, slicing deep into the Linville River Gorge and Wilson Creek, a waterfall-laden, trout-fishing venue draining Grandfather Mountain. However, its lower reaches aren't so wild. In fact, the Catawba is tamed by ten dams, the last of which is Wylie Dam. From the mountains it takes an easterly tack through the foothills before turning southeasterly, making its way through the Charlotte/Gastonia metro complex, reaching Lake Wylie. The river enters South Carolina, where this paddle takes place. It then reaches Lake Wateree, where it arbitrarily becomes the Wateree River, is dammed a final time, then flows 80 miles to meet the Congaree River southeast of Columbia, where the two waters merge to create the Santee River.

The Paddle

Wylie Dam looms large as you embark on your trip. This dam was built in 1924 on the site of a previous dam that was used to power the old cotton mill. The river stretches more than 300 feet in width here. Fewell Island is across from the put-in, just a little downstream. Birdlife is abundant here; look for herons, waterfowl, and osprey feeding near the dam. River birch and sycamore overlook the rushing, clearish-green waters. Light riffles lead you to a bend to the right at 1.0 mile. A bluff rises on river left. There's a little landing near a rock outcrop at the downstream end of the bluff. At 1.1 miles, reach the lower end of Fewell Island. Now the Catawba stretches wide and southbound.

At 2.0 miles, pass under a power line. You are being moved by a light current. At 2.4 miles, pass under another power line. Big Dutchman Creek enters on river right at this point. Ahead, the river splits around a linear island. The largest channel is river right. There's another stopping spot on the lower end of this island. Pass under the I-77 bridge at 3.0 miles, a small river-wide shoal, then under the US 21 bridge at 3.6 miles. Just past here on the right is a boat ramp and hiking trailhead at Riverwalk Carolinas. It's a planned development that includes recreation in its master plan. Riverwalk is located at the old Celanese textile site. My, how times change.

At 4.0 miles, you will encounter the biggest rapid of the trip, a river-wide shoal with a few exposed rocks, bordered by a small island. Note the old cut stones on river right here. The riverbanks remain vegetated, despite the proximity of civilization. Negotiate another rapid at 5.3 miles. At 5.7 miles, drift under the Southern Railroad Bridge and historic Nation Ford, a crossing spot since people have been crossing the Catawba. During the American Revolution and the Civil War, Nation Ford was a point of contention because of its strategic location. The Catawba narrows. Pass one last shoal at 6.0 miles, then get over to river right. Pass along River Park, then reach the River Park takeout at Manchester Creek at 6.6 miles.

8 Lower Pacolet River

Bag two rivers on this run that traces the lowermost Pacolet to meet and follow the Broad River to Lockhart.

County: Cherokee, Union, York, Chester
Start: Skull Shoals Bridge
    N34° 52.410' / W81° 31.900'
End: Lockhart Dam on Broad River
    N34° 47.844' / W81° 27.707'
Distance: 12.1 miles
Float time: 6.5 hours
Difficulty rating: Easy
Rapids: Class I
River type: Small Piedmont river and big Piedmont river
Current: Moderate
River gradient: 2.6 feet per mile
River gauge: Pacolet River near Saratt, SC, minimum runnable level: 4.0 feet, maximum: 10.0 feet

Season: Year-round
Land status: Private
Fees or permits: No fees or permits required
Nearest city/town: Lockhart
Maps: USGS Quadrangle Maps: Kelton, Wilkinsville, Lockhart
Boats used: Canoes, kayaks, johnboats
Organizations: Pacolet River Heritage Preserve, 1000 Assembly St., Columbia, SC 29201, (803) 734-3893, dnr.sc.gov/mlands/managedland?p_id=38
Contacts/outfitters: South Carolina Department of Health and Environmental Control, 2600 Bull St., Columbia, SC 29201, (803) 898-4300, scdhec.gov/environment/water

Put-in/Takeout Information

To takeout: From the intersection of SC 9 and SC 49 on the west side of Lockhart, take SC 9 north toward Jonesville for 0.7 mile to JVL Lockhart Road (there will be a sign for Lockhart School). Turn right on JVL Lockhart Road and follow it for 0.8 mile to an acute left turn for a gravel, waterside parking area. Park here, below the Lockhart Dam. The actual takeout is up the gravel road, past the parking area; no parking allowed there, near the dam, but loading is allowed.

To put-in from takeout: Follow Lockhart Road back to SC 9. Turn right on SC 9 and follow it 1.7 miles to SC 105, Mount Tabor Church Road. Turn right on SC 105 and follow it 6.5 miles to Skull Shoals Bridge. The ramp is on your right after crossing the bridge.

Paddle Summary

Any float where you can rack up two rivers on one trip is a good float. On this one you do—starting with the Pacolet River and the ending your trip on the Broad River. The Pacolet River is a tributary of the Broad. You will start at the eerily named Skull Shoals Bridge. Here, a boat ramp leads to the Pacolet just downstream of a rock said to have the face of a skull in it. You can actually paddle upstream to see this before undertaking your downstream float.

Downriver, the Pacolet flows to make an immediate big bend before assuming a southeasterly direction. Here, the treelined waterway makes for a fun trip, cruising past sandbars and astride woods. There are no big or rocky rapids to worry about. A few miles downstream, the waterway makes a series of sharp curves that provide sandy stopping spots and scenic hills. The waterway then straightens out to meet the Broad River at the intersection of three counties. Here you join the much larger mother stream of the Pacolet. Pass an island that is a favorite stopping spot before the Broad takes you on a few curves of its own.

The shores remain wooded, and eventually you are paddling through water slightly slowed by the Lockhart Dam. The takeout is on dam right. Note you have to carry your boat a short distance to a loading area. Then you will have to retrieve your vehicle a short distance down a gravel road and drive it back to the loading area, then load your vehicle before leaving. This is neither difficult nor complicated, but it is better to know such things before paddle. Do not park in the loading and unloading area—keep goodwill as a paddler.

River Overview

The Pacolet River originates in two branches, one in Polk County, North Carolina, near the community of Tryon, the other in South Carolina. In North Carolina, several tributaries form the North Pacolet River, and it flows southeasterly, entering the Palmetto State near Landrum. The North Pacolet continues its southeasterly journey through Spartanburg County, where it meets the South Pacolet River just as the South Pacolet is released from Lake Bowen. The South Pacolet River begins on the southeastern slopes of Hogback Mountain in Greenville County. It pushes easterly and is slowed in Lake Bowen, then it meets the North Fork to slow in Lake Blalock. The main Pacolet subsequently wanders through foothills and is slowed a few more times with old mill- and hydro dams. This area, along with Lawsons Fork, a major tributary, composes the Pacolet & Lawsons Fork Blueway. The 50-mile river eventually flows free below the town of Pacolet, melds into the Piedmont, then works its way to meet the Broad River 5 miles above the town of Lockhart, where this paddle ends.

The Paddle

Skull Shoals was an early ford where Revolutionary War–era South Carolinians crossed the Pacolet River. Passersby named the shoal after a rock, located near the pilings of the old bridge just upstream of the present-day span, which is said to have a skull shape. You can easily paddle upstream to find the rock. A church and small community were established at Skull Shoals at this important ford. Before bridges, shallow fords like this were important for transportation but also for defensive purposes. Upstream of here, at Grindal Shoals, was another such ford. During the Revolution, American forces camped and held Grindal Shoals before the important Battle of Cowpens.

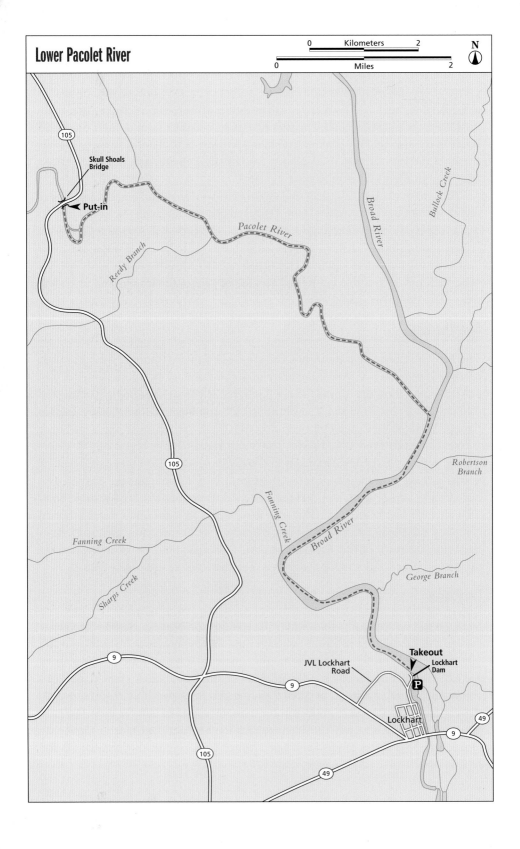

Lower Pacolet River

Kilometers 0 — 2

Miles 0 — 2

N

105

Skull Shoals Bridge

Put-in

Reedy Branch

Pacolet River

Broad River

Bullock Creek

105

Robertson Branch

Fanning Creek

Fanning Creek

Broad River

George Branch

Sharps Creek

9

9

9

49

49

Takeout

Lockhart Dam

JVL Lockhart Road

P

Lockhart

105

49

Kayakers enjoy early spring on the lower Pacolet.

Turn downstream, then join the butterscotch-tinted waterway as it flows past wooded banks, stretching over the stream and forming a partial canopy. Fallen trees extend outward, half in and half out of the water. At this point, the Pacolet spans about 140 feet across, though it narrows on curves, especially at lower water levels when sandbars are present. At 0.3 mile, the Pacolet River splits around an island, with the right channel easily being the larger channel. Just ahead, the river makes a sharp bend to the left as a cedar- and pine-clad hill, dotted with rocks, rises on river right. The riverbanks, mostly clay and/or sand, rise about 8 to 12 feet from the water. Cane thrives in ranks along bottoms. A small creek comes in on river left at 1.7 miles. Come along a bluff at 2.0 miles. The shore is free of civilization, though you do see occasional fields behind the screen of trees. At 2.9 miles, Reedy Branch, the biggest tributary of the Pacolet you will pass, comes in on your right. Just downstream, look along the shoreline on river right and you will see old stone blocks fitted to stabilize the shoreline. Their purpose is lost to time. Keep a southeasterly direction.

At 4.1 miles, the river makes a sharp bend to the right. Here a hill rises on river left, and you will see an open rock slab that makes for a fine stopping spot shaded by cedars. The current is a little fast by the rock slab, so be ready. This is the twisting section of the Pacolet. Another bluff, sprinkled with mountain laurel, rises on your left. The waterway begins curving again at 4.9 miles. Sandbars will be common in this area if you prefer that stopping option. The hills recede by 5.9 miles. At 6.7 miles, shallow sand shoals keep you moving downstream.

At 7.1 miles, meet the Broad River. Here, Cherokee, Union, and York Counties come together. It is probable that the two rivers will have contrasting colorations, depending upon recent rains and dam discharges. The Broad stretches over 200 feet in width. Immediately flow over a riffle, then pass under a power line. Your direction turns from southeast to southwest. At 7.7 miles, Robertson Branch comes in on your left. The tree-covered banks of the Broad rise about 10 feet high. You'll see a few cleared fish camps on the banks. At 8.3 miles, pass over another riffle beside a linear sandy island that is popular with campers and paddlers stopping for lunch. At 9.6 miles, Fanning Creek comes in on your right, just as the river is forced southeast by an impressive hill. Continue curving around a huge bottom. Pass a sand-dredging operation on river right at 10.4 miles; it may be a little noisy here on weekdays. George Branch enters on river left at 11.0 miles. By 11.5 miles, you round a bend and can see Lockhart Dam. Get over to the right bank. Pass under a final big hill. You will see signs indicating the dam ahead and boat takeout on river right at 12.1 miles, ending the paddle. From here, take the path beside the fence separating you from the dam to reach a gravel road. Bring your car here to load your boat.

9 Tyger River

Run this strangely named river where it is ensconced deep in the Sumter National Forest.

County: Union
Start: FR 323
    N34° 38.32' / W81° 41.78'
End: Beattys Bridge
    N34° 35.12' / W81° 35.54'
Distance: 10.5 miles
Float time: 5 hours
Difficulty rating: Easy to moderate
Rapids: Class I
River type: Sandy Piedmont hill-bordered waterway
Current: Fast
River gradient: 3.2 feet per mile
River gauge: Tyger River near Delta, SC, minimum runnable level 220 cfs, maximum 2,000 cfs

Season: Year-round
Land status: Public—national forest
Fees or permits: No fees or permits required
Nearest city/town: Whitmire
Maps: Sumter National Forest Enoree Ranger District; USGS Quadrangle Maps: Whitmire North, Whitmire South
Boats used: Canoes, kayaks
Organizations: Sumter National Forest, Enoree Ranger District, 20 Work Center Rd., Whitmire, SC 29178, (803) 276-4810, www.fs.usda .gov/main/scnfs/
Contacts/outfitters: The Tyger River Foundation, PO Box 171954, Spartanburg, SC 29301, (864) 978-6528, tygerriver.org

Put-in/Takeout Information

To takeout: From Whitmire, take US 176 west to cross the Enoree River. At 2.7 miles, pass Old Buncombe Road. Continue west on US 176 for a total of 6.5 miles from Whitmire, crossing the Tyger River, then turning left to reach the Beattys Bridge boat ramp.

To put-in from takeout: From Beattys Bridge, backtrack on US 176 east for 3.8 miles to turn right on Old Buncombe Road. Follow Old Buncombe Road for 8.6 miles to turn right on paved Minnow Bridge Road, S-44-79. At 1.3 miles, the pavement ends and the road becomes FR 323, then dead-ends in a parking circle 3.6 miles from Old Buncombe Road.

Paddle Summary

This paddling adventure skirts through the hills and bottomlands of the Sumter National Forest, staying within its confines nearly the entire 10.5-mile paddle. The trip appropriately starts at a remote national forest landing a few miles southwest of Union, near Rose Hill Plantation State Historic Site. The Tyger River will flow through flats before careening off steep hills wooded with pine and cedar. Numerous smallish creeks cut gullies, spilling into the butterscotch-tinted waterway with their own clearish flows. Much of the waterway is shallow and sandy. Bigger than its next-door neighbor—the Enoree River—the Tyger River is less subject to blockage from fallen trees, though numerous fallen and partly submerged trunks and limbs are a matter of routine along the Tyger. A swift current will push you along, but there are no rapids as such, no rocks in the river. Ample sandbars provide stopping spots. The variety of vegetation is reflected in the variety of terrain through which the river flows, from densely thicketed swamps to rock and cedar hills.

River Overview

The Tyger River is part of the Santee watershed, draining the heart of the Palmetto State. The name Tyger possibly derives from the German name "Tiekert" but the exact derivation is lost to time. The Tyger, a tributary of the Broad River, is a South Carolina native. It drains foothills just south of the North Carolina state line. Its upper branches start below Glassy Mountain, forming the North, Middle, and South Tyger Rivers. The watershed includes the town of Spartanburg and much of Spartanburg County, as well as eastern Greenville County. Anderson Mill, a 200-year-old structure, stands along the North Tyger on the site of an earlier mill, and it was where Spartanburg County's first court activities took place back in 1785. A few of the Tyger's tributaries are dammed as watershed lakes (for drinking water) in its northern reaches, impoundments such as Lake Robinson, Lymon Lake, and Lake Cooley. Fairforest Creek is a major branch of the Tyger River and merges into the main river during this paddle. The North, South, and Middle Tyger drainages flow southeasterly, melding near the town of Woodruff. Drivers on I-26 cross two branches of the Tyger River in this vicinity.

The full Tyger reaches the northwest edge of the Sumter National Forest. Most of its banks in the national forest are publicly owned, adding camping possibilities to the paddling experience. The river flows on to meet its mother stream—the Broad River—near the community of Herbert.

The Paddle

It is a short carry from a gate at the put-in parking area to the actual river. Here, you will find a riprap bank and a couple of launching spots. Despite the name Minnow Bridge Road, there is no bridge here, just some ruins. The Tyger River is flowing swiftly and begins a long bend. The river at this point is around 100 to 120 feet wide and is bordered by paper birch, willow, and sycamore. You will immediately come to the two signature features of the Tyger River—bluffs on the outsides of river bends and sandbars on the insides of river bends. Ample sandbars allow travelers to stop at their leisure. At higher water levels, these sandy spots will be submerged. Mica interspersed in the sand leaves it glittering in the sun. While floating through the national forest, look for evidence of prescribed burns, especially in the hilly, piney portions of the forest. The bottomlands are not subject to these occasional fires that are set by the forest personnel to maintain a healthy ecosystem.

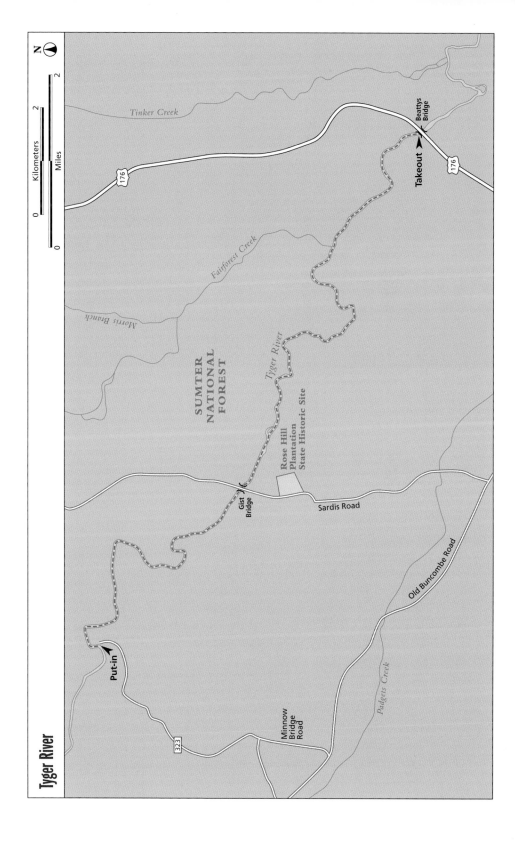

Tyger River

A kayak flotilla turns a bend in the Tyger.

The wide river is sometimes extra shallow, covered only by a thin layer of water atop shifting sands. At 0.4 mile, pass by the stone remains of the old Minnow Bridge. Bluffs continue downstream. Work easterly through a relatively large floodplain to reach a piney bluff at 1.7 miles, Here, the Tyger is forced south through the narrowing flood plain. By 2.4 miles, hills pinch in the Tyger, and it bounces off bluffs. At 2.9 miles, the Tyger makes a huge bend to the right. A narrow high-water channel shortcuts the bottoms around which the main waterway flows. The Tyger straightens out at 3.5 miles. Note the rock outcrops and cedar trees on the sloped terrain. Resume a southeasterly direction, passing under Gist Bridge on Sardis Road. There is a boat ramp on river right, off Sardis Road. Rose Hill Plantation State Historic Site is nearby; it was once the home of South Carolina governor William Gist, from whom the bridge took its name. The 44-acre state park, with its stately antebellum mansion and gardens, is well worth a visit, as is a hiking trail that leads past old slave quarters and down to the Tyger River itself.

At 5.0 miles, the Tyger River emerges from its hilly straitjacket and opens onto a floodplain. At this point, the waterway breaks up into channels between slender tree-and-debris-choked islands. Savvy paddlers will take the correct channels to avoid shallows or obstacle-forming limbs. Despite being in a wide floodplain, the river continues making numerous bends among low swampy banks. A few low hills break up the flats.

At 7.5 miles, the Tyger again breaks up into isles. The bottoms and flats end for good by 8.0 miles. From here out, paddlers will enjoy a single river channel of swift water with a clear route. Hills back the waterway on one side or the other. At 8.7 miles, Fairforest Creek, a substantial tributary with origins up in the town of Spartanburg, comes in on your left.

The river widens below Fairforest Creek and it is an easy float from here on out. A final bluff rises on your left, causing the Tyger to careen right off the rock-studded rise at 10.0 miles. From here, stay on the left bank, passing the remains of the old Beattys Bridge just before you reach the long boat ramp, near the current Beattys Bridge.

REVOLUTION ON THE TYGER: BLACKSTOCK BATTLEFIELD

Blackstock Battlefield is a Revolutionary War site where the British were defeated in 1780 by Thomas Sumter, South Carolina Revolutionary War hero, for whom the town of Sumter, Sumter National Forest, and the famed flashpoint of the Civil War—Fort Sumter—are named.

The preserved battlefield, on the banks of the Tyger River upstream of this paddle, has a hilltop monument overlooking the place where Sumter engaged Banastre Tarleton, British colonel and sworn enemy of Sumter. Today you can visit the battlefield and hike the Palmetto Trail—the state's master path—down from the battlefield to the Tyger River where it meets Hackers Creek.

This 107-acre preserved battlefield was dedicated November 19, 2005, 225 years and one day after the Battle of Blackstock, also known as the Battle of Blackstock's Plantation. On that day, ol' Thomas Sumter, the "Fighting Gamecock," from whom the University of South Carolina got its nickname, led a band of patriots against Banastre "Bloody" Tarleton. Sumter and Tarleton didn't like each other too much and had been battling off and on in the Palmetto State.

Tarleton got Sumter's ire after he decided to burn Sumter's house during one of his sweeps through the state. Sumter then rallied backwoods patriots to fight Tarleton in the Midlands and Upstate, just when many Americans were losing faith in the viability of an American revolution.

Sumter's harassment of Tarleton was the inspiration for his "Gamecock" nickname. Tarleton got the better of Sumter at Fishing Creek. Sumter was planning to attack a British force near the Little River, but he got wind that Tarleton was coming after him. Sumter immediately retreated to muster his force of 1,000 at Blackstock's Plantation, set on high ground and a good place for a defensive stand, with the Tyger River below and some five log houses and a wooden fence from which patriot sharpshooters could fire. Here, Tarleton's 400 British soldiers split and attacked Sumter, but they lost 50 men, compared to the patriots' 3 fatalities. However, Sumter was severely wounded with a shot into his shoulder and was out of commission for three months. Nevertheless, Sumter demonstrated his ragtag militiamen could stand up to the British regulars.

10 Broad River

Unlike many rivers, the Broad is bordered by public lands, Sumter National Forest.

County: Fairfield, Newberry, Union
Start: Sandy River/Broad River confluence
  N34° 34.35' / W81° 25.29'
End: Old Shelton Ferry landing
  N34° 29.31' / W81° 25.47'
Distance: 6.2 miles
Float time: 3 hours
Difficulty rating: Easy
Rapids: Class I
River type: Major waterway
Current: Moderate
River gradient: 3.0 feet per mile
River gauge: Broad River near Carlisle, SC, minimum runnable level: none, maximum: flood stage

Season: Year-round
Land status: Public—national forest
Fees or permits: No fees or permits required
Nearest city/town: Carlisle
Maps: Sumter National Forest Enoree Ranger District; USGS Quadrangle Maps: Carlisle, Blair
Boats used: Canoes, kayaks
Organizations: Sumter National Forest, Enoree Ranger District, 20 Work Center Rd., Whitmire, SC 29178, (803) 276-4810, www.fs.usda .gov/main/scnfs/
Contacts/outfitters: South Carolina Department of Health and Environmental Control, 2600 Bull St., Columbia, SC 29201, (803) 898-4300, scdhec.gov/environment/water

Put-in/Takeout Information

To takeout: From the flashing caution light at the intersection of SC 72/121 and SC 215 in Carlisle, take SC 72/121/215 east for 0.4 mile to Pinkney Street (still in Carlisle). Turn right on Pinkney Street and follow it south as it crosses railroad tracks and becomes Herbert Road. Angle left on Herbert Road and follow it a total of 5.9 miles south from SC 72/121 to St. Lukes Road. Turn right on St. Lukes Road and follow it 2.0 miles to Tyger River Road. Turn left on Tyger River Road and follow it south for 2.4 miles to Dogwalla Road. Turn left on Dogwalla Road and follow it 0.9 mile to veer left on Shelton Ferry Road. Follow Shelton Ferry Road 0.7 mile, when it turns into gravel FR 402. Stay with FR 402 for 1.9 miles to dead-end at the Broad River.

To put-in from takeout: Backtrack from the landing to rejoin Herbert Road where it meets St. Lukes Road. Head north on Herbert Road toward Carlisle. However, at 4.6 miles, before reaching Carlisle, turn right on Edwards Road and follow it 2.0 miles to reach SC 72/121. Turn right on SC 72/121 and follow it for 1.0 mile, crossing over the Broad River to turn right on Store Road (FR 406). Follow gravel Store Road for 1.1 miles, then veer right onto FR 406A and follow it 0.8 mile to dead-end at the landing on Sandy River at its confluence with the Broad.

Paddle Summary

This is a big river paddling experience in a natural setting. You will start this voyage on the Broad River, where a major tributary—the Sandy River—ends its journey.

A stern paddler enjoys the Broad River just above a Class I shoal.

The sometimes-silty Sandy River is but 50 feet wide and merges into the normally clearer and 300-plus-foot-wide Broad River. In places, a swift current flowing over big boulders will keep you moving. Significant hills rise from the bottomlands bordering the Broad. The waterway keeps a southerly course and flows over exposed stony shoals (Class I). Downstream, the waterway splits around islands, most notably Shelton Island. Fast-moving riffles keep the paddling exciting. By the time you reach the south end of Shelton Island, the trip is almost over. Pass under a historic railroad bridge and then find the confluence with the Tyger River. The primitive FR 402 takeout, Shelton Ferry, is just downstream of the Tyger.

A word of caution: Watch out for winds on this wide waterway, and before you leave the takeout, make sure and take note of where it is because the landing is not easy to spot as you are paddling down the Broad River.

River Overview

The Broad River is born on the eastern slopes of the Blue Ridge in North Carolina. It drains these Appalachian highlands easterly, gaining tributaries (namely the whitewater-frothing Green River) and momentum to enter the North Carolina

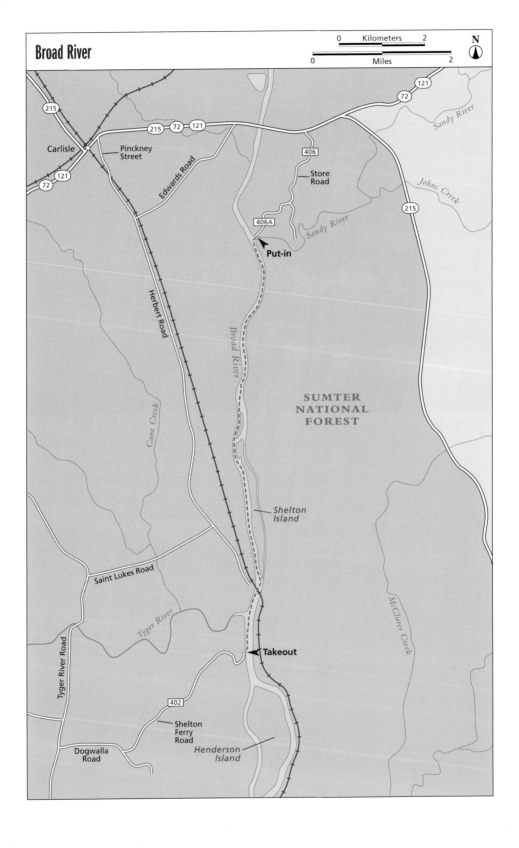

Broad River

Carlisle

Pinckney Street

Edwards Road

Herbert Road

Cane Creek

Store Road

Sandy River

Johns Creek

Put-in

Broad River

SUMTER NATIONAL FOREST

Shelton Island

Saint Lukes Road

Tyger River

Tyger River Road

McClures Creek

Takeout

Shelton Ferry Road

Dogwalla Road

Henderson Island

Kilometers

Miles

N

215

72

121

215

72

121

72

121

406

406A

215

402

foothills. The Broad maintains a stubbornly easterly direction in the Tar Heel State before entering South Carolina in Cherokee County near the town of Gaffney. At Gaffney, it is dammed, then unleashed, and heads south, forming multiple county boundaries.

The Pacolet River, a major South Carolina tributary, feeds the Broad before the Broad enters the Sumter National Forest at Lockhart. From there the Broad keeps a southerly direction through the Sumter until being tamed again at Parr Reservoir. The Broad is once again loosened and heads southeasterly to meet the Saluda River in Columbia. These two waterways meet and form the Congaree River, which flows on as the major tributary of the Santee River watershed.

The Paddle

You are expecting to enter the wide and open Broad River, but the boat ramp at that put-in actually leads to the Sandy River, a 50-foot-wide, silty stream with tall, caned banks. After just a few feet, you will open into the Broad River, itself flowing usually clearer than the Sandy, since the Broad River is impounded upstream, which lets any silt settle. The Broad here is over 300 feet wide, with low but vertical soil banks topped with hardwoods. Hills rise from the floodplain. Since the river is so expansive, you are subject to the sun the entire trip. However, I recommend sticking on one bank or the other; this way you can perhaps get a little shade and see wildlife more handily. This will also shield you from excessive wind. The shoreline is part of the Sumter National Forest, keeping the landscape native.

Your first river-wide riffle comes at 0.3 mile. Here, boulders and underwater rocks cause the waterway to speed. Depending upon the water level, these boulders may be barely underwater but prove easy obstacles to avoid. The wide river allows far-reaching views downstream of distant piney hills.

At 1.5 miles, the river speeds up again. At 2.0 miles, a pine bluff, interspersed with exposed boulders, rises on river left. The waterway narrows with exposed rocks rising from the flowing river. Slide between the exposed rocks, then come to a highlight of the trip: Here, the Broad shoots down a rock-lined Class I shoal. The exposed stone slabs make for fun mid-river stopping spots.

The Broad briefly widens again. At 2.5 miles, the river splits into islands. I recommend heading over to the right, west bank, here. The river speeds as it divides into channels. Just ahead, reach the upper end of Shelton Island, extending for nearly 2 miles in the middle of the waterway. The linear wooded isle is privately owned. Enormous piles of driftwood stand on the banks, relics of higher flows.

At 3.4 miles, come to the first of nearly continuous Class I shoals, harboring a few rocks divided by fast moving shallows. The Broad makes a good float here. Reach the sandy south end of Shelton Island at 5.2 miles.

Just downstream, the Southern Railway crosses the Broad on a high bridge. Note the stonework on the bridge pilings. At this point, get over to the right-hand bank. At 5.6 miles, the Tyger River comes in on your right. The free-flowing Tyger will be siltier than the Broad. Watch as the different-colored waterways flow side by side, eventually melding into one.

At this point be very watchful for the primitive landing at the old Shelton Ferry site. Pass a few cabins on stilts, then reach the Shelton Ferry landing at 6.2 miles, ending the paddle.

CAMPING ON THE BROAD RIVER: WOODS FERRY

The Broad River was an obstacle to travelers of times past. In 1817, Matthew Woods saw an opportunity, acquiring land upstream of this paddle; it is now a campground, Woods Ferry, in Sumter National Forest. Woods constructed a ferry for people, horses, and buggies to cross the truly broad river. During the Civil War, Confederate general Wade Hampton used the ferry while chasing Union general William Sherman during the latter's infamous March to the Sea, which effectively ended the War Between the States.

Later, the terrain, like much of the South Carolina Midlands, was logged and then unsoundly farmed, leading to soil erosion. The US Forest Service took over the depleted lands, managing them for timber and recreation. Bridges replaced the ferry both north and south of the old Woods Ferry at Lockhart and Carlisle. Today, Woods Ferry is a rustic recreation area with a quiet campground, hiking, boating, and fishing.

The campground, open April through October, is situated along a sloping valley beside the Broad River. The valley—moister than the area uplands—flourishes in a forest of pines, oaks, elm, and cedars, with a small understory of trees and bushes. Two camping loops add possibilities. Each loop has a small bathhouse with hot showers. Water spigots are seemingly everywhere in this campground, which rarely—if ever—fills.

Boaters use Woods Ferry occasionally, as do hunters, but overall the place is underused. The Woods Ferry area has a trail system used by hikers, bikers, and horses. Three loops can be made, meandering through floodplain and pine hill forests.

To reach Woods Ferry from Carlisle, cross the bridge over the Broad River, then turn left on SC 25 (Leeds Road), and follow it 2.1 miles; veer left on SC 49, crossing the railroad tracks, and keep on SC 49 for 3.6 miles to SC 574. Turn left on SC 574 and follow it for 3.6 miles to the campground.

11 Enoree River

Explore this intimate waterway that courses through the Sumter National Forest.

County: Union, Newberry
Start: FR 339 Ramp
   N34° 30.85' / W81° 36.82'
End: Brazzlemans Bridge
   N34° 25.31' / W81° 31.08'
Distance: 11.8 miles
Float time: 5 hours
Difficulty rating: Moderate
Rapids: Class I
River type: Sandy Piedmont woods-bound waterway
Current: Fast
River gradient: 2.4 feet per mile
River gauge: Enoree River at Whitmire, SC, minimum runnable level: 300 cfs, maximum: 1,800 cfs
Season: Winter, spring, early summer

Land status: Public—national forest
Fees or permits: No fees or permits required
Nearest city/town: Whitmire
Maps: Sumter National Forest Enoree Ranger District; USGS Quadrangle Maps: Whitmire North, Whitmire South
Boats used: Canoes, kayaks, occasional johnboat
Organizations: Sumter National Forest, Enoree Ranger District, 20 Work Center Rd., Whitmire, SC 29178, (803) 276-4810, www.fs.usda .gov/main/scnfs/
Contacts/outfitters: South Carolina Department of Health and Environmental Control, 2600 Bull St., Columbia, SC 29201, (803) 898-4300, scdhec.gov/environment/water

Put-in/Takeout Information

To takeout: From exit 72 on I-26 near Newberry, take SC 121 east for 5.4 miles to turn right on Old Whitmire Highway (SC 81). Follow Old Whitmire Highway for 0.4 mile to reach US 176. Keep straight, crossing US 176, now on Brazzlemans Bridge Road. Follow Brazzlemans Bridge Road 4.3 miles to cross the Enoree River. The takeout is on your right, after the bridge over the Enoree River.

To put-in from takeout: From Brazzlemans Bridge, continue northeast on Brazzlemans Bridge Road for 3.0 miles to hit a T intersection. Turn left on Maybinton Road and follow it 6.7 miles to turn left on SC 72/121. Follow SC 72/121 for 1.0 mile, turn right on US 176 West and follow it 1.0 mile, then turn left onto Old Buncombe Road. Drive 0.8 mile and then turn left onto paved Lee Cemetery Road. At 0.8 mile, FR 339 angles right as a gravel road. Continue 0.8 mile farther to dead-end at a parking circle and the boat ramp.

Paddle Summary

This paddle takes place within the confines of the Sumter National Forest, which lends it a wild aspect. Even though private inholdings in the national forest reach to the river's edge, the banks are primitive throughout, and you will not see a dwelling the entire trip, making for a continuous encounter with nature. The paddle beginning off FR 339 has a ramp. Despite being less than 2 miles from Whitmire, the Enoree River immediately delivers a wild aura. Heavily wooded banks stretch out below as well as rising to hilly bluffs. Fallen trees crowd the waterway and create obstacles around which to paddle. The river bottom is quite sandy, and you will float over tan sands on speedy riffles. Along the way, two major tributaries—Duncan Creek and Indian Creek—along with numerous other feeder streams, add their flow to the Enoree River.

The current is surprisingly fast throughout, despite there being no typical rapids, rather just a speedy flow. After passing under a railroad bridge and the US 176 bridge near Whitmire, it will be just you and nature heading southeast across a wooded remnant of the Piedmont. The second half of the paddle becomes much more convoluted, as the Enoree twists and turns around bluffs, sometimes breaking up into narrow channels winding between islands. The float ends just beyond Brazzlemans Bridge at a ramp and parking area.

River Overview

The Enoree River is part of the Santee River watershed draining the heart of the Palmetto State. The Enoree itself flows into the Broad River, coming from North Carolina. The Enoree, along with the Broad and the Tyger Rivers, form the big three streams coursing through the Enoree District of the Sumter National Forest. These three rivers and their tributaries form the aquatic veins of this undervalued Piedmont treasure, and all three are worthy paddling options. Preserved Piedmont watersheds are few in the Carolinas.

A historic waterway, the Enoree River is born in the Upstate, north of Paris Mountain above Greenville. Bunched Arrowhead Historic Park stands along its headwaters. The Enoree flows southeast, forming county boundaries nearly its entire length. It passes Musgrove Mill State Historic Site just before entering the national forest near Clinton. The Enoree then makes its run through the Sumter, passing Whitmire before making a final easterly dash to meet the Broad River just above Monticello Reservoir. Over 30 miles of paddling pleasure are available in the Sumter alone.

The Paddle

The put-in is a concrete ramp leading to a sand/mud shore at a sandy riffle. Vertical banks about 8 feet high rise from the water. Overhanging willow, paper birch, sycamore, and musclewood stretch outward from the shoreline. Beard cane grows in thickets in the bottoms. At this point, the toffee-colored Enoree River stretches about 80 feet across and is flowing swiftly over a sandy floor. Fallen dead trees become entrenched in the river, and the current works around them. Almost always, there is a navigable channel between the wooden snag; the width of the waterway prevents most river-wide logjams. At 0.4 mile, pass a water-intake station for the city

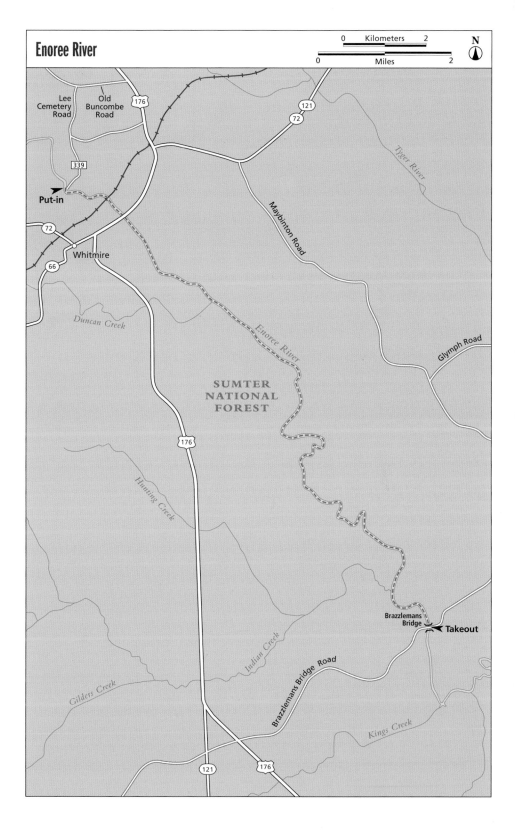

Curving around a sandbar-bordered stretch of the Enoree

of Whitmire, then the CSXT Railroad Bridge at 0.7 mile. Note the cut stone abutments. Pass under a power line just before reaching the Thorp Bridge (US 176) in Whitmire.

Wild woods continue beyond the Thorp Bridge. Resume sliding over shallow sandbars that at lower water levels will narrow the waterway. The exposed sandbars are favorable stopping spots for floaters. Sporadic hills rise from the river's edge as you keep a steady southeast course. At 2.3 miles, pass by some pastureland screened by riverside tree cover on your right. At 2.7 miles, a pine bluff rises. Occasional shoreline rocks are exposed, especially in hilly areas.

At 3.0 miles, Duncan Creek comes in on your right. The broad, shallow tributary widens the Enoree River downstream. Look for signs of beaver in the river—gnawed limbs, chewed-on stumps, and freshly cut green brush. Also, scan for deer in the bottoms; you will see their prints on the sandbars. Bird life is abundant. At 4.0 miles, a rock bluff rises on your right. At 4.6 miles, the river bends and transitions from a linear stream to a convoluted watercourse. Here, the turns in the Enoree also keep you on your guard; look ahead for fallen trees and shallows. Enjoy the next stretch of stream.

At 8.0 miles, the Enoree splits into numerous channels, slicing between teardrop-shaped islands pointing downstream. Go with the strongest channels here to avoid shallows and tree obstacles. At 9.2 miles, a big bluff rises on river left, and the Enoree curves right. Pass a second impressive bluff on river right at 9.5 miles, then enter a large bottomland with overflow swamps stretched out along the shoreline. Indian Creek enters at 10.8 miles on your right. The Enoree squeezes between pine-clad hills on its final stretch. Pass under the remains of the old Brazzlemans Bridge before taking out on river left just beyond the current Brazzlemans Bridge at 11.8 miles, ending the paddle.

BRICK HOUSE CAMPGROUND: PADDLER'S BASE CAMP

Brick House Campground makes an ideal base camp for paddling the Enoree River and other waterways passing through the Enoree District of the Sumter National Forest. It is located within easy driving distance of the Enoree, Tyger, and Broad Rivers. The serene atmosphere and quaint natural setting of Brick House will add to your paddling experience in the South Carolina Piedmont. In addition to paddling, you can also enjoy the Buncombe Trail, a 20-plus-mile network of pathways open to hikers, bikers, and equestrians. The Buncombe trailhead is within walking distance of Brick House.

The campground, open year-round, is set in a loop, where tall pines form the forest canopy. Elms, dogwoods, sweetgums, and other hardwoods grow beneath the taller evergreens. The forest floor is littered with pine needles and pointy sweetgum balls.

There is little brush between campsites, but privacy is not as much of an issue as you would think. Because this campground rarely—if ever—fills, you likely will not have a neighbor next to you. The water spigot has been dismantled, so bring your own water. Come to large, open sites on the outside of the loop. A stone marker for the Youth Conservation Corps, which rehabilitated this campground and the Buncombe Trail, is next to the road.

Notice the white-banded trees near some sites. These are where occasional horse campers can tie their animals. The terrain slopes away from the campground as the loop turns back toward Brick House Road. Some open sites lie on the inside of the loop.

To reach Brick House Campground from exit 60 on I-26 near Clinton, take SC 66 east 3.6 miles to Brick House Road. Turn right on Brick House Road, FR 358, and follow it 0.5 mile to reach the campground, which is on your right. Make sure to purchase a map of the Enoree District of the Sumter National Forest before your arrival, and you will have no problem making your way between Brick House Campground and the nearby rivers, including the Enoree.

12 Little River

This paddle is bordered by national forest lands and is the signature paddle of the Little River Blueway.

County: McCormick
Start: Calhoun Mill
 N34° 1.634' / W82° 28.655'
End: Morrah Bridge
 N33° 58.941' / W82° 26.241'
Distance: 6.4 miles
Float time: 4 hours
Difficulty rating: Easy to moderate
Rapids: Class I
River type: Piedmont creek/lake embayment
Current: Moderate
River gradient: 2.2 feet per mile
River gauge: Little River near Mount Carmel, SC, minimum runnable level: 120 cfs, maximum: 700 cfs

Season: Winter, spring, early summer
Land status: Public—national forest
Fees or permits: No fees or permits required
Nearest city/town: Mount Carmel
Maps: Sumter National Forest Long Cane Ranger District, Little River Blueway; USGS Quadrangle Maps: Calhoun Creek, Willington
Boats used: Canoes, kayaks
Organizations: Sumter National Forest, Long Cane Ranger District, 810 Buncombe St., Edgefield, SC 29924, (803) 637-5396, www.fs.usda.gov/main/scnfs/
Contacts/outfitters: Little River Blueway, littleriverblueway.org

Put-in/Takeout Information

To takeout: From McCormick, take SC 81 north to the hamlet of Willington. In Willington, turn right on Morrah Bridge Road and follow it 2.4 miles to the Morrah Bridge. The landing is on your left after the bridge; parking is on the right.

To put-in from takeout: Backtrack on Morrah Bridge Road to Willington and SC 81. Turn right, north, on SC 81 for 4.0 miles to Mount Carmel and veer right onto SC 823 toward Calhoun Mill. Follow SC 823 east 2.5 miles to the Calhoun Mill Bridge over Little River. Just past the bridge, turn right on FR 536 and follow it 0.4 mile to angle right into a parking area. From the parking area, it is about a 30-yard carry to metal stairs and the Little River.

Paddle Summary

This scenic trip is a highlight of the greater Little River Blueway, a collection of paddling opportunities near Lake Thurmond that also includes streams flowing into the impoundment. This particular paddle travels down the intimate Little River as it courses through the Long Cane District of the Sumter National Forest. The fleet and sandy stream cuts a mini valley through wooded hills before opening and slowing as it joins the impounded waters of Lake Thurmond. Though riverine in nature, the lower part of the Little River is still-water lake paddling. Therefore, you can experience

BAKER CREEK STATE PARK: BLUEWAY BASE CAMP

The official Little River Blueway map declares Baker Creek State Park to be the official base camp for paddling not only the Little River but the other streams and flat-water paddling destinations that add up to over 50 miles of water to explore. (Download the map at littleriverblueway .org.) Baker Creek State Park is a good choice for base camp. It is close to the put-ins and take-outs of the area, and it is near the town of McCormick, where you can obtain supplies.

I have used Baker Creek State Park myself in a paddling capacity. Tent campers prefer Loop 1. The hillside and lakefront camps are inviting. RVs are not allowed in Loop 1, which is set on a peninsula jutting into Lake Thurmond. Pines, oaks, hickories, and sweetgum trees shade the campsites. Dogwoods and cedars are understory trees. Loop 2, with electricity, is popular with the RV set and can be more crowded. This fifty-site camping area is set on the next peninsula over.

Situated on the shores of Lake Thurmond, Baker Creek State Park is a water-oriented destination. Anglers vie for bass, crappie, and catfish. The park has two boat ramps for motor boaters and paddlers. Swimming is popular, and you can do so at your campsite or near the park office, but no lifeguards are provided. The state park also has a 10-mile mountain-bike trail that draws visitors in, especially during spring and fall. Hikers have two short nature trails to walk at Baker Creek.

The whole park (and the whole area) slows down in summer, as it is excessively hot. April and May are the best months to visit, followed by September and October. The park is gated at night for your safety, and rangers reside on-site. Sounds like a pretty good blueway base camp to me.

both small-stream and lake paddling. In winter, and when Lake Thurmond is drawn down, the Little River may flow free the entire paddle.

It's a steep put-in, but the national forest landing is an improvement over the old landing at the Calhoun Mill Bridge. You immediately begin coursing down a narrow, speedy stream dashing over shallow sands and between fallen timbers. The float is scenic throughout, enclosed in the folds of the national forest. High hills force turns in the river, and this is where sandbars form. Eventually, the current will slow, the stream will widen, and you will experience flat-water paddling. Side streams form their own mini embayments, yet sporadic high-water events leave this lower section with sandbars as well.

River Overview

The Little River comes to be southeast of Anderson, at the Anderson County/ Abbeville County line. It begins its journey draining the northwestern reaches of

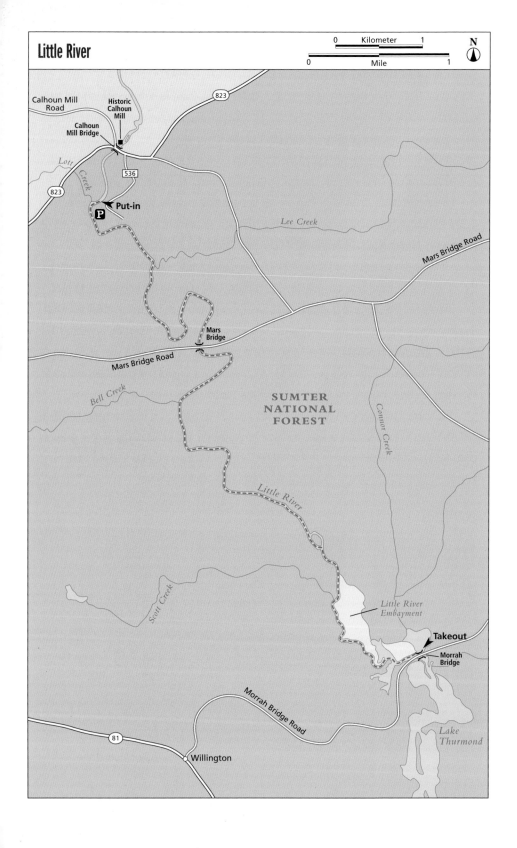

Abbeville County. It takes in a major tributary, McKenley Creek, near the town of Calhoun Falls; Calhoun Falls was a shoal on the Savannah River, now submerged under the waters of Lake Thurmond. The Little River then enters McCormick County, where Calhoun Creek adds significant flow just before reaching Calhoun Mill. The current brick Calhoun Mill building was built in 1854 on a mill site in use since the late 1700s. Wheat, grain, and corn were ground here. The old Calhoun Mill dam can still be seen from the Calhoun Mill Bridge.

From here, the Little River dances through wooded hills before being backed up as Lake Thurmond, forming a long arm of the lake, with several other embayments of tributaries, including paddleable Long Cane Creek. The Little River merges with the now-stilled Savannah River southwest of the town of McCormick.

Sandbars and steep hills characterize the banks of the upper Little River.

The Paddle

This is the highest recommended paddle put-in on the Little River. Summer and fall often find this seasonal stream too low. Make your way down the metal steps of the put-in. Rock outcrops and nearly sheer banks as high as 20 feet shield the paddler from the world beyond the cream-colored Little River. The riverbed is quite sandy and shallow in places. Thick brush and overhanging trees further create a canopy and a near tunnel effect.

Lott Creek comes in on your right just after the put-in. Sycamores, ironwood, and other streamside trees border the waterway. Sandy riffles keep the paddler moving. Fallen logs become embedded in the sand, creating boater obstacles. At 0.8 mile, Lee Creek flows in on your left. At 1.5 miles, the Little River begins a pair of U-shaped bends. The tan-colored sandbars form on the inside of these curves and overlook relatively steep bluffs. Mountain laurel is present on some of the higher bluffs. The setting remains wild as it travels through the corridor completely within the Sumter National Forest. Midstream rocks and boulders contribute to the appealing scenery. Other areas of rocks along the shore were perhaps piled there to keep the Little River somewhat navigable during the state's early days, well before Lake Thurmond's existence.

Float under the Mars Bridge at 2.3 miles. Like many other river bridges, the pilings of a previous, dismantled bridge still stand nearby. A sheer bluff, cloaked with mountain laurel, rises on your left at 2.7 miles. The riverside bluffs cease for a bit. Bell Creek comes in on your right at 3.2 miles.

From here out, the banks are low on one side or the other of the Little River. Keep a southeasterly direction. Depending on the level of Lake Thurmond, the river may or may not be slowing at this point. Sandbars and low brush, along with willow and ash trees, border the slowing water. At 5.1 miles, you will come to your first embayment off the Little River. Scott Creek comes in at 5.3 miles on your right and forms a small embayment of its own. By 5.7 miles, the banks have become low and swampy throughout. Here, the Little River makes a turn to the east. This signals yet another change in environment and enhances your possibilities for seeing wildlife.

Continue coursing through bottomland, passing a final hill on your right before reaching the Morrah Bridge at 6.4 miles. The landing is on the left just before you pass under the bridge.

13 Long Cane Creek

This is a challenging wilderness paddle set within the Sumter National Forest. Mostly stream paddling, it ends with a stretch of flat water on Lake Thurmond.

County: McCormick
Start: Long Cane Bridge (also known as Bradley Bridge)
    N34° 0.855' / W82° 20.646'
End: SC 28 Bridge
    N33° 57.689' / W82° 23.423'
Distance: 6.4 miles
Float time: 4.5 hours
Difficulty rating: Easy to moderate
Rapids: Class I
River type: Woodland wilderness stream
Current: Moderate
River gradient: 2.0 feet per mile
River gauge: No gauge on Long Cane Creek— paddlers can approximate using Little River

near Mount Carmel, SC, minimum runnable level: 150 cfs, maximum: 800 cfs
Season: Winter, spring, early summer
Land status: Public—national forest
Fees or permits: No fees or permits required
Nearest city/town: Troy
Maps: Sumter National Forest Long Cane Ranger District, Little River Blueway; USGS Quadrangle Maps: Verdery, McCormick, Willington
Boats used: Canoes, kayaks
Organizations: Sumter National Forest, Long Cane Ranger District, 810 Buncombe St., Edgefield, SC 29924, (803) 637-5396, www.fs.usda.gov/main/scnfs/
Contacts/outfitters: Little River Blueway, littleriverblueway.org

Put-in/Takeout Information

To takeout: From the intersection of SC 10 and SC 28 west side of McCormick, take SC 28 west for 5.1 miles to the SC 28 boat ramp on your right, just before the bridge over the Long Cane Creek embayment of Lake Thurmond.

To put-in from takeout: Backtrack toward McCormick for 1.3 miles, then turn left on Kennedy Road, just across from the Buffalo Baptist Church. Follow Kennedy Road for 4.1 miles to meet SC 10. Turn left on SC 10 and follow it 2.4 miles to a four-way intersection in the hamlet of Troy. Turn left on Main Street in Troy and follow Main as it soon becomes Greenwood, then Church Street. After 0.4 mile, veer right onto Puckett Town Road. Follow Puckett Town Road for 1.6 miles, then turn left on McWood Road. Follow McWood Road for 0.9 mile to reach Long Cane Road. Turn right on Long Cane Road and follow it 1.2 miles to the high bridge over Long Cane Creek. Park on your left before crossing the bridge.

Paddle Summary

This is a fine yet potentially challenging paddle. It is not because of big rapids or rough roads connecting put-in and takeout points, but rather potentially numerous fallen trees across the stream. Another problem is not having a gauge on Long Cane

Creek. However, before you say, "Not for me," how does it sound to explore pictur-esque national-forest beauty combined with solitude in one of the Sumter National Forest's most alluring watersheds, which includes the Long Cane Scenic Area? At the proper water levels, this can be a great adventure not only in the flowing upper sec-tions but also the Long Cane Creek embayment of Lake Thurmond. Luckily, there is a way to approximate the flow rate of Long Cane Creek. Simply check the gauge of the next stream to the west—the Little River. If the Little River gauge is at 150 cfs or higher, then it is likely that Long Cane Creek will be paddleable as well.

Start your trip at the Long Cane Bridge, near the historic Long Cane Church. It is a long way down a grassy bank to the water. You immediately join a serpentine stream slicing through hilly terrain and rich bottomland. Rock outcrops both in and above the water add charming value. Paddle under the remote Patterson Bridge, continuing into Sumter National Forest, deep with vegetation. Undoubtedly, a few trees will block your passage. Go light in your boat, making for easier pullovers. The shallow, sandy stream is fun if you like steering trials. Toward the end, the hills open to the Long Cane Creek embayment. The stream slows amid willow thickets that alternate with wooded hills. The embayment winds west, and you have a final mile of open-water paddling to reach the SC 28 ramp, also used by fishermen in motorboats.

River Overview

Long Cane Creek is one paddle of the greater Little River Blueway, located near the town of McCormick. The blueway is a collection of still-water and moving-water paddling destinations on Lake Thurmond and its Palmetto State tributaries; you can download the Little River Blueway map at littleriverblueway.org. Long Cane Creek starts near the town of Donalds, just inside the Abbeville County line. It flows just a short distance, then forms the Greenwood County/Abbeville County line. The stream keeps south, passing east of Abbeville, where it enters Sumter National Forest. The Long Cane Creek Scenic Area, home of the world's second-largest shagbark hickory (It has an 11-foot circumference!) is encountered. The stream then picks up significant inflow from Big Curtail Creek. A few miles and a few tributaries later, Long Cane Creek passes under Long Cane Bridge, the beginning of this paddle. The waterway then flows through pure public wildlands before being slowed by the backwaters of Lake Thurmond, forming the Long Cane Creek embayment. Long Cane Creek soon meets its mother stream, Little River, before the Little flows into the Savannah River.

The Paddle

Launch from a small sandbar on the bank of the toffee-tinted water. There was once a historic covered bridge here, but it burned in 1977. A modern bridge spans the creek at this point. River birch and sycamore overhang the 20-foot-wide waterway, which is interspersed with exposed rocks. The banks, around 8 to 12 feet high, are naturally dotted with cane, lending a name to the sand-bottomed creek. Notice how

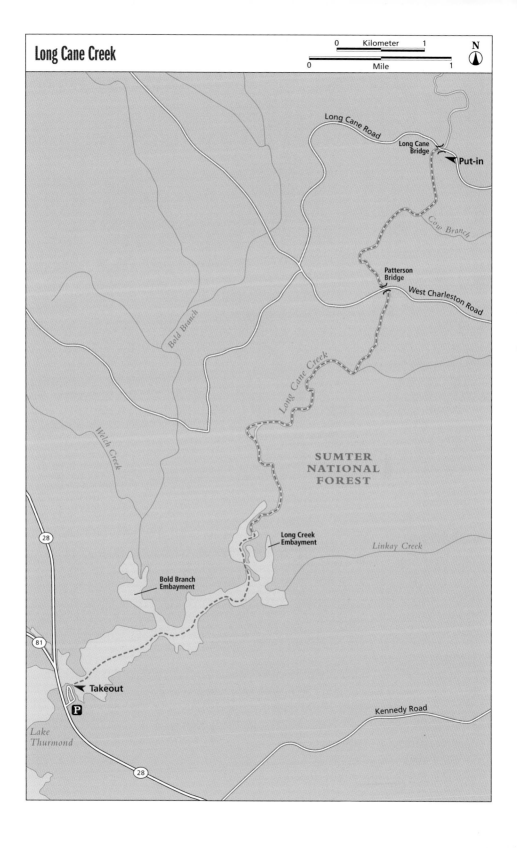

Long Cane Creek

0 Kilometer 1

0 Mile 1

N

Long Cane Road

Long Cane Bridge

Put-in

Cow Branch

Patterson Bridge

West Charleston Road

Bold Branch

Long Cane Creek

SUMTER NATIONAL FOREST

Welch Creek

Linkay Creek

28

Long Creek Embayment

Bold Branch Embayment

81

Takeout

P

Lake Thurmond

Kennedy Road

28

Long Cane Creek presents a wild corridor through which to paddle.

the waterside trees are bent downstream from high-water events. Cedars and pines rise from the hills, while hardwoods cover the bottomlands. The stream is canopied more often than not. Moss grows along the water where the shoreline faces north.

At 0.6 mile, Cow Branch comes in on your left. Long Cane Creek continues its southward journey. Shallow sand shoals keep you moving, but you will be slowed by fallen trees, such as huge loblolly pines astride the waterway. Savvy paddlers will have no problem pulling over or around the blowdowns. The key is to be patient and move slowly and methodically when approaching a fallen tree.

At 1.2 miles, Long Cane Creek makes a bend to the left, but, at higher flows, a channel also goes straight, forming an island. The channels rejoin downstream, make a few bends, then come to Patterson Bridge at 1.5 miles. The Patterson Bridge put-in is on river left as you float downstream.

At 2.2 miles, an unnamed stream comes in on your left. It is up this branch that the Long Cane Massacre grave is located. In 1760, 150 area residents fleeing from Cherokee Indians to Augusta were caught. A battle ensued, and 23 settlers were killed and then buried in a single grave. At 2.3 miles, a big bluff rises on your left. Sandbars continue to increase in size. Long Cane Creek persists, bouncing off hills. At 3.0 miles, the creek splits around an island. More islands appear ahead, and the lake effect slows the current. At 3.7 miles, the old pilings of a bridge appear on river right.

The stream morphs into a serpentine lake embayment bordered by willows. Fallen trees no longer pose a challenge. At 5.0 miles, the Linkay Creek embayment stretches out to your left. At 5.6 miles, the main embayment narrows and squeezes between piney hills. The SC 28 bridge comes into view as you pass the Bold Branch embayment on your right. Now it is an open-water paddle to the SC 28 boat ramp that you reach at 6.4 miles.

LONG CANE SCENIC AREA

Long Cane Scenic Area is located in the Sumter National Forest, upstream of this paddle, and offers a chance to explore the upper Long Cane valley as well. The Long Cane Trail starts at Parson Mountain Recreation Area, undulating among piney ridges and hardwood bottomlands. The area is home to wildflowers aplenty and South Carolina's champion shagbark hickory. The trail is shared by hikers, bikers, and equestrians.

It is 2.2 miles to Long Cane Creek, then the trail passes over a historic iron bridge to reach the scenic area. Here, you will find the big shagbark hickories. If you continue the trail, it follows the Old Charleston Road, which once connected the port city to the Upstate. Beyond here, the Long Cane Trail continues a huge 20-plus-mile loop.

If you aren't into hiking, consider a stay at Parsons Mountain Recreation Area, where the Long Cane Trail begins. It offers boating, swimming, and fishing, along with an excellent campground in a rustic and well-kept setting.

The roots of the recreation area were planted decades ago, when the Civilian Conservation Corps dammed Mountain Creek and developed the resulting shoreline, including the campground. The historic part of the recreation area, including the stonework, was left intact even after the area was modernized. Sweetgum, dogwood, pine, cedar, and elm compose the twenty-three-site campground forest.

The size keeps the campground generally quiet, but it's not so small that it fills too quickly. However, Parson's Mountain does fill on ideal spring and early summer weekends. At 28 acres, Parson's Mountain Lake is also just the right size. No gas motors are allowed, and paddlers will be pleased to know that the lake has a boat ramp. The primary day-use area has a designated swim beach and a large picnic shelter.

To reach the campground from the SC 28 boat ramp on this paddle, follow SC 28 west toward Abbeville to Parson's Mountain Road. Turn left on Parson's Mountain Road, and follow it 1.4 miles to FR 514. Turn right on FR 514, and follow it 0.8 mile to the recreation area.

14 Turkey Creek/Stevens Creek

This is simply one of the most beautiful trips in the Palmetto State. Paddle a clear stream interspersed with lively shoals under the canopy of huge cypress and sycamore trees of the Sumter National Forest.

County: Edgefield, McCormick
Start: Key Bridge
  N33° 47.671' / W82° 8.784'
End: SC 23 Bridge
  N33° 43.784' / W82° 10.960'
Distance: 7.8 miles
Float time: 4.5 hours
Difficulty rating: Moderate
Rapids: Class I+
River type: Wilderness stream with some rapids
Current: Moderate
River gradient: 1.3 feet per mile
River gauge: Stevens Creek near Modoc, SC, minimum runnable level: 120 cfs, maximum: 750 cfs

Season: Winter through early summer and following summer storms
Land status: Public—national forest
Fees or permits: No fees or permits required
Nearest city/town: Parksville
Maps: Sumter National Forest Long Cane Ranger District; USGS Quadrangle Maps: Parksville, Clarks Hill
Boats used: Canoes, kayaks
Organizations: Sumter National Forest, Long Cane Ranger District, 810 Buncombe St., Edgefield, SC 29924, (803) 637-5396, www.fs.usda.gov/main/scnfs/
Contacts/outfitters: South Carolina Department of Health and Environmental Control, 2600 Bull St., Columbia, SC 29201, (803) 898-4300, scdhec.gov/environment/water

Put-in/Takeout Information

To takeout: From the flashing yellow light in Parksville, take US 221 South/SC 28 East for 4.0 miles to Modoc and SC 23. Turn left on SC 23 and follow it for 1.3 miles to the parking area on your left, about 80 yards before the bridge over Stevens Creek. Alternate directions: From the town square in Edgefield, take SC 23 west for 16.5 miles to the takeout parking, which is on your right, after the bridge over Stevens Creek.

To put-in from takeout: Drive east on SC 23 and follow it over Stevens Creek bridge for 2.5 miles to Cold Springs Road. Turn left on Cold Springs Road and follow it 2.8 miles to Key Road. Turn left on Key Road and follow it 3.0 miles to FR 614, just before the bridge over Turkey Creek. Follow FR 614 left for 0.25 mile, where it reaches a parking area and trailhead. A short road splits left from this parking area and soon dead-ends. Park here; a trail leads down to metal steps and a gravel bar launch on Turkey Creek.

Paddle Summary

This is simply one of the finest paddles around. Set in the Sumter National Forest, Turkey Creek and Stevens Creek flow through hilly terrain from which grow incredible forests, including huge streamside cypresses with their queer knees. Rock outcrops not only add to the landscape but they also provide surprisingly fun Class I+ rapids to shoot. Impressive hills and bluffs rise from the waterways in contrast to the thickly vegetated bottomlands. The clear waters reveal gravel stream bottoms and submerged trees that add paddling challenges. Numerous tributaries contribute their flow and often form little noisy waterfalls as they meet the main streams.

You will start out below the historic Key Bridge, now a trail bridge, on Turkey Creek (the current Key Bridge is just upstream of the historic Key Bridge). The slender watercourse snakes its way south, passing bluffs and flowing over rocky shoals. A little less than halfway through the trip, you will float into larger Stevens Creek, doubling the fun and scenery. The huge cypresses continue to impress, and frequent shoals keep the paddling interesting. The national forest shoreline delivers eye-pleasing Carolina woodland wonder. All too soon you are at the SC 23 Bridge and a steep takeout marked with a metal stairway. From there, you have to tote your boat to the road. However, you will agree that this takeout was more than worth the paddling trip that I consider one of the finest in the Southeast, much less the Palmetto State.

River Overview

Turkey Creek is a tributary of Stevens Creek. Turkey Creek and its feeder streams are formed southwest of the town of Saluda, primarily draining the eastern edge of Edgefield County. The two primary tributaries (with interesting names by the way) that together form Stevens Creek—Hard Labor Creek and Cuffytown Creek—flow south from the town of Greenwood. Much of the Stevens Creek watershed is within the Long Cane District of the Sumter National Forest. These wooded waterways result in a relatively clear stream that is Stevens Creek.

Turkey Creek becomes paddleable 4 miles above Key Bridge at the SC 283 Bridge. Then comes this 7.8-mile section to the SC 23 Bridge, during which Turkey Creek ends its journey and joins Stevens Creek. Below this, Stevens Creek continues southeast, partly in the national forest, with limited public access, then flows into the Savannah River just above the Stevens Creek Dam near North Augusta, South Carolina.

The Paddle

Leave the landing below historic Key Bridge. Turkey Creek is about 30 to 40 feet wide, flowing clear over a rock and gravel bottom. You will immediately notice the regal cypress trees bordering the waterway. These aren't the only huge trees; syca-mores also reach mammoth proportions along high, steep banks. Experience the beauty great and small, notably mussel shells in the water and waterside flowers in the warm season.

Sidle alongside the first big bluff after 0.25 mile. Many more are to come. At 0.6 mile, Turkey Creek makes a sharp U-shaped bend to the right, turned by a high

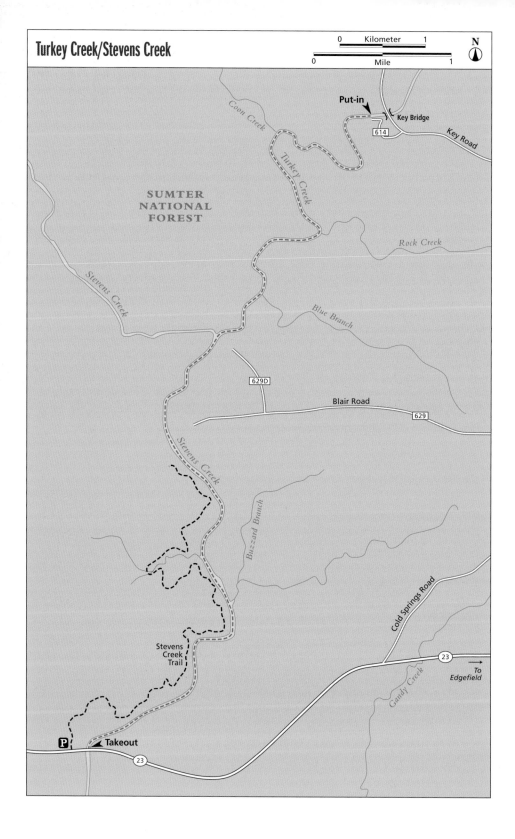

Turkey Creek/Stevens Creek

Coon Creek

Put-in

Key Bridge

614

Key Road

Turkey Creek

SUMTER
NATIONAL
FOREST

Rock Creek

Stevens Creek

Blue Branch

629D

Blair Road

629

Stevens Creek

Buzzard Branch

Cold Springs Road

23

To
Edgefield

Gandy Creek

Stevens
Creek
Trail

P   Takeout

23

Rapids like this add spice to paddling Turkey Creek.

bluff scattered with mountain laurel. At 1.0 mile, float through your first rocky shoal, dropping about 1.5 feet. A short straight drop occurs at 1.2 miles. Coon Creek comes in on your right at 1.4 miles. At 1.6 miles, pick your way across a stream-wide rock riffle. Wide-reaching limbs canopy the waterway; combined with the high banks, they leave you feeling as if you're in a mini canyon. Expect to work over one or two downed trees in Turkey Creek. Rock Creek flows in on your left at 2.2 miles. At this point Turkey Creek is making a big bend to the right and presents a sizeable sandbar.

At 3.1 miles, Blue Branch enters on the left. There is a rocky rapid here. At 3.6 miles, Turkey Creek meets its mother stream, Stevens Creek, which is wider. There is a rough access on river left just as Turkey Creek meets Stevens Creek. Downstream, Stevens Creek doubles in width and slows in a big pool. At 4.2 miles, riffles and drops resume. You dance among stream-wide upturned bluish rocks. At 4.6 miles, pass another shoal and some long rocky riffles. Slow into another pool, floating over submerged rocks. Cypresses continue, sporting their strange knees.

At 5.8 miles, Stevens Creek divides around an island. The right channel is clearly wider. Get ready for a pair of rocky drops at the tail end of the island. At 6.1 miles, Buzzard Branch flows in on your left. At 6.3 miles, curve right past the highest bluff on the paddle. Rocks line the shore at the bluff base. The stream narrows and keeps south-west, flowing over submerged stones. At 7.8 miles, watch for the old SC 23 Bridge pilings and get to the right side of the creek. Ahead, you will see the current bridge. As you reach the metal steps leading from the creek, take out and end the paddle.

HIKE, BIKE, AND PADDLE STEVENS CREEK

The Stevens Creek Trail starts at the takeout for this paddle on SC 23. This well-maintained path, open to hikers and mountain bikers, travels the steep bluffs and rich bottomlands of Stevens Creek and steep-sided valleys that feed Stevens Creek. Perhaps its most noteworthy feature is the size and preponderance of jack-in-the-pulpit wildflowers, which grow in this valley like I have never seen anywhere else.

Jack-in-the-pulpits are normally green to whitish, and sometimes adorned with stripes, making them much less showy than other colorful wildflowers. However, once you notice them, they are everywhere, blooming in numbers that will stagger. Its prime bloom time here in Stevens Creek is mid-April to mid-May. "Jack" is the nodule that sits in the middle of the pulpit, which is called a spathe. The actual wildflower is inside the pulpit, clustered at "Jack's" base. These wildflowers sometimes will have a carrion-like odor, indicating they are pollinated by flies.

Leave the parking area and immediately enter rich hardwoods of white oak, sugar maple, and beech above a ferny forest floor. Cross the first of many wooden bridges that span feeder branches. The trail winds around to minimize trail gradients. All these meanderings can be explained by the trail's increased popularity with mountain bikers, though the path is still well used by hikers.

At 2.1 miles, reach a junction. Here, a spur trail leads left, uphill to an alternative parking area on FR 632. The Stevens Creek Trail leaves the junction and works onto the side of a sheer bluff. You can look through the trees below to see tan sandbars and rocky riffles.

At 3.6 miles, the trail turns west and climbs onto a pine-dominated ridge that is mixed with a few cedars. At this point, the path reaches its highest elevation, just above 300 feet. Descend to the largest expanse of bottomland yet. This is good deer country; you may see a deer here in early morning or late evening.

Work back onto another sheer bluff. Stevens Creek can be seen below, rushing over rapids. Leave the bluff and wind amid more hollows before reaching the Stevens Creek Trail's official end at private property at 5.6 miles. This is a good place to turn around and retrace your steps to the trailhead, combining a hike with your paddle.

15 Rapids of the Savannah River

Navigate the fun shoals of the Savannah River as it descends the fall line near North Augusta.

County: Edgefield, Aiken
Start: Savannah Rapids Park
  N33° 32.876' / W82° 2.221'
End: North Augusta Boat Ramp
  N33° 29.638' / W81° 59.416'
Distance: 5.4 miles
Float time: 3 hours
Difficulty rating: Moderate
Rapids: Class I–II at normal flows
River type: Dam-controlled big river
Current: Moderate to swift
River gradient: 6.9 feet per mile
River gauge: Savannah River at Augusta, GA, minimum runnable level: 5,000 cfs, maximum runnable level: 15,000 cfs
Season: Mar through Nov

Land status: Private, some park and preserve land
Fees or permits: No fees or permits required
Nearest city/town: North Augusta
Maps: USGS Quadrangle Maps: Martinez, North Augusta, Augusta East
Boats used: Kayaks, canoes until below fall line, then motorboats also
Organizations: Savannah Riverkeeper, Inc., PO Box 14908, Augusta, GA 30909, (877) SRK-7711, savannahriverkeeper.org
Contacts/outfitters: Savannah Rapids Kayak Rental, Savannah Rapids Park, Martinez, GA 30907, (706) 832-5323, kayakaugustacanal.com

Put-in/Takeout Information

To takeout: From exit 1 on I-20 in North Augusta, take SC 230 south for 2.4 miles to Hammond Avenue. Turn right on Hammond Avenue and follow it 0.4 mile to turn left on West Woodlawn; follow it for 0.2 mile. Turn right on Fairfield Avenue to enter Riverview Park. Keep straight for 0.5 mile until you reach a traffic circle and the park's activities center. Veer left from the traffic circle and shortly reach Hammond Ferry Road. Turn right here and follow it to dead-end at the North Augusta Boat Ramp.

To put-in from takeout: Backtrack on Hammond Ferry Road to the first intersection. Turn right on Georgetown Road and follow it a few hundred feet, then turn right on Buena Vista Avenue and follow it for 0.8 mile to Georgia Avenue. Turn right on Georgia Avenue, cross the river, and follow Georgia Avenue 0.8 mile into Georgia to turn right on Reynolds Street (GA 104 West). Follow GA 104 west as it becomes Riverwatch Parkway. Drive for 6.1 miles on Riverwatch Parkway, then turn right on Stevens Creek Road and follow it 2.1 miles to Evans-to-Locks Road. Turn right on Evans-to-Locks Road and follow it 1.0 mile to enter Savannah Rapids Park. From here, follow the one-way loop road to the unloading spot near the Augusta Canal. Do not put in the canal, but carry your craft over the pedestrian bridge spanning the canal, then proceed down steps to a floating dock on the Savannah River.

Paddle Summary

This aquatic adventure slaloms through the fun rapids of the Savannah River as the big river dips off the fall line near North Augusta, South Carolina. Of course, the Savannah River forms the boundary of South Carolina and Georgia. You will start on the Georgia side at Savannah Rapids Park, one of the finest preserves in the region. Here, you can launch your craft on the big Savannah or the paralleling Augusta Canal (not detailed here). Our trip joins the rocky Savannah and immediately begins a fun excursion through moderate shoals to pass under the I-20 Bridge. From there, bluffs rise on the South Carolina side of the waterway, including the protected Savannah River Bluffs Heritage Preserve. More rapids lie ahead, including a long stretch of Class I–II rapids. On the far left at the base of this rapid set lies Hammond Rapid, a borderline Class III shoal that can be avoided by staying away from the far left shore. Beyond this final set of rapids, the Savannah River is below the fall line. From here, make an easy cruise to North Augusta Boat Landing and Riverview Park, a large developed park on the Palmetto State side of the river. Both these parks have trails. A bike shuttle can easily be made using almost all greenways and a road crossing of the Savannah River.

River Overview

The Savannah River is one of South Carolina's biggest waterways. Born at the confluence of two large rivers, the Tugaloo and the Seneca, which themselves drain the mountains north of them, the Savannah then flows southeasterly, forming the boundary between South Carolina and Georgia for its entire distance. Much of the upper river is dammed as Richard B. Russell Lake and also Lake Thurmond. Finally released from bondage, the Savannah flows through the towns of North Augusta and Augusta. Downstream the Savannah morphs into a surprisingly remote big river. Finally, as it nears the town of Savannah, tidal influence slows the river, and it enters the Atlantic Ocean.

The Paddle

There is a paddler put-in on the Augusta Canal that does not access the Savannah River. Instead, head over the pedestrian bridge connecting to the Levee Trail. Stairs lead down to a landing on the much larger Savannah River. The waterway is a good 500 to 600 feet across, and rocky rapids begin just below the put in. This initial set of shoals is mild and easy and is a good warm-up run. This area is known as Ninety Nine Islands. A V-shaped dam and the Augusta Canal headgates are upstream. Begin picking your way through the mix of islets and shoals. The rapids are mostly Class I with a few rocks thrown in, and they extend river wide. At higher flows, there will be more pure water surge and less stony segments. The state of Georgia rises to the right of the clear river, and South Carolina is on your left. Spider lilies can be found among the rocks. A quarry-turned-dump mars the Georgia side of the river.

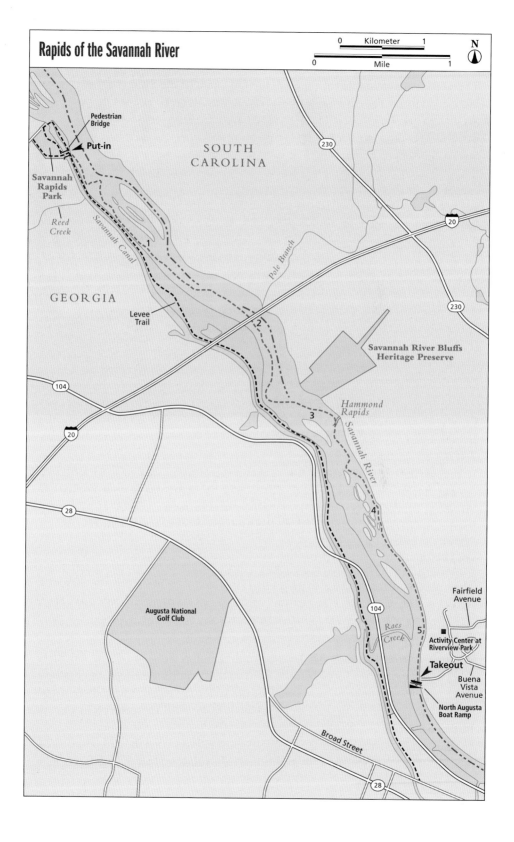

Rapids of the Savannah River

SOUTH
CAROLINA

Pedestrian
Bridge
Put-in

Savannah
Rapids
Park

Reed
Creek

Savannah Canal

GEORGIA

Levee
Trail

230

20

230

Pole Branch

Savannah River Bluffs
Heritage Preserve

Hammond
Rapids

Savannah River

104

20

28

Augusta National
Golf Club

104

Raes
Creek

Fairfield
Avenue

Activity Center at
Riverview Park

Takeout

Buena
Vista
Avenue

North Augusta
Boat Ramp

Broad Street

28

1

2

3

4

5

A gnarled tree stands guard over rapids of the Savannah River.

You are through the first set of rapids after 0.5 mile. However, now the river divides into a series of channels moving between long linear islands, allowing for numerous route possibilities. The I-20 Bridge looms in the distance. Nearby, aquatic vegetation sways in the current, while boulders and sand form a still contrast on the river bottom. The water keeps moving through stony shallows upstream of the interstate bridge. At 1.0 miles, the linear isles are behind you. The Savannah flows as one wide sheet. Agricultural fields stand to your left.

Pass under the I-20 Bridge at 2.0 miles. Wooded bluffs scattered with houses rise on the South Carolina side of the river. More rapids and rocky isles stand in the Savannah. While having fun running these shoals, you will likely miss Savannah River Bluffs Heritage Preserve, a South Carolina flora-and-fauna sanctuary of 83 acres with 1,076 feet of riverfront. A hiking trail runs through the preserve and can deliver a different perspective of the waterway below. You will see a sign for the preserve while driving to the takeout from I-20. The preserve is just off Plantation Road.

Meanwhile, on the Savannah River, the rapids and isles continue almost unabated. Not all of the exposed rock is naked; however, some mid-river islands are fully

A grassy area near the Levee Trail overlooks the wide Savannah River.

vegetated with brush and trees that, undoubtedly, are periodically inundated. Conversely, at low water, the river can seem nothing but a minefield of rocks.

At 2.5 miles, you will see a clearing, a restroom, and the Levee Trail on your right. This makes for a convenient break spot. The river is so wide at this point that if you are on one side of it, you will not be able to utilize, appreciate, or enjoy whatever is on the other side. The shoals fall like stair steps beyond the clearing and are Class I–II. If you do not want to go down the most difficult rapid, Hammond Rapids, stay away from the far-left shoreline while descending. Instead, pick your way down another route. Do not be afraid to stop and scout, though as long as there is enough water, a paddler of moderate skills will be able to get through here—and have fun doing it.

Islands and shoals continue. The wide river and different water levels could allow a different route every trip. At 3.8 miles on river right, you will see the big brick building of the old Augusta Waterworks. The rapids cease by 4.0 miles; you are now officially below the fall line. Like Columbia and other cities, Augusta came to be on the fall line for two reasons: It was as far upstream as boat traffic could travel from the ocean due to rapids, and secondly, those very rapids could be harnessed for industrial uses.

By 4.7 miles, you have passed the last of the islands. The Savannah is one channel again. The current slows, and the absence of rocks and rapids allows boats of every stripe—from pontoons to jet skis—to ply the Savannah. Suddenly, self-propelled paddlers are in the minority. Raes Creek comes in on your right at 5.1 miles. Ahead, you will see the fishing pier and floating dock of the North Augusta boat ramp. Paddle over to river left and takeout at 5.4 miles. The ramp has two launches, but it can be busy on weekends.

16 Savannah River

Paddle a big river bordered with wild banks.

County: Barnwell, Allendale
Start: Stony Bluff Landing
N33° 2' 34.6" / W81° 33' 23.0"
End: Burtons Ferry Landing on US 301
N32° 56' 11.4" / W81° 30' 15.8"
Distance: 14.0 miles
Float time: 6 hours
Difficulty rating: Easy
Rapids: Class I
River type: Dam controlled big river
Current: Moderate to swift
River gradient: 0.8 feet per mile
River gauge: Savannah River at Burtons Ferry Branch near Millhaven, GA, no minimum runnable level, maximum runnable level flood stage

Season: Mar through Nov
Land status: Private, some government land also
Fees or permits: No fees or permits required
Nearest city/town: Allendale
Maps: USGS Quadrangle Maps: Millett, Martin, Burtons Ferry Landing, Bull Pond
Boats used: Powerboats, johnboats, canoes, kayaks
Organizations: Savannah Riverkeeper, Inc., PO Box 14908, Augusta, GA 30909, (877) SRK-7711, savannahriverkeeper.org
Contacts/outfitters: South Carolina Department of Health and Environmental Control, 2600 Bull St., Columbia, SC 29201, (803) 898-4300, scdhec.gov/environment/water

Put-in/Takeout Information

To takeout: From Allendale, take US 301 south 13 miles to cross the Savannah River into Georgia. Reach the left turn to Burtons Ferry boat landing, just after the bridge over the Savannah River. Follow the two-lane road, Old US 301, to the actual landing with a boat ramp.

To put-in from takeout: Return to US 301, then head on US 301 north toward Sylvania, GA, passing the Georgia Welcome Center. A short distance beyond the welcome center, turn right onto Oglethorpe Trail and follow it for 7.2 miles to Stony Bluff Landing Road. Turn right onto Stony Bluff Landing Road and follow it to 0.2 miles to dead-end at a boat ramp.

Paddle Summary

Have you ever wanted to paddle a really big river? Here's your chance. Don't let the distance of this day paddle scare you, as the Savannah is quite swift and will immensely aid your downstream progress under normal conditions. The Savannah River drains over 10,000 square miles, and much of this waterway is still wild, despite being dammed upstream of Augusta. Starting at Stony Bluff Landing, this paddle travels the boundary between Georgia and South Carolina past thickly wooded shores that are remote and wild. Expect little to no company most of the time, as this stretch of river is used almost exclusively by locals, and then usually during warm, pleasant weather.

River Overview

The Savannah River is one of South Carolina's biggest waterways. Born at the confluence of two large rivers, the Tugaloo and the Seneca, which themselves drain the mountains north of them, the Savannah then flows southeasterly, forming the boundary between South Carolina and Georgia for its entire distance. Much of the upper river is dammed as Richard B. Russell Lake and also Lake Thurmond. Finally released from bondage, the Savannah flows through the town of Augusta and changes to a surprisingly remote big river, and is the part where this paddle takes place. Finally, as the river nears the town of Savannah, tidal influence slows it, and it enters the Atlantic Ocean.

ELI WHITNEY AND THE COTTON GIN

Eli Whitney is one of America's great inventors. It was on the banks of the Savannah River, downstream of this particular paddle near the city of Savannah, where Eli Whitney invented the cotton gin.

Born in Massachusetts, Whitney graduated from Yale University, then made his way down to the Savannah River valley to study law at Mulberry Grove, the plantation home of the widow of ex-Revolutionary War leader Nathanael Greene. Cotton was being grown here but was not well utilized simply because the seed was so hard to separate from the cotton.

Seeding had to be done by hand and was extremely slow and so labor-intensive as to be prohibitive. During this time, Whitney made some minor but effective changes in the ways Mrs. Greene operated her plantation, causing her to believe Whitney could solve the vexing problem of separating the seed from the cotton. Before starting, Whitney had to make his own iron tools and other items to construct the gin. Unfortunately, his invention was caught up in lawsuits, as its success inspired copiers and the outright theft of his idea. Whitney was eventually recognized as the inventor of the cotton gin, but the money he spent on his invention, as well as the lawsuits, cut mightily into the profit. However, in the early 1800s, cotton exports from the United States grew to over forty times their previous level from the early 1790s.

Whitney was also one of the first to use interchangeable parts in manufacturing. He signed a large contract with the US government to build muskets and created a firearms factory, helping to develop mass production and the factory concept. The Mulberry Grove property, the site on the Savannah River where he first made the gin, was burned by the Union's General Sherman on his infamous and brutal march at the end of the Civil War.

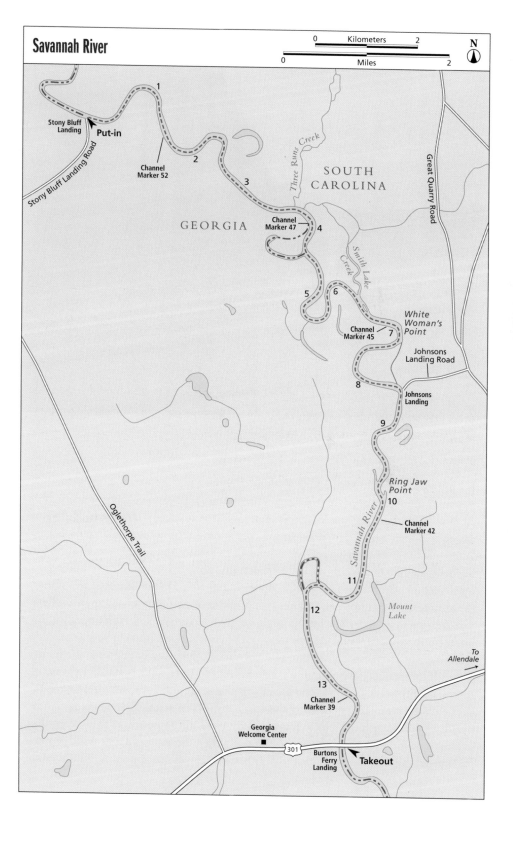

Wing dams recall the days when the middle Savannah River was used by barges.

The Paddle

At Stony Bluff Landing, the Savannah River is about 200 feet wide, flowing between thickly wooded banks. Just downstream, note some channel aids—wooden berms known as wing dams or weirs that extend in the water, deepening the channel for big boats, despite the dearth of commercial traffic here. Barges once went all the way up to Augusta from the coast. Rock riprap is also along the banks. You will notice the channel marker numbers, another legacy of the Army Corps of Engineers, which manages not only the river but the dams upstream. Vertical soil bluffs occasionally hover on the outside of bends, but most of the river's edge is thickly vegetated with willows, river birch, and sycamore. The vegetation gives way enough on the inside of bends to have an ever-changing combination of gravel, sand, and soil for landing spots. The current is fairly swift and tends to boil in places, but it is no threat to the alert paddler; it's merely exhibiting the characteristics of a large river. The Savannah may have a brownish tint but is actually fairly clear, as the upstream dams keep the sediment down. Pass a few shacks on the right, then the river remains wild, despite passing old Browns Landing on the South Carolina side of the river. Sturdy oaks and pines occupy the high bluffs, rising 25 feet or more above the water. Occasional cypress trees are mostly relegated to the back sloughs, which occasionally spur off the main river.

Pass channel marker 52 at 1.5 miles. The Savannah widens in excess of 200 feet in places. At 2.7 miles, the river begins a long straightaway. You may notice the sign on river left that states "130." That is river mile 130 and indicates you are now 130 miles upstream from the Atlantic Ocean. The river mileages are signed every 10 miles. The left bank is now Department of Energy property, part of the Savannah Nuclear Facility. That shore is obviously off limits. At 3.8 miles, near channel marker 47, Lower Three Runs Creek comes in from the South Carolina side. The Savannah begins another series of bends. Ahead, the old river curved right and made a big oxbow, but you travel through a cut created by the Army Corps of Engineers when they straightened parts of the river for commercial traffic. You are paddling with South Carolina on both shore-lines. At 6.4 miles, a large slough leads toward the South Carolina side. This is actually Smith Lake Creek. There is an island in mid-river as well. Below the island and slough, the Savannah temporarily widens, and you pass a large beach on river left and channel marker 45. The Department of Energy property has ended. There is also a boat ramp here, on the South Carolina side, at a place known as White Woman's Point.

The river narrows again, then curves to reach a boat ramp on the South Carolina side at 8.6 miles. This is Johnsons Landing, and can be used as an alternate access to shorten this paddle. Sloughs increase near Ring Jaw Point. Pass some wing dams and channel marker 42 at 10.4 miles. Ahead, the Savannah River curves right and narrows and splits around an island. McDaniel Creek comes in on the far side of the island, draining nearby Georgia uplands. Pass river mileage mile marker 120 at 12.6 miles. Downstream, channel marker 39 precedes a curve to the right, then the US 301 bridge and your takeout comes into view. Note the current US 301 bridge with the old bridge just beyond it. The old roundhouse bridge swiveled in the middle to let river traffic pass by. Burtons Ferry boat ramp will be on your right.

17 Lower Saluda River

This paddle combines distance, scenery, and rapids in and near Columbia on a state scenic river.

County: Lexington
Start: Metts Landing
  N34° 2.75' / W81° 11.47'
End: West Columbia Riverwalk at Gervais Street Bridge
  N33° 59.700' / W81° 3.145'
Distance: 10.2 miles
Float time: 6.5–7.5 hours
Difficulty rating: Moderate (assuming portage of Mill Race Rapids)
Rapids: Class I–II
River type: Dam-fed cold water river with shoals
Current: Moderate
River gradient: 5.9 feet per mile
River gauge: Saluda River near Columbia, SC; minimum flow: 450 cfs, maximum flow: 3,500 cfs

Season: Year-round
Land status: Public landings, public and private shoreline
Fees or permits: No fees or permits required
Nearest city/town: Columbia
Maps: Lower Saluda Scenic River; USGS Quadrangle Maps: Irmo, Columbia North, Southwest Columbia
Boats used: Canoes, kayaks, johnboats on upper stretch
Organizations: South Carolina Department of Natural Resources, Rembert C. Dennis Building, 1000 Assembly St., Columbia, SC 29201, (803) 734-9100, dnr.sc.gov/
Contacts/outfitters: Adventure Carolina, Inc., 1107 State St., Cayce, SC 29033, (803)796-4505, adventurecarolina.com

Put-in/Takeout Information

To takeout: From exit 3 on I-126 in Columbia, head south on Huger Street for 0.6 mile to Gervais Street. Turn right on Gervais Street, cross the Congaree River, and just after the crossing at 0.5 mile, turn left on Alexander Street, then immediately turn left again into the West Columbia Riverwalk parking area. The boat landing is below the small amphitheater here.

To put-in from takeout: Head north onto Alexander from the landing and immediately hit Gervais Street. Turn left and go just a few feet, then make a quick right onto Sunset Boulevard (US 378 West). Follow US 378 west for 5.9 miles, then veer right onto Corley Mill Road. Follow Corley Mill Road for 3.1 miles to Hope Ferry Road and turn right, follow it 0.4 mile to dead-end at Metts Landing.

Paddle Summary

This excellent all-day river trip ends in downtown Columbia and is easily accessible for all residents of South Carolina's capital city. Start at James R. Metts Landing, a fine put-in, to enter the dam-chilled Lower Saluda, a state-designated scenic river. A trout fishery is supported by the icy, crystal-clear waters flowing from beneath the Lake

Murray Dam. Your easterly direction takes you ever closer to downtown Columbia, but first you will paddle through some attractive scenery. Several large feeder streams add their flow to the river by the time you reach the Gardendale access. The river then takes on a more urban aspect as it passes under two interstate bridges. The Saluda River changes character while dropping through several rapids and cutting its way through the fall line. At normal water levels, these are straightforward Class I–II rapids—except for Class III Mill Race Rapids. This shoal has a steep, elongated drop and is irregular because a former dam collapsed here; the dam's sharp-cut blocks tumbled into the shoal and add a level of danger unseen in natural rapids. A portage trail on river left will take you around Mill Race Rapids. More shoals lay ahead, all Class I–II, and add splashing fun to the adventure. The Saluda merges with the Broad just above downtown Columbia amid a jumble of islands and little rapids, and together they form the Congaree. The last mile of the trip is on the Congaree River. End at the West Columbia Riverwalk landing just below the historic Gervais Street Bridge.

River Overview

The Saluda River drains the highest reaches of Greenville County below the North Carolina state line. There are three prongs of the upper Saluda, all gorgeous mountain tributaries, especially the Middle Saluda, the aquatic pulse of Jones Gap State Park. The Middle flows to meet the South Saluda and together they join with the North Saluda a few miles above Saluda Lake. After leaving the foothills, the 200-mile-long waterway keeps southeasterly, forming county boundaries, slowing at remnant-textile milldams. A big dam forms Lake Greenwood, then the Saluda flows only to slow again at popular Lake Murray. From there it makes its way into Columbia, culminating in rocky shoals before the Saluda meets the Broad River. Together they form the Congaree River. This lowermost part of the river is where this paddle takes place.

The Paddle

There is a standard boat ramp as well as a walk-down put-in at Metts Landing. On a warm summer day, fog will form atop the dam-chilled water, which runs very clear. This cool air and cooler water is welcome on a hot summer day, for a dip in the Saluda below Lake Murray is guaranteed to chill your bones. Aquatic grasses sway in the current below your boat. The river is about 250 feet wide at this point and is flowing easterly. These last 10 miles from Lake Murray to its confluence with the Broad are a state-designated scenic waterway. The banks are heavily wooded, with an occasional house on the south bank, but the north bank is all natural within the confines of Saluda Shoals Park, which also has a boat ramp and is a developed park, but there is an entry fee.

Hit your first rocky riffle at 0.3 mile. Pass under a major power line at 0.5 mile. At 0.9 mile, cloudier and warmer Rawls Creek comes in on river left. At 1.1 miles, come to Corleys Island. Here a narrower channel splits left around a rock outcrop

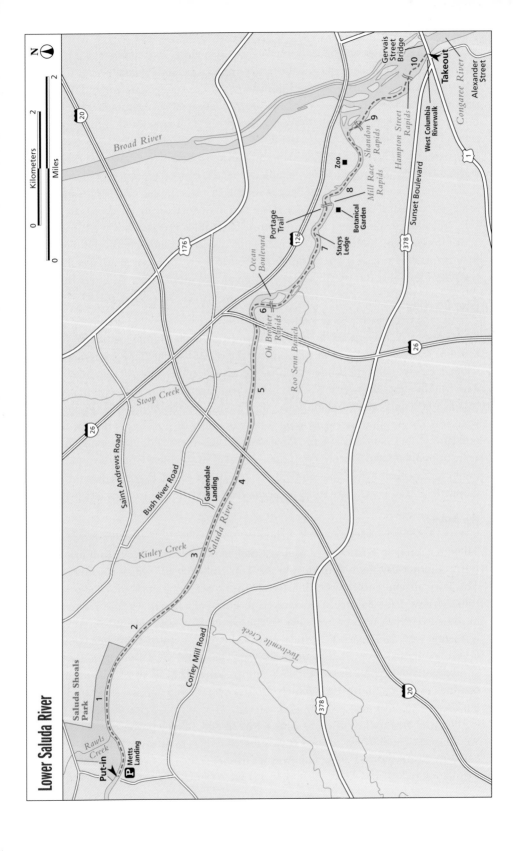

Lower Saluda River

N

Kilometers
0   2

Miles
0   2

Broad River

20

176

26

Saint Andrews Road

Stoop Creek

Bush River Road

Kinley Creek

Gardendale Landing

Saluda River

Corley Mill Road

Twelvemile Creek

378

20

Saluda Shoals Park

Rawls Creek

Put-in

Metts Landing

1

2

3

4

5

6

7

8

9

10

Ocean Boulevard

Portage Trail

125

Oh Brother Rapids

Roo Senn Branch

Stacys Ledge

Botanical Garden

Zoo

Mill Race Rapids

Shandon Rapids

Hampton Street Rapids

Sunset Boulevard

378

26

West Columbia Riverwalk

Congaree River

Gervais Street Bridge

Takeout

Alexander Street

1

Happy paddler after running a rapid on the lower Saluda River

while the main channel of the Saluda River flows on the right. The left bank is still within the confines of Saluda Shoals Park. Continuing downstream you will see the private landing of a planned community on your right. At 1.5 miles, the channel that went around Corleys Island reunites with the main channel of the Saluda. A small shoal gurgles at the lower end of Corleys Island. Pass an old water-intake station, then the Saluda Shoals Park tube takeout at 1.7 miles. This marks the end of Saluda Shoals Park, but the banks remain forested on both sides, with only sporadic houses.

At 2.3 miles, big Twelvemile Creek comes in on your right. At normal flows, you can paddle up this stream a bit. Smaller Kinley Creek comes in on your left at 3.1 miles. Continuing downstream, reach the marked Gardendale Landing on your left at 3.5 miles. It is a carry landing for hand-propelled craft, with about a 25-yard haul from the parking lot to the Saluda River.

Continuing downstream, your next significant marker is the I-20 Bridge at 4.3 miles. The Saluda keeps easterly. Stoop Creek enters on river left at 5.2 miles. Pass under the low I-26 Bridge at 5.8 miles. Here, the Saluda makes a sharp right turn and becomes rocky, then splits around an island. Shoals form. The shoals on the right of the isle are named Oh Brother, and the one on island left is Ocean Boulevard. Both are longish Class I–II rapids. More islands appear. At 6.4 miles, the river becomes a single large channel. Roo Senn Branch enters river right at 6.5 miles.

River-wide Class II Stacys Ledge appears at 7.1 miles. There are three main channels: left, right, and middle. Each will take you over the rapid. There is a portage trail around the ledge on river right. Pay close attention now. The river is keeping southeasterly, and you come to Mill Race Rapids at 7.5 miles. You will see the steep drop of the Saluda and the broken walls of the old dam on each side of the river. Additionally, the head of the rapids is beneath a cleared power line. A trail goes to the botanical garden on river right, but I recommend the portage trail on river left, as you face downstream. Pull up to the grassy landing, then carry your boat past a concrete relic, over an intermittent ditch, then down some boulders to reach the base of the rapid after a 10-minute carry. Take your time and be careful. Don't try to shortcut halfway in the rapid; go to the bottom. In the future, there may be paddler parking here, in which case you could end your trip above the rapids. In addition, whitewater paddlers in play boats are known to run Mill Race Rapids, carry their kayak up, and run it repeatedly. In a normal canoe or kayak, one portage will likely sate your desire for toting boats. Return to the river and immediately shoot Class II Popup Hole, a short straightforward drop.

The river slows as you paddle beneath the pedestrian bridge linking the Columbia botanical garden and zoo at 8.3 miles. At 8.8 miles, the Saluda curves right and reaches the Class II Shandon Rapids, a longer shoal with a good splash. Take the far right channel. There is a portage trail on river right. Beyond here, the clear, cold Saluda merges with the warmer Broad. Stay right and pass through Class I White House Rapids, then easy Hampton Street Rapids. Stay on the right-hand side of the river, reaching the takeout and historic Gervais Street Bridge at 10.2 miles, ending the adventure.

18 Broad River at Columbia

This paddle in the heart of Columbia dances through fun shoals to join the Congaree River at its end.

County: Richland, Lexington
Start: Riverfront Park
  N34° 1.979' / W81° 4.068'
End: West Columbia Riverwalk at Gervais Street Bridge
  N33° 59.700' / W81° 3.145'
Distance: 3.3 miles
Float time: 1.5–2.5 hours
Difficulty rating: Easy
Rapids: Class I–II
River type: Wide Piedmont river with rocky shoals
Current: Moderate
River gradient: 6.2 feet per mile
River gauge: Broad River near Columbia, SC, minimum flow: 1,200, maximum flow: 4,000

Season: Year-round
Land status: Public landings, private shoreline
Fees or permits: No fees or permits required
Nearest city/town: Columbia
Maps: USGS Quadrangle Maps: Columbia North, Southwest Columbia
Boats used: Canoes, kayaks
Organizations: South Carolina Department of Health and Environmental Control, 2600 Bull St., Columbia, SC 29201, (803) 898-4300, scdhec.gov/environment/water
Contacts/outfitters: Adventure Carolina, Inc., 1107 State St., Cayce, SC 29033, (803) 796-4505, adventurecarolina.com

Put-in/Takeout Information

To takeout: From exit 3 on I-126 in Columbia, head south on Huger Street for 0.6 mile to Gervais Street. Turn right on Gervais Street, cross the Congaree River, and just after the crossing, at 0.5 mile, turn left on Alexander Street, then immediately turn left again into the West Columbia Riverwalk parking area. The boat landing is below the small amphitheater here.

To put-in from takeout: Backtrack across the Gervais Street Bridge, then turn left on Huger Street, still backtracking. However, instead of rejoining I-126, veer right at 0.7 mile onto Elmwood Avenue. Follow Elmwood Avenue 0.7 mile to turn left onto Main Street. Follow Main Street 0.5 mile, then veer left onto River Drive. Follow River Drive a total of 1.5 miles, then turn right into Riverfront Park just before River Drive crosses the Broad River. Enter Riverfront Park and follow the road 0.4 mile to dead-end at a parking area. From here, you must carry your boat up and across the Broad River Canal, then down to the Broad River below the diversion dam.

Paddle Summary

This is a great half-day float through the heart of Columbia. Not many state capitals can claim such fun paddle routes so close to downtown. Moreover, being scenic and historic on top of its ease of opportunity makes it all the better!

It is a carry to reach the put-in, but you will enjoy the views of the river before jumping in your boat at a rapid and instantaneously doing some rock dodging. The float on the aptly named Broad River is a truly urban paddle, right through the heart of Columbia. But that doesn't mean it isn't scenic. Rocky shoals add visual and auditory beauty. Bridges mark your passages. Downstream you pass under the Timmerman Bridge, then enter a series of islands with multiple passages, depending on water level. Amid these islands, the waters of the Broad River merge with those of the dam-chilled, clear waters of the Saluda River, and together they form the mighty Congaree.

More shoals lie ahead, mild Class I–II drops. The river is wide, and you must pick your routes. The best bet is to get river right, as the Congaree is very wide, and your takeout is on the right (west) side of the Gervais Street Bridge.

River Overview

The Broad River rises on the eastern slopes of the Blue Ridge in North Carolina. It drains the Appalachian highlands easterly, gaining tributaries—namely the whitewater-frothing Green River—and momentum to enter the North Carolina foothills. The Broad maintains a stubbornly easterly direction in the Tar Heel State before entering South Carolina in Cherokee County near the town of Gaffney. At Gaffney, it is dammed, then unleashed, and it heads south, forming multiple county boundaries.

The Paddle

The put-in is historic. Here, at the diversion dam crossing the Broad, a canal was created, and the water was used for the world's first electrically operated textile mill. The hydroelectric plant is the oldest in South Carolina. Riverfront Park is poplar for fishing, and the levee between the Broad River and the Columbia Canal has a walking trail that runs 2.5 miles along it. Combine this trail with a little sidewalk walking, and you can hike or bike this shuttle.

But when launching from the gravel put-in below the diversion dam, you will be thinking of how to navigate the first rapid. You start in the middle of it. It is an easy Class I–II, and you are soon through the rocks and shoals, now with time to consider the river. Here, the Broad stretches in excess of 400 feet and usually has a green-brown coloration with a slightly cloudy tint. Mostly wooded banks rise from the moderate current. At 0.5 mile, paddle under the River Drive Bridge. More exposed rocks rise from the waters, meaning swifter water. At 0.8 mile, a small linear island points downstream. The Broad River Canal is flowing parallel and unseen, divided by the trail-topped levee, atop which you see occasional hikers, bicyclists, and joggers.

Interestingly, spider lilies are found in the open, rocky shoals of Broad River, here in the heart of Columbia, at 1.3 miles on this paddle. Even if you don't catch their late

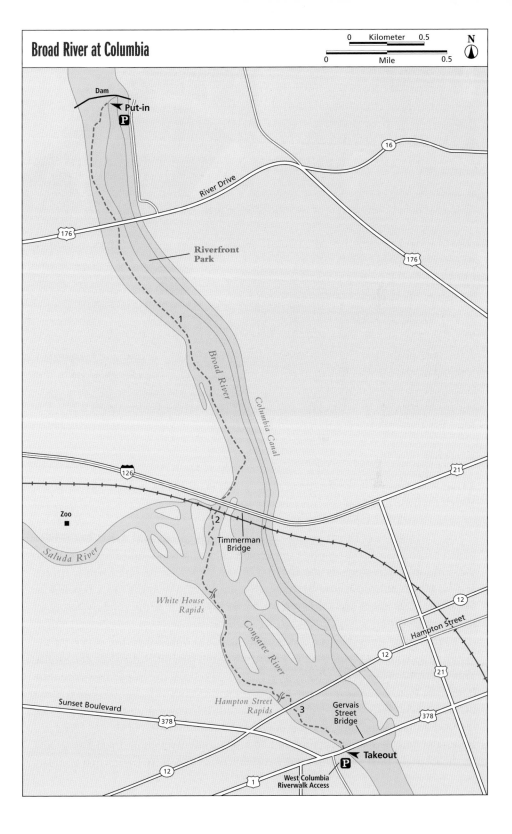

Broad River at Columbia

Dam
Put-in
P

16

River Drive

176

176

Riverfront Park

1

Broad River

Columbia Canal

126

21

Zoo ■

Saluda River

2

Timmerman Bridge

White House Rapids

Congaree River

12

Hampton Street

12

21

Sunset Boulevard

378

Hampton Street Rapids

3

Gervais Street Bridge

378

12

1

Takeout
P

West Columbia Riverwalk Access

0   Kilometer   0.5
0   Mile   0.5

N

This paddle ends under the historic Gervais Street Bridge.

spring bloom, you will see the green plants rising in mid-river, bordered by boulders. Watch for herons and other birds perching on these rocks. On shore, gravel bars can be found near these rapids and make preferred stopping spots.

By 1.4 miles, the Broad begins dividing around islands and meets the Saluda, which has come from the tiptop of the Upstate, at the North Carolina state line. Work through some light shoals as you near I-126, passing under the Timmerman Bridge at 1.9 miles. A railroad bridge immediately follows. Now you can see a timeline of South Carolina travel: first water, then rail, and now roads as the primary means of transportation.

I recommend moving over to the right here, not only to see the waters of the Saluda meld with the Broad but also to best access the takeout. Paddle into the Saluda. You will be surprised at the chill compared to the Broad, as the Saluda flows from the bottom of Lake Murray upstream. A mini maze of islands stretches to your left and makes for fun exploration possibilities and avails different routes should you repeat this paddle. Continue downstream, now on the uppermost point of the Congaree River, and float through the tame White House Rapids. By 2.3 miles, paddlers should be on the right bank of the Congaree. Look toward downtown; observant paddlers will see the domed top of the South Carolina statehouse on the horizon. Pass through the mild Hampton Street Rapids, then at 2.9 miles paddle beneath the Hampton Street Bridge. The Gervais Street Bridge is ahead. A final set of easy rapids speeds you along. Do a good job snaking among the rocks here, for a walking trail leads up from the takeout to these shoals, and you will likely be paddling for an audience. At this point all paddlers should hug the right shore. A final drop under the Gervais Street Bridge leads you to the West Columbia Riverwalk access. Haul your boat up some steps and around the amphitheater to the parking area.

THE COLUMBIA CANAL

Back in the 1820s, Columbia's residents used water for transportation. Freight and passengers could be taken from the coast up the Santee and Congaree Rivers as far as Columbia, and there they reached the fall line. Rocky rapids prevented passage to the Upstate. A canal with locks was built on the Columbia side of the Congaree and Broad for a stretch of 3.0 miles, bypassing the rapids of the fall line.

The canal was also used for waterpower to operate mills. However, by the 1840s, railroads had reached the state capital, making water transportation tenuous. The Columbia Canal seemed defunct for good. But, in 1891, a portion of the Columbia Canal was redug and designed. A diversion dam was built. The new canal powered a large mill.

Canal water also fueled a power plant that is still in operation today. Furthermore, a significant portion of Columbia's water is taken from the Columbia Canal and processed at the Columbia Canal Water Treatment Plant, though it is supplemented by another water plant at Lake Murray. So when you cross the diversion dam above the canal on the way to the put-in, look down and realize that you may drinking that water, and it will also power your home.

19 Congaree River at Columbia

This paddle starts in downtown Columbia and explores the surprisingly natural yet historic banks of the mighty Congaree.

County: Richland, Lexington
Start: West Columbia Riverwalk at Gervais Street Bridge
    N33° 59.700' / W81° 3.145'
End: Cayce Landing
    N33° 56.957' / W81° 1.749'
Distance: 3.7 miles
Float time: 2–3.5 hours
Difficulty rating: Easy
Rapids: Class I
River type: Wide Piedmont river with a few shoals
Current: Moderate
River gradient: 2.8 feet per mile
River gauge: Congaree River at Columbia, SC, no minimum flow, maximum flow flood stage

Season: Year-round
Land status: Public landings, public and private shoreline
Fees or permits: No fees or permits required
Nearest city/town: Columbia
Maps: Congaree River Blue Trail; USGS Quadrangle Maps: Southwest Columbia; *Delorme: South Carolina Atlas & Gazetteer,* P.36 2-F, G
Boats used: Canoes, kayaks
Organizations: Congaree Riverkeeper, 1001 Washington St., 2nd Floor, Columbia, SC 29201, (803) 760-3357, congareeriverkeeper.org
Contacts/outfitters: Adventure Carolina, Inc., 1107 State St., Cayce, SC 29033, (803)796-4505, adventurecarolina.com

Put-in/Takeout Information

To takeout: From exit 2 on I-77 south of Columbia, head north on 12th Street Extension for 2.0 miles, then turn right on Godley Street and follow it for 0.2 mile, then turn right on New State Road. Follow New State Road for 0.5 mile, then veer right onto Old State Road and follow it for 0.8 mile. Turn left toward the Thomas E. Newman Landing, at the same turn for the Cayce water plant. Dead-end at the boat ramp at 0.2 mile. Newman Landing is known alternatively as Cayce Landing.

To put-in from takeout: From Cayce Landing/Newman Landing, backtrack to 12th Street Extension. This time, turn right (north) on 12th Street. Follow 12th Street for 1.7 miles to Knox Abbott Drive and a traffic light. Turn right on Knox Abbott Drive and follow it east for 1.0 mile to turn left on Alexander Street (the road going right at this four-way intersection is Axtell). Follow Alexander Street for 0.6 mile to the parking area and entrance into West Columbia Riverwalk on your right. If you reach Gervais Street from Alexander, you have gone a little too far. *Note:* This is a viable bike shuttle using a few roads at the takeout and the Three Rivers Greenway.

Paddle Summary

Columbia is very fortunate to have a canoe and kayak launch in the heart of downtown. Here, you can paddle the uppermost waters of the Congaree, where the Gervais

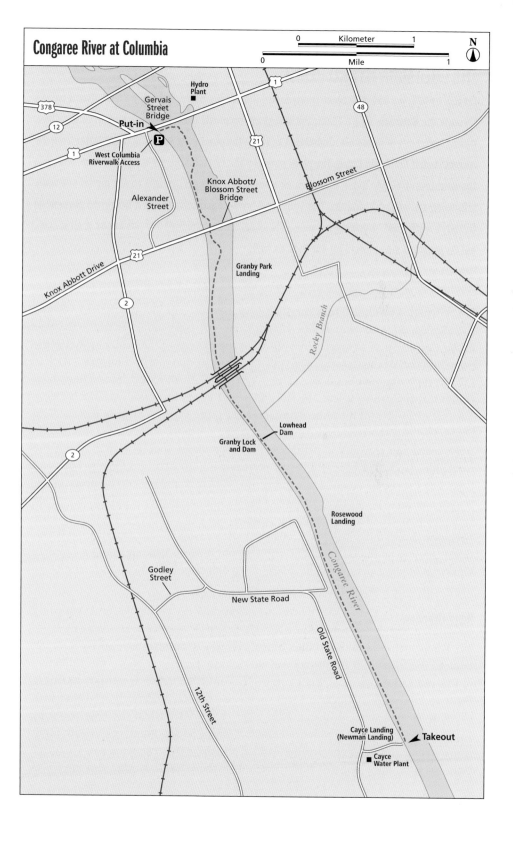

Congaree River at Columbia

378

12

Hydro
Plant ■

Gervais
Street
Bridge

Put-in

P

West Columbia
Riverwalk Access

1

Knox Abbott/
Blossom Street
Bridge

Blossom Street

Alexander
Street

48

21

21

Knox Abbott Drive

21

Granby Park
Landing

2

Rocky Branch

2

Lowhead
Dam

Granby Lock
and Dam

Rosewood
Landing

Godley
Street

Congaree River

New State Road

Old State Road

12th Street

Cayce Landing
(Newman Landing)   Takeout

Cayce
■ Water Plant

THE COLUMBIA HYDRO PLANT

On this paddle, you have the opportunity to see the outflow of the Columbia Canal after it passes through the Columbia Hydro Plant, the oldest continuously operating power plant in the state, owned by the city of Columbia. Completed in 1896, the plant used (and still uses) water from the reconstructed Columbia Canal. The plant powered the city's textile mills, light system, and even the downtown trolleys. Today, it powers all manner of electrical systems in our digital age while still using the original turbines. The stone-and-brick construction adds a historical element to the city's waterfront, providing not only a visual delight for paddlers and passersby of all stripes, but its practical side powers up our lives as well.

Street Bridge crosses it. From the West Columbia Riverwalk—a worthy waterside trail destination in its own right—launch your craft and paddle easterly at the base of the Gervais Street Bridge. Here you will see the arches of the bridge as well as the stone outflows of the historic hydro plant on the east side of the Congaree.

The float trip then heads downriver, skittering through rocky shoals. Downtown Columbia stands to your left. The river takes you along surprisingly natural banks, as one side or another of the river is protected as a greenway and/or park. It is not long before you pass the Granby Park launch on the northeast shore. A few more mild riffles speed you atop the sometimes shallow but always wide waterway. Ahead, the rumbling sounds you hear will be the river flowing over the old Granby Lock and Dam. The dam is but a low-head spillover; however, rock and rebar make floating over it a less than ideal proposition. Instead, enjoy shooting through the old concrete-lined lock. Just beyond, there is a stopping point where you can access the Three Rivers Greenway. Beyond the lock, the Congaree makes a wide straightaway, passing Rosewood Landing on the far bank. This trip ends at Newman Landing, more commonly known as Cayce Landing, where a long ramp and large parking area accommodate many a motorboater, paddler, and picnicker.

River Overview

For being such a wide and voluminous river, the Congaree is relatively short in distance. Formed from the Broad and the Saluda Rivers just above the beginning of this paddle in Columbia, the Congaree begins its existence as a major waterway. From Columbia, the Congaree heads southeast, entering a relatively wild land with overflow swamps on both banks. Things get even wilder when the river passes by Congaree National Park, a protected preserve with a large stand of old-growth forest rising among an interconnected network of waterways. After flowing past Congaree National Park, the Congaree River runs under the US 601 Bridge, also known as

The last part of the paddle passes through a now-defunct lock.

Bates Bridge, the first developed landing in 47 miles! Beyond here, the Congaree soon meets the Wateree River, and together they form the massive Santee River, which in turn, is quickly dammed as Lake Marion.

The Paddle

It is a short carry down to the river from the parking area, as you pass around a small riverside amphitheater. Trails of the local greenway system go both directions along the Congaree. From the landing, you can admire the arches of the Gervais Street Bridge, a symbol of Columbia and listed on the National Register of Historic Places. It was the only bridge spanning the Congaree until 1953. The Gervais Street Bridge was opened in 1928, replacing a bridge built in 1870, which replaced the first bridge over the Congaree from 1827. Paddle in the shadow of its arches across the Congaree, aiming for the far bank. Now check out the outflow of the hydro plant and its stone construction. The water noisily churns from the plant and creates a powerful current that makes the hydro plant a challenge to reach. This also adds water taken away from the Broad River in its last few miles (via the Columbia Canal) before meeting the Saluda.

Splash through some easy shoals just downstream of the bridge. The Congaree stretches a good thousand feet across at this point, making it a fairway for winds. I suggest picking one bank or another, not only to diminish the winds but also to enjoy the riverside scenery. At this point, both banks are relatively natural. Pass under the Knox Abbott Road/Blossom Street Bridge at 0.7 mile. Now, you have Granby Park to your left and the Three Rivers Greenway to your right, creating a protected park corridor on both sides of the Congaree. Rocks are scattered in the river here, creating light shoals. At 1.0 mile, you will pass the Granby Park boat launch and park access on your left. This is a simple carry versus the developed boat ramp at the takeout at Casey/Newman Landing.

At 1.5 miles, float under a pair of railroad bridges. Beyond here, begin moving over to the right bank. Rocky Branch comes in on the left bank at 1.8 miles. You will begin to see a large concrete structure along the right-hand bank ahead. This is the old Granby Lock. Head for it and avoid the lowhead dam. Aim for the channel between the old lock walls. This passage is an easy 40 feet wide, and the water speeds through it. The lock and dam were built in 1905 to raise water levels to navigate upstream shoals. When the Congaree was low, mobile wickets would be raised along the river bottom, bringing the Congaree up as much as 10 feet, so that boats could make it to the Gervais Street Bridge landing in Columbia and unload their goods. Proposals have been made to remove what is left of the dam, but nothing has happened yet.

Just beyond this lock, you can beach your canoe or kayak and reach the Three Rivers Greenway. Climb atop the lock and soak in a fine view of the valley. Continuing downriver, pass Rosewood Landing at 2.5 miles, on river left. Beyond there, the Congaree makes a long straightaway. The I-77 Bridge (no access) stands in the distance. Dance over some fast-moving shallows before reaching the Cayce/Newman Landing at 3.7 miles. It's a long double ramp used by powerboaters, so take out quickly on busy weekends.

20 Congaree Creek

This intimate waterway provides instant access for a remote swamp paddle.

County: Lexington
Start: Charleston Highway, US 21/176/321
N33° 56.259' / W81° 4.630'
End: 12th Street Extension access near SCANA headquarters
N33° 56.548' / W81° 2.713'
Distance: 3.3 miles
Float time: 1.5–2.5 hours
Difficulty rating: Moderate
Rapids: Class I
River type: Narrow, swift swamp creek with obstacles
Current: Moderate to fast
River gradient: 4.0 feet per mile
River gauge: None

Season: Sept through May
Land status: Public—state preserve
Fees or permits: No fees or permits required
Nearest city/town: Cayce
Maps: Congaree Creek Heritage Preserve;
USGS Quadrangle Maps: Southwest Columbia
Boats used: Canoes, kayaks
Organizations: Congaree Creek Heritage Preserve, South Carolina DNR, 1000 Assembly St., Columbia, SC 29201, (803)734-3893, scgreatoutdoors.com/park-congareecreek heritagepreserve.html
Contacts/outfitters: Adventure Carolina, Inc., 1107 State St., Cayce, SC 29033, (803) 796-4505, adventurecarolina.com

Put-in/Takeout Information

To takeout: From exit 2 on I-77 south of Columbia, head north on 12th Street Extension for 0.6 mile to a traffic light. Turn left on SCANA Parkway, then immediately turn right into Congaree Creek Canoe Access. Reach a parking lot and spur to the creek. Park here.

To put-in from takeout: Return to 12th Street Extension and head south, back toward I-77. Drive 0.5 mile, then turn right on Saxe Gotha Road. Travel 1.1 miles, then turn right on Dixiana Road. Follow Dixiana Road for 1.1 miles to reach Charleston Highway. Turn right on Charleston Highway and head north for 0.2 mile, then look right for an undeveloped parking area just past the bridge over Congaree Creek. This is a viable bike shuttle.

Paddle Summary

A paddling trip down Congaree Creek instantaneously transitions you from suburban Columbia to the back of beyond when your boat slips away from Charleston Highway. Congaree Creek is a tributary of Congaree River, but the two Columbia-area waterways share little else besides a name. Congaree Creek is a swift, narrow, dark, shady swamp stream, versus the massive, open Congaree River. It isn't long before you enter the boundaries of the Congaree Creek Heritage Preserve, a state-designated wild sanctuary. Gum and cypress trees, as well as oaks and bay trees, create

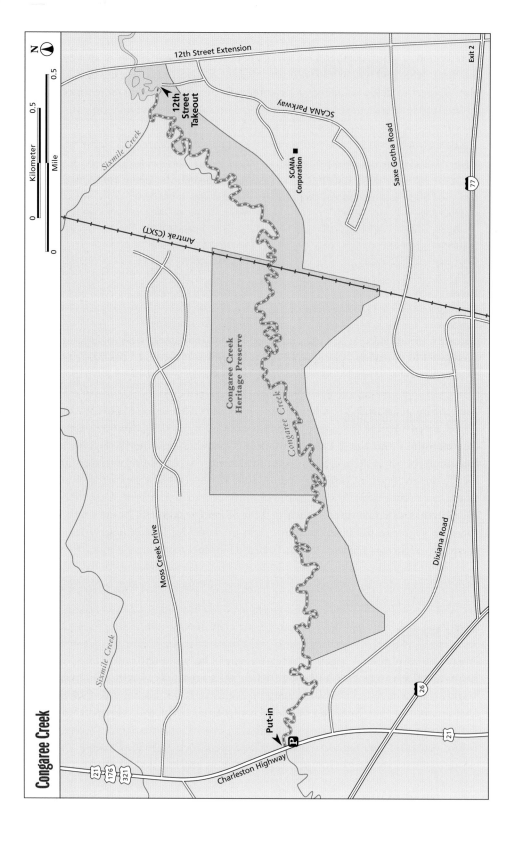

Congaree Creek

N

Kilometer

0   0.5   0.5

Mile

0   0.5

12th Street Extension

Exit 2

SCANA Parkway

SCANA Corporation

Saxe Gotha Road

77

12th Street Takeout

Sixmile Creek

Amtrak (CSXT)

Moss Creek Drive

Congaree Creek Heritage Preserve

Congaree Creek

Sixmile Creek

Dixiana Road

26

Put-in

Charleston Highway

21

21 176 321

a continuous canopy overhead. Of special note is the Atlantic white cedar tree, rare for these parts, and one of the reasons for the heritage-preserve status in the first place. Expect to deftly maneuver your watercraft, seemingly turning more times than a NASCAR driver in a 500-mile race. Throw in some fallen trees and you will come away from your trip with your steering skills challenged.

The small stream provides an intimate paddling experience and will make you consider the paddling potential of every small stream you encounter. The heritage preserve keeps the banks untamed and provides a visually appealing corridor. However, stopping spots are few—an occasional tiny sandbar—but the short distance of the trip makes break points less necessary.

Being close to Columbia combined with easy access makes this an ideal after-work or half-day paddling trip. The takeout is as fine and developed as the put-in is rough, more of a fisherman's locale. The put-in should be turned into an official paddling access.

River Overview

Congaree Creek flows from hills in Richland County west of Edmund, alternately seeping through swamps and slipping through narrower drainages. After the addition of Red Bank Creek and First Creek near the Styx State Fish Hatchery, Congaree Creek then speeds under I-26 and reaches Charleston Highway. Paddlers put in just downstream of an artificial spillway on the east side of Charleston Highway. This area is frequented by bank fishermen who have created trails along the first portion of the waterway. From there, Congaree Creek courses through the heritage preserve, emerging at the 12th Street Extension canoe launch. The waterway widens as it flows southeasterly and passes under Old State Road, where there will be an official paddler access one of these days. The stream turns south, then passes under I-77 and feeds its mother stream, the Congaree River. For those wishing to float this lowermost section, you currently must paddle all the way down to the US 601 access on the Congaree River, 44 miles downstream.

The Paddle

The put-in can be unkempt, as the fishermen and others who stop there sometimes leave their trash. You may have to carry your craft downstream a little to reach the bank, and you certainly want to put in below the spillway, just on the downstream side of the Charleston Highway Bridge. There will be no break-in time to test your paddling skills, as Congaree Creek starts its convolutions amid overhanging vegetation and sporadic fallen trees. Take note that outfitters and creek paddlers keep the canoe trail cut open. The South Carolina DNR website states that they also clear out the waterway yearly.

Nevertheless, you will be ducking and dodging while simultaneously admiring the watery world into which you have escaped as instantaneously as switching

Morning sun reveals the shallow bottom of Congaree Creek.

channels on a television screen. Look for the evergreen Atlantic white cedars. Tea-colored water takes you on an aquatic ride through an overflow swamp forest. Congaree Creek is about 20 to 25 feet wide at this point, but the effective paddling area will be much smaller. It isn't long before anglers' foot accesses are left behind, making it an exclusive paddler's world. The heritage preserve provides a wildlife corridor for deer, bobcats, and avian life, which you will hear aplenty, including a woodpecker or two. I've seen deer back here myself.

By 0.3 mile, you will have come to your first stream division. And when already small Congaree Creek divides into channels, it makes finding the correct route key, but you will not go far if you've gone the wrong way, as vegetation and low water will prevent passage. Congaree Creek is continually curving and creating oxbows as it eventually shortcuts its own bends, just as swamp streams are wont to do. By the way, there is no gauge, so a visual check at the accesses is your best bet. Consider using the Cedar Creek at Congaree National Park gauge as a very rough correlation, proceeding if Cedar Creek is 3.0 or above.

Since this is a short paddle, take your time, relax, and soak in the scenery. Congaree Creek maintains an overall easterly direction, despite its cacophony of curves. At

1.3 miles, a low bluff rises on right. Pines and the back of a building reveal themselves before you turn back into overflow floodplain. The abundance of shade makes this a viable early morning paddle even in the swelter of a South Carolina summer.

At 2.3 miles, pass under the CSXT railroad bridge and then through a power-line clearing at 2.8 miles. The brightness of the power-line clearing contrasts mightily with the dark paddling path. Quickly return to the gums, cedars, and cypress. Look for Sixmile Creek coming in on your left.

Atlantic white cedars thrive here. They grow in an irregular, mostly coastal belt from Mississippi all the way to Maine, thriving in wet soils along streams and in swamps. Atlantic white cedars are coveted as a long-lasting wood for log cabins, from the floors up to the shingles. Atlantic white cedars resemble cypress trees; however, their brownish-gray bark grows in vertical strips, and you won't find "knees" rising around the trunks, as cypresses have. In winter, the still-green Atlantic white cedars are easy to spot.

At 3.3 miles, Congaree Creek opens into another power-line cut, then curves into the signed landing on the hill below the 12th Street Extension parking area. In the future, expect to easily extend your trip to a developed landing on Old State Road. Even today, paddlers make their way down to Old State Road and use the Timmerman Trail, a path that links the 12th Street parking area to reach the currently undeveloped steep access on Old State Road.

CONGAREE CREEK HERITAGE PRESERVE

Congaree Creek Heritage Preserve is a 627-acre swath of land that protects not only the immediate Congaree Creek waterway but also adjacent lands. Aboriginals occupied this area for thousands of years, as is evidenced by tools, pottery shards, and mining digs. Clay was dug here at one time for making pottery. A pathway linking the mountains to the sea, known as the Old Cherokee Trail, traversed the preserve.

The English arrived here in 1718, establishing Fort Congaree. Settlers soon followed and created a community known as Saxe Gotha, located very near this paddle's takeout. Lands were platted out, and at one time hundreds of people lived in Saxe Gotha. Repeated Indian incursions scared the settlers into abandoning these lands.

The Congaree Creek area was also the site for Revolutionary and Civil War forts. Interestingly, the same clay that attracted Indians later attracted the nearby Guignard Brickworks to mine for clay in the early 1900s. These clay pits now function as wildlife ponds within the heritage preserve. The Guignard Brickworks Trail takes you on a 2.5-mile loop through the preserve. The path is accessible via Old State Road. For more information, visit the Congaree Creek Heritage preserve page on the South Carolina DNR website, dnr.sc.gov.

21 Cedar Creek

This paddle at Congaree National Park delivers a superlative experience.

County: Richland
Start: Bannister Bridge Access
　　N33° 50.414' / W80° 51.632'
End: South Cedar Creek Access
　　N33° 49.125' / W80° 47.275'
Distance: 6.9 miles
Float time: 4–5 hours
Difficulty rating: Moderate
Rapids: Class I
River type: Remote swamp creek
Current: Moderate to fast
River gradient: 1.0 feet per mile
River gauge: Cedar Creek at Congaree NP near Gadsden, SC, minimum runnable level: 4.0 feet, maximum: 7.0 feet

Season: Sept through May
Land status: Public—national park
Fees or permits: No fees or permits required
Nearest city/town: Gadsden
Maps: Congaree National Park; USGS Quadrangle Maps: Gadsden
Boats used: Canoes, kayaks
Organizations: Congaree National Park, 100 National Park Rd., Hopkins, SC 29061-9118, nps.gov/cong
Contacts/outfitters: Adventure Carolina, Inc., 1107 State St., Cayce, SC 29033, (803) 796-4505, adventurecarolina.com

Put-in/Takeout Information

To takeout: From exit 5 (Bluff Road) on I-77 south of Columbia, take SC 48 east for 8.4 miles to Old Bluff Road. Veer right onto Old Bluff Road and follow it for 6.5 miles (passing Bannister Bridge put-in and the entrance to Congaree National Park on the way) to a T intersection at South Cedar Creek Road. Turn right onto South Cedar Creek Road and follow it for 1.8 miles to reach the South Cedar Creek paddle access on your right.

To put-in from takeout: Backtrack from the takeout 1.8 miles north to Old Bluff Road. Turn left on Old Bluff Road and follow it 4.1 miles to the Bannister Bridge put-in, which will now be on your left. It is a small shady parking area with a 50-yard boat carry to Cedar Creek.

Paddle Summary

A trip down Cedar Creek—at the proper water levels—delivers a trip into some of South Carolina's finest natural environments at underappreciated Congaree National Park, located within easy striking distance of greater Columbia. This park, first protected as a national monument in 1976, conserves part of the Congaree River floodplain, where massive old-growth trees will amaze. Cedar Creek, a tributary of the Congaree, enters the national park at Bannister Bridge then delves into a protected

Cedar Creek

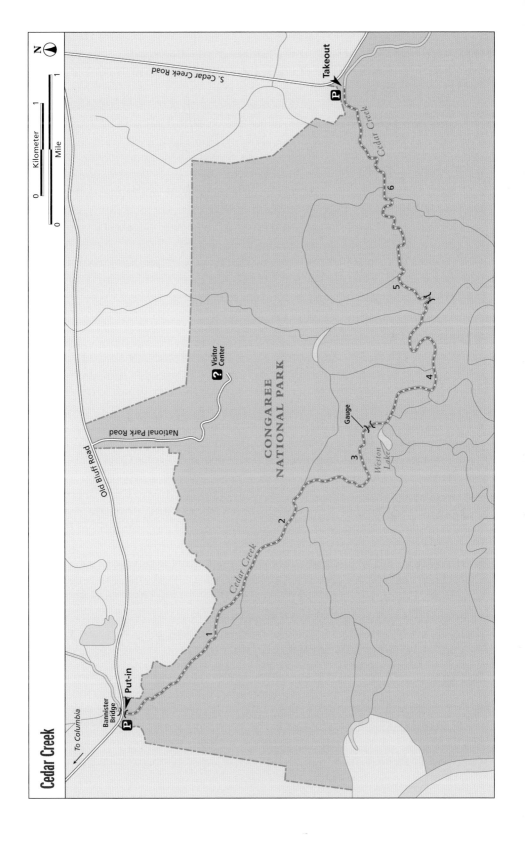

wildland of huge forests, where massive hardwoods rise above a periodically flooded forest floor, where birdsong echoes among the leaves, and where sunlight filters onto the darkened waters of the surprisingly swift stream.

This paddle tests your steering skills from the outset, as Cedar Creek twists and turns, making 180-degree turns and splitting into channels, but not so many as to be confusing—unless you are on the river above recommended levels when the main stream spills into the adjacent floodplain and becomes very hard to follow. Cedar Creek passes under two hiking-trail bridges, which help gauge your position. About halfway through, the creek widens, and turns become less abrupt, but be ready for a few blowdowns; however, the park service keeps fallen trees cut more than your average swamp stream. The takeout is marked by yet another hiker bridge, and if you don't get out here, it is 20 miles downstream to the next access on the Congaree River. Don't attempt this trip outside the recommended water levels, for the stream disperses when too high, and when too low you will be pulling over more logs than you want. Furthermore, in summer, the heat and mosquitoes can make paddling Cedar Creek a decidedly negative experience. *Note:* This paddle offers a viable bike shuttle.

River Overview

Cedar Creek is born in the hills of Fort Jackson, then flows south. It becomes paddleable—and accessible—where this paddle starts at Bannister Bridge. Here, Myers Creek adds its volume. Cedar Creek then winds its way southeasterly toward its mother stream, the Congaree River, by quite a convoluted course. Within the park, intermittent streams such as Tennessee Gut, Hammond Gut, Wise Lake, and other swamp rivulets add—and sometimes take away—flow from Cedar Creek. The channels running through Congaree National Park form a complicated plumbing system, especially considering the ten or so annual overflows of Cedar Creek and other tributaries of the Congaree River, as well as the Congaree itself, that make charting the flow patterns of this stream confusing. That being said, the main stem of Cedar Creek then flows easterly, nearing the park visitor center, where it passes through the heart of the park hiking-trail system. Beyond South Cedar Creek Road access, Cedar Creek keeps southeasterly then reaches Mazyck's Cut, which is used to access the Congaree River. Beyond Mazyck's Cut, Cedar Creek is a paddler's no-man's-land, with log-choked channels eventually flowing into the Congaree River about 7 miles above the US 601 access on the Congaree River. Paddlers going on Cedar Creek downstream of Mazyck's Cut do so at their own peril.

The Paddle

After making the 50-or-so-yard portage to the put-in, immediately enter a dark, wild world after putting in on Cedar Creek. The dim tannic water flows swiftly around small submerged sandbars under cypress, magnolia, holly, and sweetgums. Vines tangle themselves in the trees. It isn't long before Cedar Creek splits into channels, but the

Cedar Creek flows beneath forest primeval.

main way is evident. Look for sawn logs along the water's edge for route confirmation. The creek is less than 20 feet wide at this point. Look for wild hogs along the banks or in the waterside woods. They will present themselves at some point during your paddle. The continually curving creek will keep you focused on the water ahead, especially for the first couple of miles.

Cedar Creek is taking a southeasterly tack, though you wouldn't know it by the twists and turns. Firm, dry ground is hard to find, as a look around reveals the entire area as a massive overflow swamp, cloaked in beard cane. The waterway is canopied nearly its entire distance, creating a shady paddle. To appreciate the woods most, I recommend paddling here between spring leafing and June, or in fall after things cool down but before the leaves have fallen. However, having the right water level is paramount above all other considerations.

Cypress and gum trees line the hairpin turns as you head deeper into the national park, where wild banks only get wilder, recalling the clichéd term *brooding swamp*. Occasional park-service signs reassure you that you are on the right water trail.

At 2.5 miles, Cedar Creek widens. The majestic tree canopy rises still higher, held aloft by buttressed trunks. The banks rise a bit, and a main channel is more evident. At

3.2 miles, pass a river gauge on your left. Curve left and a hiker bridge spans Cedar Creek. This is a popular stopping spot. Consider adding a hike to your paddle. Trail maps are available online and at the park's visitor center. Pass under the hiker bridge and curve right. Weston Lake is to your right through the cypress and gum, and is worthy of exploration. Meanwhile, Cedar Creek continues easterly under higher banks and a still higher tree canopy. Look for waterside loblolly pines and cypress with impressive girths.

Weston Lake Loop Trail parallels the left bank at this point. In fall, ample acorns from oaks will splash into the stream around you. These acorns are nectar to the park's wild pigs. You will see their waterside rootings, which disturb the banks. At 4.9 miles, pass under a second hiker bridge over Cedar Creek, part of the Oak Ridge Loop. This is a shorter, less elaborate span, but it serves to mark your passage and is another hiking opportunity. Now, the Kingsnake Trail meanders the right bank for the next mile plus.

A 5.9 miles, look right for a hiker bridge crossing a draw on the right bank. From here, the Kingsnake Trail turns away from Cedar Creek. Continue easterly, ducking under an occasional tree outstretched over the water. A bluff rises on your left just before reaching South Cedar Creek Road takeout, marked with yet another hiker bridge spanning Cedar Creek. You can land your craft on a natural bank just before the bridge on your left or on concrete steps, also on your left, just after the hiker bridge.

HIKING CONGAREE NATIONAL PARK

The 2.4-mile boardwalk loop leaving from Congaree National Park Visitor Center is a must-do hike in the Palmetto State. Walk above the floodplain and beneath the canopy of an incredible forest, the perfect complement to your paddle. The hike leaves the visitor center breezeway to join a boardwalk. Take the "Low Boardwalk," which is eye level with wide, buttressed, moss-covered cypress and tupelo trees that thrive in this wetland. Continue south along the Low Boardwalk and reach an intersection: The Low Boardwalk Loop leaves left. Notice piles of debris banked against trees. This occurs when the floodplain is inundated, and leaves, brush, and other fodder are pushed up by the current and then left behind when the waters recede.

Just ahead meet the Elevated Boardwalk. Don't bypass the overlook of Weston Lake before continuing away from the lake on the high boardwalk. Head north, looking from a 10-foot-or-so perch into the forest. It's a great place to photograph the landscape before returning to the park's visitor center.

22 Wateree River

This big water run starts below the Lake Wateree Dam and takes you down a wide waterway. A few shoals spice up the float.

County: Kershaw
Start: Lugoff Access
    N34° 19.993' / W80° 42.001'
End: Patriots Landing near Camden
    N34° 14.704' / W80° 39.233'
Distance: 7.4 miles
Float time: 3.5 hours
Difficulty rating: Easy to moderate
Rapids: Class I
River type: Dam-controlled tailwater river
Current: Fast when generating
River gradient: 1.7 feet per mile
River gauge: Duke Energy Water Release Schedule: duke-energy.com/lakes/scheduled -flow-releases.asp. Scroll to find Wateree.

Release schedules are posted 72 hours in advance. As long as they are generating, the river is a go, barring flood conditions.
Season: Year-round
Land status: Private
Fees or permits: No fees or permits required
Nearest city/town: Camden
Maps: Wateree River Blue Trail; USGS Quadrangle Maps: Rabon Crossroads, Lugoff
Boats used: Canoes, kayaks, johnboats
Organizations: Wateree River Blue Trail, water eeriverbluetrail.blogspot.com
Contacts/outfitters: Congaree Land Trust, congareelt.org

Put-in/Takeout Information

To takeout: From the intersection of US 521 and US 1 in downtown Camden, take US 1 south toward Lugoff for 3.0 miles, crossing the Wateree River. Turn left just after crossing over to the west side of the bridge to Patriots Landing. The gravel road curves left and passes under the US 1 bridge.

To put-in from takeout: Leave Patriots Landing and head left (west) out of the boat ramp, onto US 1 south toward Lugoff. Follow US 1 for 0.6 mile then turn right on Longtown Road. Follow Longtown Road for 5.1 miles, then veer right on Wateree Dam Road and follow it for 2.7 miles to turn right, still on Wateree Dam Road, at a sign for Wateree Dam. Continue 0.6 mile, then turn right on Tailrace Road. Follow Tailrace Road for 0.9 mile to end at the boat ramp below Wateree Dam.

Paddle Summary

This section of the Wateree River makes for an ideal recreational day trip for paddlers. Starting at the boat ramp at the foot of Wateree Dam, you enter swift-moving water generated by releases from the dam. If Duke Energy is not generating, the river may be too low and boney—that is, rocky—to float. So, go when Duke Energy is generating. Wateree Dam looms large above you, yet the current takes you downstream over very mild Loves Shoals. The water remains fast, and downstream the Wateree River splits around a couple of islands. The noisiest rapid is at an island. Most paddlers take the water left fork. Multiple channels offer clean routes. Campers can sometimes be seen on this island.

From here, the Wateree River makes an almost due-south course, flowing wide under the open sky. The fast water keeps you moving, yet there is little in the way of rapids. The river curves back to the southeast, and you can look downstream at the US 1 Bridge and at your takeout in the distance. Several creeks feed the Wateree River in this segment, most notably Twenty Five Mile Creek, which you pass just before the takeout on river right.

River Overview

The Wateree River starts as a big waterway and is essentially a continuation of the Catawba River coming from North Carolina. The Catawba enters Lake Wateree and then emerges as the Wateree River. The Wateree Dam is the last of eleven Duke Energy dams on the Catawba/Wateree River system. The dam and lake name comes from area Indians and Big Wateree Creek and Little Wateree Creek that flow into Lake Wateree. Once it emerges from Wateree Dam, the Wateree River Blue Trail starts an 80-mile stretch of river that is very wild for its size and is the longest free-flowing segment of the entire Catawba/Wateree system. After the takeout at US 1, it is 44 miles until the next bridge (at US 378) and boat ramp on the Wateree. That is a remote stretch of river, with ample sandbars for those wanting to camp. Make sure and plant yourself high on a sandbar in case of big releases from Wateree Dam. The river winds through remote areas bordered by swamps while passing east of Columbia. The last 4 miles of the Wateree border Congaree National Park. The Wateree then meets the Congaree River to form the Santee River just above Lake Marion.

The Paddle

A concrete ramp astride a large open field with a few scattered trees leads to the Wateree. Ample parking is available for boaters and anglers who like to fish from shore. When the dam is generating power, you immediately enter fast water. The river is divided by an island at the launch, making the course narrower at the beginning, about 160 feet wide. The channel on the other side of the island is the old Wateree Canal. Banks of sycamore, ash, paper birch, magnolia, and cedar clad the shore. Fast-moving generated water keeps river rubble to a minimum, though you will have sporadic exposed rocks and fallen trees directly along the shore. The route shortly passes over Loves Shoals, a former rocky impediment to traveling upstream on the Wateree—and one reason that the Wateree Canal was dug. The shoals are submerged when Duke Energy is generating.

The first stream coming in to the Wateree is the interestingly named Grannies' Quarter Creek. It is on the far shore, and you will likely pass right by without coming

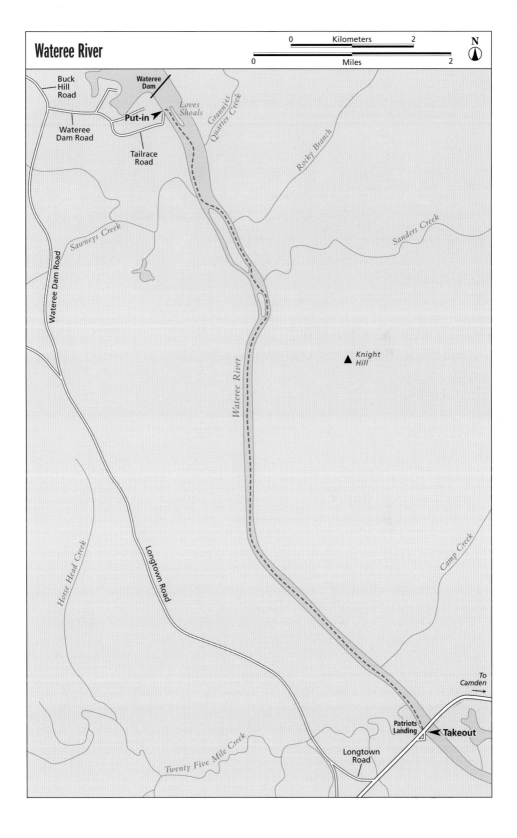

Wateree River

Kilometers
0   2

Miles
0   2

N

Buck Hill Road

Wateree Dam

Put-in

Loves Shoals

Grannies Quarter Creek

Rocky Branch

Wateree Dam Road

Tailrace Road

Wateree Dam Road

Sawneys Creek

Sanders Creek

Knight Hill

Wateree River

Horse Head Creek

Longtown Road

Camp Creek

To Camden

Patriots Landing

Takeout

Twenty Five Mile Creek

Longtown Road

A local paddling club enjoys a relaxing afternoon on the Wateree.

too close. After 0.5 mile, the water slows. Sawneys Creek comes in on your right at 1.1 miles. Ahead, the Wateree splits around a few more linear islands. A steady current keeps you moving, whether you want to or not.

At 1.5 miles, Rocky Branch comes in on your left. At 1.9 miles, the river speeds, and Sanders Creek adds its flow to the Wateree River. The watercourse then splits around an island shoal at 2.2 miles. This is the biggest rapid on the river, and it is just a Class I. However, there are a few rocks to avoid but multiple channels to choose. Most paddlers stay to the left of this island.

From here on out the trip is an easy float on a wide river. The stout current pushes you along. However, strong head winds on the now 300-plus-foot-wide waterway can slow your progress. At 2.5 miles, Knight Hill rises on river left, and you are pushed to the right but are still maintaining an almost due southerly course.

At 3.0 miles, enjoy a direct downriver sweep. Flats stretch out from both banks under a big sky. You may see anglers in anchored-down johnboats, trying to catch a few fish. Small unnamed tributaries feed the Wateree. Pass under a power line at 4.4 miles. The river begins curving left and takes a southeasterly direction. Once again, you have a long straightaway with a far-reaching view downriver. The US 1 bridge becomes visible in the distance, but enjoy your experience, relaxing as the Wateree pushes your craft downstream.

At 7.1 miles, Twenty Five Mile Creek comes in on your right. This is the largest feeder stream you will pass. Get over to the right-hand bank and reach the Patriots Landing boat ramp and a floating dock on your right just before passing under the US 1 bridge. Be prepared for a fast current as you pull into the dock. This is a popular ramp for johnboats. On nice weekends, boaters will be pulling the trailers up and down the long ramp. Try to land on the dock and get your boat up the walkway and out of the ramp area as quickly as possible.

THE ERA OF CANALS ON THE WATEREE

With the success of the many canals up north and in the Lowcountry of the Palmetto State, it was only a matter of time before canals were used in interior South Carolina. In the early 1800s, overland roads were few and in rough shape. If they weren't overwhelmed by dust, fallen trees, and ceaseless growth, they were mired in mud and plagued by stream fords and infrequent bridges. It was difficult getting people and products to market. Therefore, rivers were used for transportation. In the Midlands, where the fall line created opportunities to harness river power—which is the reason many cities were established where they were, the same rapids were obstacles to river transportation. Therefore, canals were built around rapids. Where this paddle takes place, the Wateree Canal extended for 5 miles and was part of the Catawba/Wateree River navigation system. This canal had seven locks, raising boats a total of 52 feet. The canal, 80 feet wide and 10 feet deep, was completed in 1821. The waterway was in operation for seventeen years before exorbitant startup, operating costs, and rebuilding costs, as well as the coming of the railroads, closed the canal.

23 Big Pine Tree Creek Canoe Trail

Paddle through the cypress swamps at Goodale State Park.

County: Kershaw
Start: Goodale State Park ramp
   N34° 17.035' / W80° 31.421'
End: Goodale State Park ramp
   N34° 17.035' / W80° 31.421'
Distance: 3.0 miles
Float time: 2.5 hours
Difficulty rating: Easy
Rapids: None
River type: Cypress-covered lake and swamp creek
Current: None to slow
River gradient: 0.3 feet per mile
River gauge: None, dam-controlled pond

Season: Year-round, park open 9 a.m. to 6 p.m daily; closed Mon through Thurs from Dec through mid-Mar
Land status: Public
Fees or permits: No fees or permits required
Nearest city/town: Camden
Maps: Goodale State Park; USGS Quadrangle Maps: Camden North
Boats used: Canoes, kayaks, johnboats
Organizations: Goodale State Park, 650 Park Rd., Camden, SC 29020, (803) 432-2772, southcarolinaparks.com
Contacts/outfitters: South Carolina Department of Health and Environmental Control, 2600 Bull St., Columbia, SC 29201, (803) 898-4300, scdhec.gov/environment/water

Put-in/Takeout Information

To takeout: From the intersection of US 1 and US 521 in downtown Camden, take US north for 3.1 miles, then turn right on Old Stagecoach Road. Follow Old Stagecoach Road for 2.5 miles, then turn left on Park Road. The park entrance is on your right after 0.2 mile. Enter the park and shortly turn right, then follow the road through the park picnic area to reach Adams Mill Pond and a sandy put-in.
To put–in from takeout: Put-in and takeout are the same.

Paddle Summary

This is one of those "why don't more people paddle here?" places. The Big Pine Tree Creek Canoe Trail, located at N. R. Goodale State Park near Camden, presents an opportunity to paddle a cypress swamp, winding your way amid hardwoods rising from the coffee-colored waters of 140-acre Adams Mill Pond, which is fed by Big Pine Tree Creek. After working your way across the open waters of Adams Mill Pond, you will find the marked Big Pine Tree Creek Canoe Trail. The signed paddling path twists and turns up the old channel of Big Pine Tree Creek, while watery swamp extends to hilly, pine-clad shores. It's comforting to know the signs are there, allowing you to absorb the land and waterscape, where alligators ply, birdlife is abundant, and an altogether engaging adventure awaits.

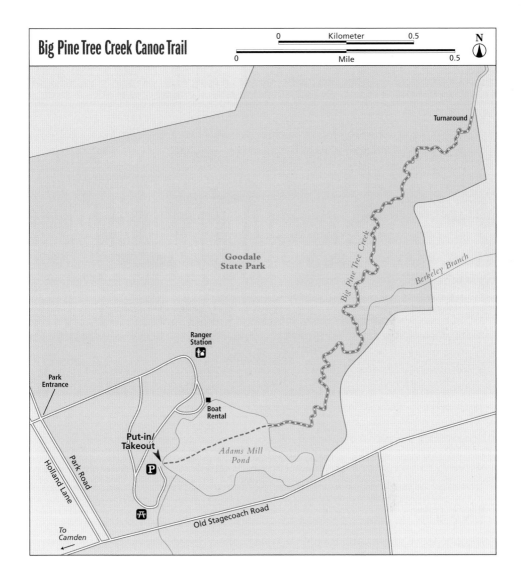

Kilometer 0.5

Mile 0.5

N

Turnaround

Goodale
State Park

Big Pine Tree Creek

Berkeley Branch

Ranger
Station

Park
Entrance

Boat
Rental

Put-in/
Takeout

P

Adams Mill
Pond

Holland Lane

Park Road

Old Stagecoach Road

To
Camden

As you paddle to the head of Adams Mill Pond, feel the current of Big Pine Tree Creek pushing against you. Underwater grasses sway in the current. The wetland narrows until eventually the only potential paddling area is directly up the stream. Numerous sharp turns and dense vegetation make the paddling exciting. Eventually you will reach the park boundary, marked with a sign by the creek and a small piney hill that allows for a break. From there, make your way back down the stream pushed by the current until it slows.

The trail is marked with a sign indicating the paddle trail as you are heading away from the put-in and a "State Park" arrow while heading back toward the put-in to keep you from being turned around. That being said, there are other waters to explore

Wood duck boxes are situated along the canoe trail.

in addition to the marked trail. A GPS will help your confidence both on the paddle trail and if you decide to explore other waters of Adams Mill Pond.

River Overview

Big Pine Tree Creek is a tributary of the Wateree River. It originates in eastern Kershaw County, near the town of Cassatt. Unlike most South Carolina waterways, Big Pine Tree Creek flows southwesterly, picking up a few tributaries, including Berkeley Branch, just as it becomes slowed by Adams Mill Pond. The pond here at Goodale State Park was originally created when Big Pine Tree Creek was dammed to power a mill back in the mid-1800s. It was one of several milldams on the stream. From Goodale State Park, Big Pine Tree Creek continues its southwesterly journey and is stopped one more time at big Hermitage Mill Pond, just southeast of Camden. The stream courses through wetlands, then meets its mother stream, the Wateree River, just south of Camden.

The Paddle

The boat ramp—just a sandy spot leading from the dam area to the water—is next to

Adams Mill Pond spillway. This is a popular fishing spot for shoreline anglers, so don't be surprised if there are cars and people crowded around the put-in. As you look out, the park's boat rental area and large pavilion are on the shoreline to your left. An open stretch of water lies before you, though a scattering of cypress trees is nearby. Since Adams Mill Pond is dammed, the water level remains stable under normal conditions. Leave the put-in and head easterly through a channel bordered by cypress trees toward a large white sign marking the beginning of the Big Pine Tree Creek Canoe Trail.

Nesting boxes for wood ducks are scattered throughout the paddling trail. You will see the wooden boxes atop posts, with a circular galvanized-metal barrier on the post below the box to foil predators such as raccoons or rat snakes; they will go after the duck eggs or even the nesting hen if given the opportunity. Wood ducks are one of the few reproducing waterfowl in South Carolina. In the East, they are found from Minnesota to Florida and Texas. South Carolina is doing its part to help wood ducks, as the Department of Natural Resources, along with Ducks Unlimited, has helped provide funding for over 30,000 wood-duck nesting boxes over the last two plus decades.

Reach the big white sign starting the official paddling trail. It explains that you follow the diamond-shape trail signs on your outbound journey and the arrows marked with "State Park" on your return. You go out and back on the same trail, though there is no rule against exploring. After 0.25 mile, enter a watery corridor bordered by swamp trees. The trail signs are obviously the best way to stay on track, but you can also observe aquatic vegetation in the water. There'll be more vegetation on and under water that is not being paddled than the trail itself, which will be freer of lily pads and such.

At 0.4 mile, the trail begins twisting and turning worse than a snake. You can see pine hills, signifying dry land in the distance. Though you're keeping a generally northeast direction, the fast turns keep paddlers on their toes and require full cooperation if two people are in the same boat. Shorter kayaks are preferred on this trail.

GOODALE STATE PARK

Goodale State Park was opened in 1955 and named for a local florist who was the force behind acquiring the land for the 763-acre park. Paddling is the centerpiece of the park activities. The park rents canoes, kayaks, and johnboats quite inexpensively. Only electric trolling motors are allowed, keeping park waters tranquil. There is also fishing on Adams Mill Pond. Anglers will be vying for bass, bream, and catfish. The picnic shelters at the park are popular for family and church gatherings. Other land-based recreation includes a 1-mile hiking trail that explores the hills beside Adams Mill Pond. The town of Camden is just a few miles away, and the park is less than an hour's drive from Columbia. It should be easy to make a day of it paddling, hiking, and picnicking at Goodale State Park.

Flowering aquatic plants grow along Big Pine Creek.

A variety of vegetation grows on the buttressed tops of the cypress trees standing atop the water, including carnivorous pitcher plants and small Atlantic white cedars. The cedars were once common in Palmetto State swamps, but their numbers have dwindled because many were cut for their fine aromatic wood, and much of their native habitat has been lost. This state park is a good place to harbor the evergreens.

At 0.7 mile, you will skirt against dry land off to your right. Wooded hills screen Old Stagecoach Road in the distance. Continue winding past lily pads, duck moss, and varied aquatic vegetation. Fallen logs are regularly cut on the trail; look for them to help you discern the correct route. At 1.1 miles, come near a piney shore, this time on your left. The pond continues to narrow, and a current is detectable—that is, it is working against you—in the canoe-trail channel that is now in the flow of Big Pine Tree Creek. Cypresses rise high for the sky. The farther you go, the more narrow the channel and the stronger the current. At 1.5 miles, reach a sign indicating the park boundary. Here, a small landing on a wooded hill presents an opportunity to get out of your boat. From this point, it is a 1.5-mile backtrack to the landing. Look for the arrows imprinted with "State Park" to guide your return.

Adams Mill Pond avails open and wooded waters to explore. Big Pine Tree Creek upstream of the park boundary has a lure as well, but you may find blown-down trees an impediment. Either way, feel free to test the boundaries of what lies beyond the trail.

24 Cheraw State Park Paddle

Explore a picturesque lake, a cypress swamp, and the stream that feeds the lake, all at a historic state park.

County: Chesterfield
Start: Cheraw State Park ramp
N34° 38.457' / W79° 53.602'
End: Cheraw State Park ramp
N34° 38.457' / W79° 53.602'
Distance: 5.9 miles
Float time: 4 hours
Difficulty rating: Moderate
Rapids: None
River type: Cypress-covered lake and swamp creek
Current: None to slow
River gradient: None
River gauge: None, lake

Season: Year-round
Land status: Public
Fees or permits: No fees or permits required
Nearest city/town: Cheraw
Maps: Cheraw State Park; USGS Quadrangle Maps: Cheraw, Cash
Boats used: Canoes, kayaks, johnboats
Organizations: Cheraw State Park, 100 State Park Rd., Cheraw, SC 29520, (843) 537-9656, southcarolinaparks.com
Contacts/outfitters: South Carolina Department of Health and Environmental Control, 2600 Bull St., Columbia, SC 29201, (803) 898-4300, scdhec.gov/environment/water

Put-in/Takeout Information

To takeout: From Cheraw, take US 1 South /US 52 East to where they split. At the road split, stay left on US 52 East and follow it for 1.0 mile to the park entrance on your right. Continue past this main entrance for 0.3 mile farther, then turn right into the campground/boat ramp entrance and follow the road for just a short distance to reach a right turn to the boat ramp and parking area.

To put-in from takeout: Put-in and takeout are the same.

Paddle Summary

This state park paddle presents a little bit of everything. For starters, it is set in a scenic location, within the confines of Cheraw State Park, a large recreation area located in the sand hills near the town of Cheraw, developed in the 1930s by the Civilian Conservation Corps. The paddle begins at a convenient boat ramp, then cruises 360-acre Lake Juniper, an impoundment of Juniper Creek. Part of the lake is open, and part of it is dotted with cypress stands, creating a swamp labyrinth through which you can paddle. Make your way up the south shoreline as it curves past pine hills and through shallows. Float around an island, then enter eerie swamp woods, still paralleling the shoreline. After paddling to an old bridge abutment, you begin stroking up Juniper Creek, free flowing at this stage. After paddling up the creek to your heart's desire, you then backtrack to the lake and explore its northern shore. Revel in more swamp paddling among

EXPLORING THE LAND ECOSYSTEMS OF CHERAW STATE PARK

Cheraw State Park seemingly offers something for everyone, including two interconnected loop trails for hikers that provide interpretive information, a restored red-cockaded woodpecker habitat, and a visit into the valley of Juniper Creek before arriving at a scenic overlook of Lake Juniper.

The Cheraw Nature Trail and the Turkey Oak Trail leave as one from the trailhead. Enter pine woods that have been restored to their natural state. At one time, the park suppressed fires here, resulting in a heavy undergrowth of turkey and blackjack oaks. Eventually, many of the small oaks were cut, opening the longleaf pine woods to their natural habitat with a primary understory of wiregrass. It is important that Cheraw State Park restore and preserve this habitat. The purposes of state parks are numerous—preservation, recreation, and wildlife habitat.

The trail enters a nesting area for the red-cockaded woodpecker. As this forest was being restored to its natural state, park personnel actually created artificial nesting cavities in the longleaf pines and brought woodpeckers to the area. They stayed, and the bird reintroduction has been successful. Reach a trail junction here, at 0.9 mile. The Cheraw Nature Trail continues left, but the Turkey Oak Trail turns right. Stay right here, following the red blazes and traveling over piney sand hills, which contrast with the wetter lowlands around them.

The wet lowlands grow thick with bay trees and ferns, dense as the longleaf/wiregrass forest is open. The longleaf/wiregrass ecosystem once covered more than 50 million acres in the Southeast and now grows in less than 3 million acres. These pine flatwoods are easy to develop or alter and thus have been cut over, changed, or allowed to evolve into other forest types after fire suppression.

The path begins dipping into the Juniper Creek valley and a moister environment, but not quite a wetland. And with the change come different trees: loblolly pines, dogwoods, and more mature oaks. Reach a trail junction on an old roadbed at 2.6 miles. Here, walk right along the old roadbed to find an overlook of Lake Juniper. A bench offers a resting and reflection spot. You can see this bench on your paddle.

The Turkey Oak Trail now heads away from the lake on the old roadbed, gently rising from Lake Juniper. Continue climbing away from the lake to cross a wide, sandy old road at 3.6 miles. Pinewoods dominate beyond the sand road, and you are in very open country pocked with tall longleaf pines. Before you know it, the Cheraw Nature Trail and Turkey Oak Trail meet. Backtrack to the trailhead, completing your loop at 4.2 miles and adding a hike to your paddle.

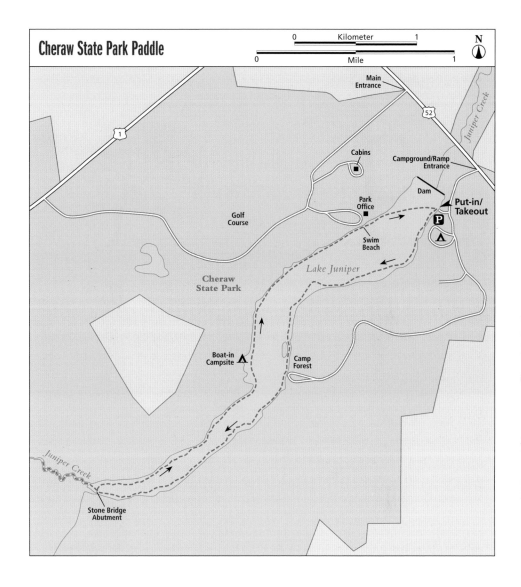

the cypresses. Come near many of the park facilities, including a boat-in campsite, before returning to the boat ramp. Here at Cheraw, a large state park at over 7,300 acres, not only do they have a paddling lake, but they also have a campground, fishing, swimming and hiking, a golf course, and even trails for mountain bikers and equestrians. Don't forget the rental cabins for those who want to make roughing it a little easier.

River Overview

Juniper Creek has its headwaters deep in the Sand Hills State Forest, in the shadow of Sugarloaf Mountain. The waterway flows eastward, roughly parallelling US 1,

Cypresses rise eerily against a dark and cloudy sky.

then nears Cheraw National Fish Hatchery before slowing as it enters Lake Juniper and Cheraw State Park. Here it is dammed as part of the state park, before continuing easterly and picking up its biggest tributary—Thompson Creek—then winding a short distance to enter the Great Pee Dee River. Juniper Creek remains entirely within the boundaries of Chesterfield County, nearly stretching from one end of the county to the other before meeting its mother stream, the Great Pee Dee River.

The Paddle

Leave the boat ramp and begin heading southwesterly along the shoreline. You will immediately paddle past the park campground, where campers may be relaxing along the shore, perhaps throwing in a line. At 0.2 mile, cruise by an old floating dock. The park's swim beach and office are across the lake. Continue paddling in open water. The shoreline is super shallow, and you have to avoid sunken stumps. At 0.5 mile, come to an island. Scattered cypresses are between you and the shoreline, but paddlers can thread their way through, and return to open water.

At 0.8 mile, the lake curves to the southwest. Stay along the wooded shoreline, from which Cypress trees creep. At 1.1 miles, you sneak past a small island and the shore, a precursor to the paddle ahead. At 1.3 miles, pass Camp Forest, part of the park. A small grassy landing here avails a stopping point. Continue down the narrowing lake. Enter the area of cypress. Competent paddlers will easily be able to wind their way among the trees rising from the water. Dare yourself to stay as close to the shore as possible while working your paddling magic. Solid shoreline is always identifiable by the pines.

At 2.2 miles, visit the embayment of a small tributary. At 2.6 miles, the paddling area is squeezed in by the stone abutments of an old bridge crossing Juniper Creek. This is a palatable stopping spot. Be apprised there is another stopping spot, the other side of the old roadbed. At this point, continue up Juniper Creek. Though bordered by still swamp, there is a channel and movement to the stream at this point. Continue following the waterway as it narrows further until finally there is nothing but the stream itself to follow. The current becomes swifter but is easy to overcome with a little arm muscle. Expect to see a beaver lodge or two in this area. The stream continues to twist and turn sharply, pushing your steering skills as well as your ability to duck under overhanging vegetation.

At 3.1 miles, solid ground rises on river right and affords a potential stopping spot. Otherwise, turn around and backtrack to the bridge abutment, then join the north shoreline. You will quickly pass a contemplation bench, part of the Turkey Oak Trail, detailed in the sidebar. Squeeze betwixt more cypresses, looking for pitcher plants perched on the tree bases.

Pass a few small islands, then reach the boat-in campsite at 4.7 miles. It offers a fire ring, picnic table, and open-sided shelter. Ahead, you will see part of the golf course. The lake continues to open. Paddle near the swim beach and park office at 5.5 miles. Beyond here, aim for the boat ramp, completing the paddle at 5.9 miles.

The Lowcountry

The author takes off as an early morning autumn sun illuminates Awendaw Creek (paddle 33).

25 Little Pee Dee River

Wind your way on a swift smallish stream through a lush swamp forest in the shadows of Dillon.

County: Dillon
Start: Stafford Bridge Landing
N34° 26.846' / W79° 20.540'
End: Dillon County Landing
N34° 22.122' / W79° 21.234'
Distance: 8.3 miles
Float time: 4 hours
Difficulty rating: Moderate
Rapids: Class I
River type: Twisting swamp stream
Current: Moderate to swift
River gradient: 1.7 feet per mile
River gauge: Little Pee Dee River at Galivants Ferry, minimum runnable level: 2.0 feet, maximum 9.0 feet

Season: Year-round
Land status: Private
Fees or permits: No fees or permits required
Nearest city/town: Dillon
Maps: Little Pee Dee Trail Guide; USGS Quadrangle Maps: Dillon East, Fork
Boats used: Kayaks, canoes, a few johnboats
Organizations: South Carolina Department of Natural Resources, Rembert C. Dennis Building, 1000 Assembly St., Columbia, SC 29201, (803) 734-9100, dnr.sc.gov/
Contacts/outfitters: South Carolina Department of Health and Environmental Control, 2600 Bull St., Columbia, SC 29201, (803) 898-4300, scdhec.gov/environment/water

Put-in/Takeout Information

To takeout: From exit 193 on I-95 near Dillon, take SC 57/SC 9 (Radford Boulevard) south for 1.1 miles to a traffic light and US 301. Turn right here and follow US 301 south for 0.9 mile to a traffic light and Main Street in Dillon. Turn left here and follow Main Street for 0.8 mile, then veer right onto SC 57 south and follow it for 2.9 miles, and then turn left on Pee Dee River Access Place. The sand road dead-ends at the landing after 0.2 mile.

To put-in from takeout: Backtrack from Dillon County Landing all the way through Dillon and to the intersection of US 301 and SC 57/SC 9 (Radford Boulevard), near I-95. Now, continue north on US 301 beyond the intersection with Radford Boulevard for 1.8 miles, crossing the Little Pee Dee River. Just after the bridge over the Little Pee Dee, turn right on Kentyre Road and immediately turn right again onto the gravel road leading to the landing.

Paddle Summary

This is a fun trip on a scenic waterway—literally, as it is one of nine state-designated scenic rivers in the South Carolina. The paddling trip down the Little Pee Dee River takes place just east of Dillon, though you would never know the town is so close while you are on the water. The river meanders back and forth through a wide

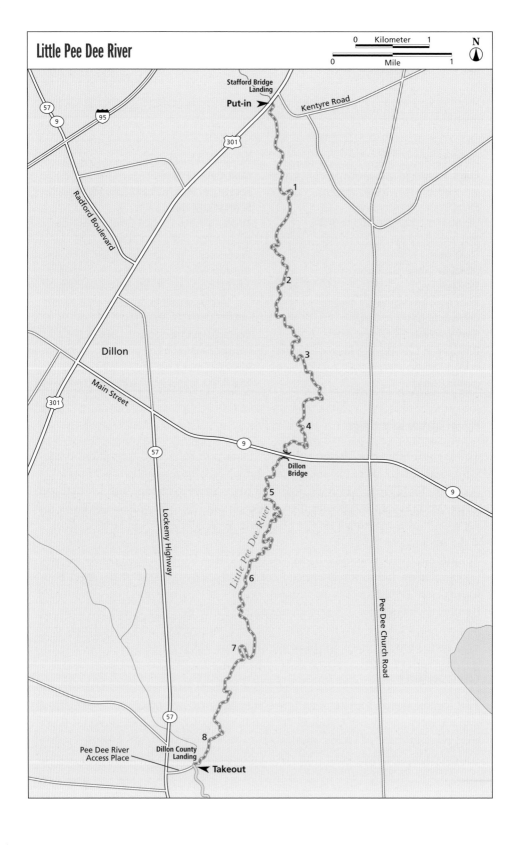

floodplain that is dense with cypress and tupelo trees. Beyond this swampy bank—normally well out of sight from the paddler—rises an elevated terrace where civilization begins.

Leave the Stafford Bridge Landing and commence swiftly down this blackwater stream, dodging occasional fallen trees under a canopy of vegetation. The Little Pee Dee rarely goes straight; it is usually curving in this section. Occasionally, the river will divide into channels, and you must choose your way. However, the correct route will be evident with a cut and cleared channel, whereas the wrong route will almost always clog up with vegetation. You will see a few houses on adjoining sloughs but not very many. You will likely see more wildlife than people. A little over halfway through, pass under the SC 9 Bridge. Though it does not have an official landing, people use it as a bank fishing spot and boat throw-in. Leave civilization again to resume your meandering through this linear swamp. River bends are fewer on the lower part of the paddle, but streamside vegetation is every bit as thick. The trip ends at the Dillon County Landing, a sandy stopping point with a boat ramp that has been historically used as a landing, fishing, and (especially) swimming spot for over a century.

River Overview

The headwaters of the Little Pee Dee River flow south from Marlboro County, at the confluence of South Carolina's Beaverdam Creek and Gum Swamp Creek, which begins in Scotland County, North Carolina. These two streams come together near Red Bluff, South Carolina. From here, the river runs southeasterly near the state line and begins its 120-mile journey to meet its mother stream, the Great Pee Dee River. This upper section is tough for paddling but becomes commonly used just a few miles north of Dillon at Moccasin Bluff Landing. The next major landing is at Stafford Bridge, where this paddle starts. The river then continues its southerly quest and passes by Little Pee Dee State Park. Near the town of Mullins, its major tributary—the Lumber River—enters from North Carolina. The Lumber River is a fine paddling stream itself, though only a little over 10 miles of the Lumber flow in South Carolina, and it is arguably bigger than the Little Pee Dee. From this confluence, the Little Pee Dee turns southwesterly as a much bigger waterway and continues flowing through a wide swamp valley bordered by higher, drier terraces. Public lands and preserves border portions of this lower waterway. Though remote, occasional landings are decently interspersed and provide good access. Finally, the Little Pee Dee meets the Great Pee Dee a bit north of the hamlet of Bucksport.

The Paddle

Jump in your boat and immediately shoot swiftly down a classic blackwater stream. These upper reaches of the Little Pee Dee River are narrow and interspersed with partly submerged trees that require vigilance while paddling. This regularly

Make a quick escape to nature on this waterway on the outskirts of Dillon.

paddled stretch of river is cleared by local boaters. The waterway stretches about 30 feet and is under a canopy. It isn't long before the Little Pee Dee breaks into channels or splits around islands. Most of these isles are small groupings of tightly knit cypress trees.

The thickness of the bordering swamp forest effectively creates a visual wildland, belying the nearness of Dillon and underscoring the fact that this stretch of river in Dillon County is a state scenic river, designated as such in 2005. Landings such as this one at Stafford Bridge were subsequently established and/or improved. Old river meanders and high water channels create routes of exploration. Cypress knees by the thousands extend away from the river and through the swamp. At 0.4 mile, the river makes a mean bend and you pass your first sandbar. These ideal stopping spots will be submerged at higher water levels. The current hastens through sandy shallows or where it becomes constricted by fallen trees.

At 1.0 mile, the Little Pee Dee passes a piney bluff. This is one of the few places where the river curves to the edge of its greater floodplain. Downstream, the bluff continues for 0.5 mile, then the Little Pee Dee turns again. Watch for water lilies blooming here in season.

On the slightest stretches of higher ground, you may spot rough fish camps, seemingly encircled by swamp woods and water. At 3.7 miles, pass under a power-line clearing. Sloughs aplenty, formed from old river channels, are found below here. Pass a short stretch of high ground before floating under the SC 9 Bridge, also known as the Dillon Bridge, at 4.5 miles. Bank fishermen are often seen watering their line and relaxing by the river. You can throw in your boat using the old, closed bridge, adjacent to the current bridge.

Downstream, the wooded floodplain widens. There are more small islet clusters in the stream, and thus more route decisions, though the primary route is obvious more often than not. However, the Little Pee Dee does cut through sharp bends, and logjams will reroute the river as well. Look for cut logs from previous paddlers. The forest rises, and in places, the plethora of moss hanging in the trees adds to the jungle effect of the landscape. At 6.4 miles, the Little Pee Dee bends left, then keeps a relatively straight course for almost 0.5 mile before resuming its curvaceous ways. At 7.6 miles you come along some actual high, dry ground on river right. Here, you see a few houses on still higher ground back from the river. Reach the boat ramp and sand stop at Dillon County Landing at 8.3 miles, ending this trip.

CONSERVATION: A CLEANER RIVER

The South Carolina Department of Natural Resources offers a set of suggestions for those interested in keeping the Palmetto State's waterways cleaner and more natural. Here are some of them:

- Reduce polluted runoff.
- Properly use and dispose of all chemicals and oil.
- Properly control animals and their waste.
- Repair leaking vehicles and boat motors.
- Do not use storm drains for disposal.
- Inspect septic systems and pump them out regularly.
- Properly dispose of human waste while camping along the river.
- Pick up trash, do not litter, and volunteer to help with river sweep events.
- Manage stormwater flow.
- Capture runoff and let the water soak into the soil before allowing it to reach the river.
- Follow best management practices to protect water, soil, and wildlife.
- Use better building practices.
- Reduce unnecessary pavement or use permeable materials where possible.

Everyone's property eventually drains into a river. Consider some of the above practices on your stretch of South Carolina stream, keeping it a paddler's paradise.

26 Waccamaw River

Take a trip down the upper part of this federally designated blue trail.

County: Horry	**Season:** Year-round
Start: Worthams Ferry Landing	**Land status:** State heritage preserve, some
N33° 55.463' / W78° 40.285'	private land
End: Anderson Memorial Landing	**Fees or permits:** No fees or permits required
N33° 54.674' / W78° 42.904'	**Nearest city/town:** North Myrtle Beach
Distance: 6.0 miles	**Maps:** Waccamaw River Blue Trail; USGS Quad-
Float time: 3.5 hours	rangle Maps: Longs
Difficulty rating: Easy to moderate	**Boats used:** Kayaks, canoes, some johnboats
Rapids: None	**Organizations:** American Rivers, 1101 14th St.
River type: Blackwater river	NW, Ste. 1400, Washington, DC 20005, (877)
Current: Moderate	347-7550, americanrivers.org
River gradient: Less than 1 foot per mile	**Contacts/outfitters:** South Carolina Depart-
River gauge: Waccamaw River near Longs, SC,	ment of Natural Resources, Rembert C. Dennis
minimum runnable level: 100 cfs, maximum:	Building, 1000 Assembly St., Columbia, SC
flood stage	29201, (803) 734-3893, dnr.sc.gov

Put-in/Takeout Information

To takeout: From the on/off ramp of SC 31 expressway and SC 9 just north of North Myrtle Beach, take SC 9 north just a short distance to a traffic light and an intersection, with SC 57 leaving left and Wampee Road leaving right. From here, keep straight on SC 9, bridging the Waccamaw River. Just after the long bridge, at 2.6 miles, turn left into the Chris Anderson Memorial Landing. There is a large two-lane boat ramp, a parking lot, and picnic tables here.

To put-in from takeout: Backtrack on US 9 south 2.6 miles to Wampee Road. Turn left here, heading northeast for 2.2 miles to turn left on Highway 111, also known as Little River Road. Follow Highway 111 for 1.2 miles to reach a stop sign. Keep straight here, as the road changes names to Granger Road. Shortly dead-end at Worthams Ferry. This is a small public gravel launch with limited parking. Please be considerate when parking your vehicle.

Paddle Summary

This is a trip down one of the most interesting blackwater rivers in the South. For starters, the river runs southwesterly, paralleling the Atlantic Ocean. This section of the Waccamaw is entirely freshwater and is above tidal influence, whereas most South Carolina rivers flow southeasterly from the mountains to the sea. The river has just entered the Palmetto State from North Carolina. The Waccamaw makes a serpentine

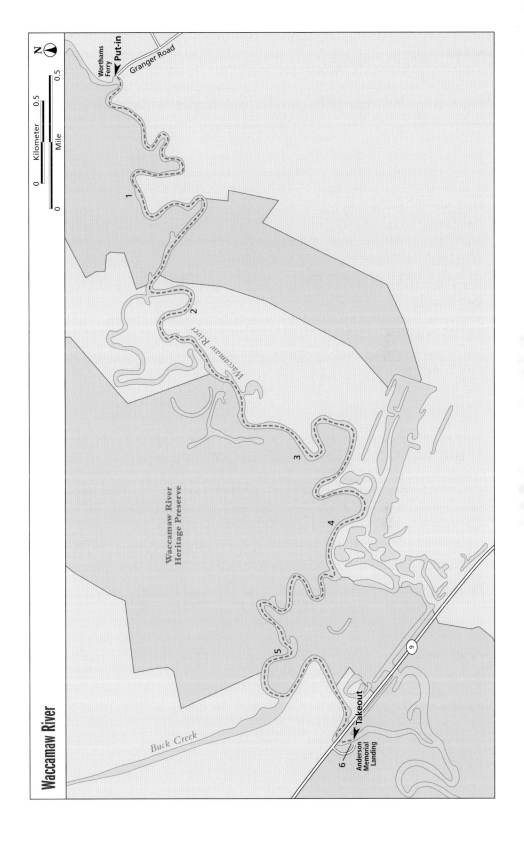

Waccamaw River

Worthams Ferry Put-in
Granger Road

1

Waccamaw River

2

Waccamaw River Heritage Preserve

3

4

5

Buck Creek

6

Takeout
Anderson Memorial Landing

9

N

Kilometer
0   0.5
Mile
0   0.5

course through a wide floodplain but occasionally curves against a bluff on its south-east side, a natural berm lying between it and the Atlantic coast. An aerial view reveals old oxbows, and you will experience the current incarnation of the river and its turns. Much of the bank is protected as part of a South Carolina heritage preserve, which keeps it wild.

The relatively swift waterway is small enough to be intimate, yet not so small that you have blowdowns blocking the course. Extensive forested wetlands border the river, creating habitat for flora and fauna of the coastal plain. Interestingly, the heritage preserve and other public lands create a wildlife corridor for mammals, including black bear, as well as a refuge for songbird migrations. Paddlers will find sandbars for stopping on the insides of river bends. The undulations continue throughout the paddle, but the river maintains its overall southwesterly direction. Finally, the noise of SC 9 lets you know the end is near. After passing under the SC 9 Bridge, the ramp is reached on your right. It does have a floating dock in addition to two ramps.

River Overview

The Waccamaw River exhibits unusual characteristics even at its birthplace in Lake Waccamaw, an unusual body of water known as a Carolina bay. These natural lakes stretch from Florida to New Jersey, but they are most prominent in the Carolinas. Bay lakes are usually oval in shape, pointed on a northwest to southeast axis, and are usually no deeper than 10 feet. Theories about the origin of these lakes range from meteors crashing into the earth to gigantic prehistoric whales carving holes in ancient shallow seas with their tails. Their origins remain a mystery to this day.

From Lake Waccamaw, the 140-mile-long, paddleable river heads south through swamps, merging with other swamp streams until it comes reaches the Atlantic coastal ridge at the South Carolina state line after 50 miles. From here, the Waccamaw aims more southwesterly, still within a swampy floodplain. It gets wide by the time it reaches Conway and continues a now tidally influenced course for the sea. Its lower portion, formerly rice plantation country, becomes part of the Intracoastal Waterway before finally emptying into the Atlantic near Georgetown, at Winyah Bay.

The Paddle

As you enter the river at Worthams Ferry, there are a couple of houses on river left. However, the right bank is part of the Waccamaw River Heritage Preserve. The preserve starts a few miles upstream at the North Carolina state line. Being a small landing, Worthams Ferry is infrequently used and does not accommodate larger boats. The blackwater river is about 50 feet wide here and churns on its frequent turns, where sandbars can be found. At 0.5 mile, the river comes back to the bluff on the southeast side of the wooded floodplain. Live oaks, river birch, and sweetgum stretch over the Waccamaw. The constant companion of blackwater rivers—cypress—stands guard at the water's edge. At 1.0 mile, work around a small island in the river. Other

The Waccamaw makes a serpentine course through a wide floodplain.

small tree islands will be seen. Pass a low pine bluff on river right at 1.1 miles. The natural berm quickly falls away to wooded wetland.

Bump into the bluff on river left again at 1.3 miles. Pass a large slough at 1.6 miles. It is part of an oxbow, once the primary channel of the Waccamaw. Just ahead, the heritage preserve is briefly interrupted. However, with the numerous bends and ample sand, there is always a place to stop and land your canoe or kayak.

At 2.4 miles, heritage-preserve property resumes on the right bank for almost the rest of the trip. The banks here are low but defined, a natural berm with wetlands behind them. At 2.5 miles, watch for a large slough on river left. At 3.0 miles, the now-narrowing river resumes more extreme bends. At 3.3 miles, the river bumps against the bluff that is the Atlantic coastal ridge one last time. There is a private landing and dock on river left at 3.9 miles. It was an amenity of a now-failed housing venture.

At 4.2 miles, there is a sandy campsite on river left. Here a slough goes forward and leads into a series of dug lakes. However, the Waccamaw River makes a hard right. Stay with the stronger flow. Watch for more oxbows ahead. At 5.3 miles, channelized and perhaps muddy Buck Creek enters on river right, as the Waccamaw turns left.

Even though the SC 9 Bridge is humming nearby, the Waccamaw still has some river bending to do, and it does, turning almost north, then due south, then west before finally passing under the road span. Note the USGS river gauge here; this is the gauge used for judging paddleability for this stretch of the Waccamaw. Get over to the right here, for the landing is a short piece below the bridge, at 6.0 miles. This can be a busy ramp on weekends, so unload as quickly as you can; use the floating dock, keeping the ramps clear.

WHAT IS A BLUE TRAIL?

In 2009, the 90 miles of the South Carolina portion of the Waccamaw River was declared a national water trail—a blue trail, a route for paddlers like us. The national water trails system brings together a host of existing and newly identified blue trails into one cohesive unit. Two of its primary goals are to "protect and restore America's rivers, shorelines, and waterways and conserve natural areas along waterways, and increase access to outdoor recreation on shorelines and waterways."

Designated by the US Secretary of the Interior, these blue trails are managed by local entities. Designation as a blue trail increases visibility in the community and helps gets river landings established, increases chances for protection of the water resource, increases ecotourism of the waterway, and provides a venue for more people to get out in nature and exercise a little.

The mission statement for the Waccamaw River Blue Trail is to "connect communities along the Waccamaw to their hometown river, encourage stewardship of this important natural, cultural and historical resource, and be a local economic driver. Protection of the Waccamaw and its surrounding lands is of critical importance as the river provides clean drinking water, opportunities for outdoor recreation, and is home to many rare plants and animal species, some of which are found nowhere else on earth."

A practical result of the establishment of the Waccamaw as a blue trail is the thirty-page online booklet about the Waccamaw River, aptly entitled *Waccamaw River Blue Trail*. This booklet has useful maps and information about river landings, mileage, and fascinating facts about South Carolina's only federally designated blue trail. It can be found at bluetrailsguide.org/rivers/waccamaw.

27 Great Pee Dee River

This truly large state scenic waterway pushes a strong current through wild Carolina.

County: Marion, Florence
Start: Bostic Landing
    N33° 56.228' / W79° 28.990'
End: Allison Landing
    N33° 53.056' / W79° 24.597'
Distance: 9.3 miles
Float time: 4 hours
Difficulty rating: Easy to moderate
Rapids: None
River type: Very large floodplain river
Current: Moderate to swift
River gradient: 1.1 feet per mile
River gauge: Pee Dee River at Pee Dee, SC, no minimum runnable level, maximum: flood stage
Season: Year-round

Land status: Mostly state heritage preserve and wildlife management area
Fees or permits: No fees or permits required
Nearest city/town: Kingsburg
Maps: South Carolina DNR Wildlife Management Area Map 8; USGS Quadrangle Maps: Gresham
Boats used: Johnboats, canoes, kayaks
Organizations: South Carolina Department of Natural Resources, Rembert C. Dennis Building, 1000 Assembly St., Columbia, SC 29201, (803) 734-3893, dnr.sc.gov
Contacts/outfitters: Naturally Outdoors, 2519 W. Palmetto St., Florence, SC 29501, (843) 665-1551, naturallyoutdoors.com

Put-in/Takeout Information

To takeout: From the intersection of US 378, SC 51/SC 41, and Old River Road in the hamlet of Kingsburg, head south on SC 51/SC 41 and follow it 0.2 mile, passing Kingsburg Baptist Church. Turn left on Kingsburg Loop and follow it 0.2 mile to Poston Road. Turn right on Poston Road and follow it 1.4 miles to turn left on Allison Landing Road; follow it for 1.2 miles to dead-end at the large parking area and boat ramp with floating dock.

To put-in from takeout: Backtrack to the intersection of US 378, SC 51/SC 41, and Old River Road. This time head north on Old River Road and follow it for 4.0 miles to turn right on Bazen Road. Follow Bazen Road 0.3 mile to dead-end at Bostic Landing with its double boat ramp.

Paddle Summary

The Great Pee Dee is deserving of having "Great" in its name. It exudes a large size, depth, and power of current while driving through a wild corridor protected by a wide floodplain forest. This paddle courses through two South Carolina Wildlife Management Areas, keeping the scenery natural. Even where the banks are private land, nary a house can be found. It is some fine scenery. Lush junglesque shores of willow occasionally give way to sandbars. These sandbars make for convenient

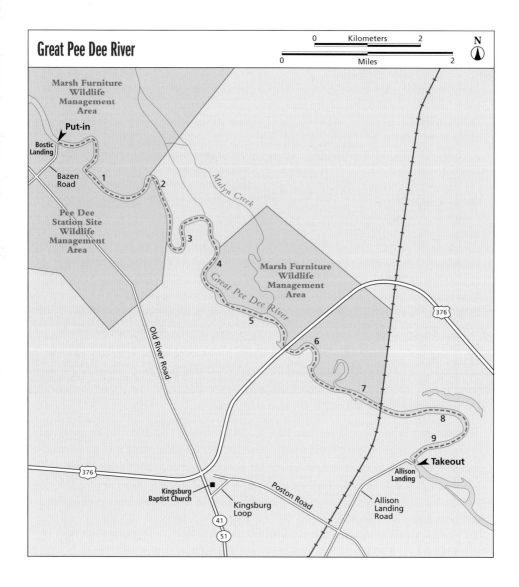

0   Kilometers   2

0   Miles   2

N

Marsh Furniture
Wildlife
Management
Area

Put-in

Bostic
Landing

Bazen
Road

1

2

Mulyn Creek

Pee Dee
Station Site
Wildlife
Management
Area

3

4

Marsh Furniture
Wildlife
Management
Area

Great Pee Dee River

5

6

376

Old River Road

7

8

9

Takeout

Allison
Landing

376

Kingsburg
Baptist Church

Kingsburg
Loop

Poston Road

Allison
Landing
Road

41

51

stopping spots. In still other places, rocky bluffs overlook the swirling waters pushing toward the coast from the mountains of North Carolina. The Pee Dee is traveling southeasterly with an extended hillside running along the southwest side of its flood-plain. In the course of the float, the river curves through the floodplain, occasionally returning to this same linear hillside. Even the takeout is located on this bluff.

The current is powerful throughout the entire paddle, never falling as rapids but neither stilling in pools. It just keeps pushing. Being a big river, even its bends are large. The arcs of the Great Pee Dee sweep in multiple directions. The waterway remains wide throughout, raising the potential problem of winds. A little over halfway you will float under the US 378 bridge. From there, the Great Pee Dee has its longest

The swirling waters of the Great Pee Dee push past a fallen tree.

straight stretch. It makes one final bend before reaching Allison Landing, located at the downstream end of a picturesque bluff and curve that offers both upstream and downstream panoramas of the truly Great Pee Dee.

River Overview

The Great Pee Dee River is paddleable throughout South Carolina and presents an opportunity to float a large yet often remote waterway. Its headwaters begin on the east side of the Blue Ridge, way up in the mountains of North Carolina, as the Yadkin River. It gathers tributaries of the Pisgah National Forest, works easterly into the foothills near Winston-Salem, then turns south and becomes impounded in a series of lakes. The 232-mile official Great Pee Dee begins when the Yadkin and Uwharrie Rivers meet at Lake Tillery. The Great Pee Dee is dammed one last time just above the South Carolina state line and is then set free to flow through land of the Pee Dee Indians, from whom it drew its name. Its drops off the fall line near Cheraw and then enters a wide floodplain, keeping the banks wild. The river takes on major South Carolina tributaries such as the Lynches and Little Pee Dee, entering the domain of the Swamp Fox—Francis Marion—who used these river corridors to surprise and elude the British during the Revolutionary War. The lowermost part of the Great Pee Dee becomes tidally influenced freshwater marsh, where rice cultivation once took place. Finally the Great Pee Dee meets the Waccamaw River at salty Winyah Bay, then gives up its waters to the Atlantic Ocean.

The Paddle

Leave the Bostic boat ramp to enter the Great Pee Dee. You will immediately notice its tan tint, reflective of draining clay soils of the Piedmont in North Carolina, as opposed to the blackwater of most waterways in this part of South Carolina. Willow, sycamore, and oak border the river, which stretches 250 feet wide. There will be tree snags in the river, but the wide waterway prevents complete blockage for the paddler. Brush and vines form a tangle with shoreline trees. During the lower water levels of summer and fall, sandbars will be present inside bends, like the one you pass at 0.4 mile. The Little Pee Dee Station Site Wildlife Management Area occupies the right bank, while the Marsh Furniture Wildlife Management Area protects the left bank. The sheer banks are soil. The water churns and gives an appearance of boiling when it is constricted in curves. This poses no hazard to the paddler.

A beech-covered bluff rises on river right at 1.0 mile. These hillsides present additional floral variety of oak, hickory, and, of course, beech trees. Birdlife is abundant, from woodpeckers to herons. Leave the bluff and eventually make a bend to the right at 1.9 miles. The next big bend comes at 2.8 miles, and you are curving left. A power line runs near the right-hand bank. Willow thickets flank much of the shoreline. At 3.5 miles, a branch of Mulyn Creek comes in on your left. Ahead, pass under the aforementioned power line. At 4.5 miles, the Great Pee Dee has returned to the bluff. This stretch of hillside is sheer, rocky, and steep. Paddle up close and you will even see overhanging sections of stone strata. It is surprising to see 40-foot bluffs so deep into the coastal plain.

Beyond this bluff, the Great Pee Dee River heads southeasterly, the aforementioned bluff line keeping the river in check. Another branch of Mulyn Creek enters on river left at 5.2 miles. Bend to the right and pass under the tall US 378 bridge at 5.6 miles. The river has narrowed and curves yet again at 6.0 miles. It seems to keep returning toward the bluff to the southwest, as it does yet again at 6.4 miles. At 7.2 miles, you will pass under an old railroad bridge. Note that when the Great Pee Dee was used for transportation and tall boats needed clearance, this bridge swiveled. Boats used to come from the coast as far up as Cheraw, where rapids prevented further upstream navigation. At 8.2 miles, the river makes its final big bend to the right. After this elongated turn, look for the bluff where Allison Landing is located. Curve below the bluff to find the two-ramp landing and dock on your right at 9.3 miles.

SOUTH CAROLINA SCENIC RIVERS PROGRAM

South Carolina's scenic river program is administered through the state Department of Natural Resources (DNR). This program is designed to protect the unique and outstanding portions of waterways flowing through the Palmetto State. Just a small fraction of the total mileage of waterways is under protection as state scenic rivers. Portions of the Ashley River, Black River, Broad River, Catawba River, Little Pee Dee River, Saluda River, Middle Saluda River, Lynches River, and, of course, the Great Pee Dee River are designated as state scenic rivers.

The DNR uses specific criteria to designate a state scenic river—including the presence or quality of plant and animal life, animal habitat, scenery, recreation, wetlands, and cultural and historical components. The state then requests input from interested persons, from landowners to anglers, farmers, loggers, and paddlers like us. Then the agency comes up with a management plan that factors in the comments and issues about a particular river.

A river is then classified as natural, scenic, or recreational. Almost all scenic rivers have special components, whether flora, fauna, or historical significance. When this designation has been finalized, a state-appointed board works with various parties to keep the unique features of a waterway unharmed. This way we can all enjoy the gorgeous waterways that make paddling in South Carolina so special.

28 Lynches River

This state scenic river offers alluring—and historic—paddling.

County: Florence	**Season:** Year-round
Start: Lynches River County Park	**Land status:** County park, private
N34° 2.02' / W79° 47.44"	**Fees or permits:** No fees or permits required
End: Jeffords Landing	**Nearest city/town:** Effingham
N34° 1.052' / W79° 42.797'	**Maps:** Revolutionary Rivers PDF; USGS Quad-
Distance: 8.4 miles	rangle Maps: Effingham, Evergreen
Float time: 4 hours	**Boats used:** Kayaks, canoes, a few johnboats
Difficulty rating: Moderate	**Organizations:** Lynches County Park, 5094
Rapids: Class I	County Park Rd., Coward, SC 29530, (843)
River type: Swamp river	389-0550, lynchesriverpark.com
Current: Moderate	**Contacts/outfitters:** Riverrats Canoe Rentals,
River gradient: 0.9 feet per mile	2740 Indigo Landing Rd.,Scranton, SC 29591,
River gauge: Lynches River at Effingham,	(843) 389-4656, riverratscanoerentals.com
minimum runnable level: 3.0 feet	

Put-in/Takeout Information

To takeout: From the intersection of US 301 and US 52 in Effingham, take US 52 east toward Lake City. Drive for 3.2 miles to turn left on Old Georgetown Road (New Hope Road is the right turn). Follow Old Georgetown Road for 2.3 miles to Jeffords Road on your left. Follow sandy Jeffords Road shortly to dead-end at a sand landing on your left.

To put-in from takeout: Backtrack out of Jeffords Road and Old Georgetown Road to US 52. Turn right on US 52 west back toward Effingham, then turn left onto Old Highway 4 at 2.0 miles. Follow Old Highway 4 for 1.8 miles to Lynches County Park. Enter the park and follow County Park Road for 0.7 mile, then veer left to the large parking area with the signed river access and canoe launch just beyond it. The launch is on a hill, and you tote your boat a short ways to the water.

Paddle Summary

This paddle explores a favorable part of the Lynches River, a state-designated scenic waterway, one of only nine in the state. Here, the Lynches makes an arc as it heads toward the coast. Begin the adventure at Lynches River County Park, a fine preserve with a campground, trails, and a unique universally accessible paddler launch that you have to see to believe. After leaving the park, you will swiftly twist and turn your first mile before the kinks in the river loosen. The waterway then passes under the US 52 bridge and another of the many boat landings on the paddleable part of the

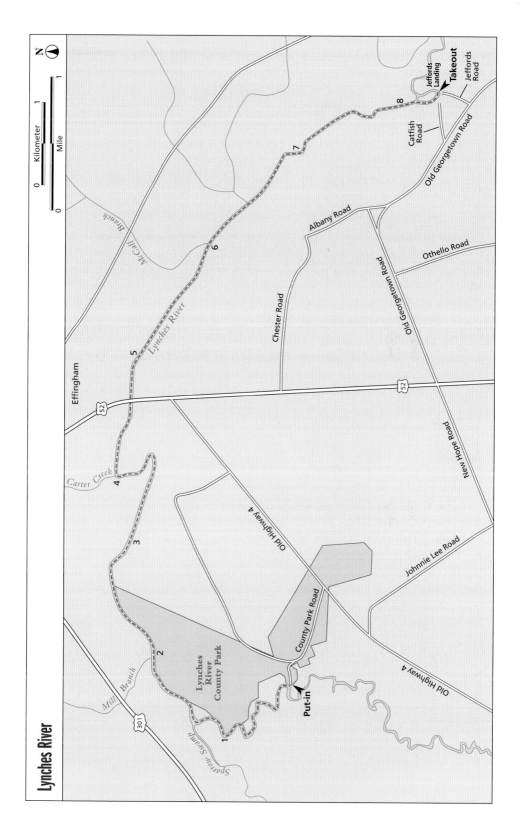

Lynches River

river. It then curves southeasterly, winds less, and slows in places. McCall Branch and other tributaries enter the Lynches. The arc of the river continues, and you head fully south before the main river turns sharply east and north as it cuts across an old bend. Here, paddlers must take the old bend to reach a pair of simple landings, the second of which is your takeout.

River Overview

The Lynches River is born just across the border in Union County, North Carolina. It enters South Carolina east of Lancaster, where it keeps a steady southeasterly direction and forms county boundaries. The Little Lynches River enters near the town of Bethune. It is this area, from the US 15 Bridge near Bishopville all the way to Lynches River County Park, that became the first official state scenic-river segment of the Lynches back in 1994. This includes the river portion flowing through Lee State Natural Area. Near Bishopville is where the Lynches becomes regularly paddled and is interspersed with landings. In 2008, the Lynches—downstream all the way to its confluence with the Great Pee Dee River—was added to the state scenic-river register, creating 111 miles of state scenic waterway. This lower segment takes on several swamp-stream tributaries before meeting the Great Pee Dee. Every segment of these 111 miles can be enjoyed in a canoe or kayak. This river is served by a competent outfitter in Riverrats, situated at Indigo Landing in Florence County. The swamps along the Lynches and its feeder streams are noteworthy as a former hideout for runaway slaves and the site of the state's last duel.

The Paddle

Lynches River County Park is a fun destination in and of itself, so consider adding time to visit the Environmental Discovery Center or stroll the waterside boardwalk and trail before launching your craft. You could make more than a day of it and overnight at the park campground.

The launch is elaborate and accommodates not only disabled paddlers but also all paddlers at differing water levels. This is done via is graduated, multilevel entrances. Pretty nifty. Enter the tannin-darkened Lynches River at a bend. The water flows swiftly here, passing regal and thickly rooted cypresses and tupelo, along with oaks on higher ground. Trees canopy the water's edge. Lynches River County Park and its riverside boardwalk rises on the right shore above the 40-foot-wide waterway. The Lynches is shallow where swift, and fallen trees form aquatic hurdles, but they do not completely block the river. This initial section has many bends with small sandbars on their insides.

The left bank is private land, and you will pass a few houses here and there, especially where low bluffs rise from the swampy shore. Take note of rock outcrops along the water level around these bluffs. At 1.3 miles, pick your route around an island. There is a large sandbar here on river right. Part of Lynches River County Park, it

This elaborate paddler access at Lynches River County Park is designed to handle varied water levels.

makes for a popular stopping spot. Just downstream on river left, Sparrow Swamp adds its flow to the Lynches River. Watch for small unnamed branches noisily falling into the main waterway.

The twists ease up, and Mill Branch enters on river left at 2.0 miles. Bluffs form with regularity. Leave Lynches River County Park at 2.6 miles. At 3.7 miles, the river makes a sharp bend to the left. The Lynches narrows and speeds. At 4.0 miles, Carter Creek enters on the left. At 4.6 miles, you will come to the US 52 boat landing on river right. There are three bridges here—the old US 52 bridge, the new US 52 bridge, and a railroad span.

Thus far, the Lynches has gone northwest, north, east, and now turns southeast, continuing its long arc. A long bluff runs on river left. The river is broader here. Bay Branch and McCall Branch add their respective flows, though these tributaries are less easily detected because of the many sloughs along the Lynches. By 7.5 miles, the banks of the river have lowered, and overflow swamp borders the waterway. At 8.1 miles, the main river curves left and has shortcut an old bend. A lesser channel keeps straight, and this is your route. This lesser channel is kept clear by boaters using

Jeffords Landing and Catfish Landing. Keep straight here with the lesser channel and float a shallow waterway bordered with more brush and fallen vegetation than the main river. You will see Catfish Landing and a slender canal just before coming to the takeout at Jeffords Landing on river right.

Since the takeout is on the old main channel of the river and thus is not completely apparent—though water does move through the old channel at water levels above 3.0—consider either marking the Jeffords Landing on your GPS or physically paddling to the main channel of the Lynches to look at the turn spot.

SOUTH CAROLINA'S LAST DUEL

Did you know that, until 1954, public officials in South Carolina had to swear that they had not been in a duel? This strange pledge was born out of the state's last duel, which occurred on Shannon Hill, just east of the US 15 crossing of the Lynches River. See, a pair of former Confederate soldiers, one Colonel E. B. C. Cash and the other William Shannon, clashed with pistols on July 5, 1880. Cash fatally shot his onetime friend through the heart.

Apparently, the wife of Cash and the wife of Shannon got into a dispute over the division of property. A court case ensued that went all the way to the South Carolina Supreme Court. Just a few months later, Colonel Cash's wife passed away, and Colonel Cash decided to avenge William Shannon for dragging Mrs. Cash through court, thus hastening her death.

Cash, described as a "bold and desperate fighter" during the Civil War, was known to have a short fuse, and after an exchange of letters, the much older William Shannon accepted the challenge to a duel. The death of Mr. Shannon caused an uproar throughout the state, whereupon the legislature passed an anti-dueling law, along with the aforementioned pledge for state officials.

By the way, Colonel Cash was arrested for both murder and dueling. His first hearing ended in a mistrial. Nevertheless, he was tried yet again and was acquitted of all charges. The colonel died at home in 1888, the last duelist in the Palmetto State.

29 Black River

This paddle features narrow, fast channels as well as wider, slow segments on a state-designated scenic river.

County: Williamsburg
Start: Ervin Landing
    N33° 31.664' / W79° 37.014'
End: Reds Landing
    N33° 29.208' / W79° 32.742'
Distance: 10.4 miles
Float time: 6 hours
Difficulty rating: Easy to moderate
Rapids: None
River type: Alternating swift and slow blackwater river
Current: Moderate
River gradient: Less than 1 foot per mile
River gauge: Black River at Kingstree, SC, minimum runnable level: 80 cfs
Season: Year-round

Land status: Private
Fees or permits: No fees or permits required
Nearest city/town: Andrews
Maps: USGS Quadrangle Maps: Warsaw, Andrews
Boats used: Kayaks, canoes, some johnboats
Organizations: South Carolina Department of Natural Resources, Rembert C. Dennis Building, 1000 Assembly St., Columbia, SC 29201, (803) 734-9100, dnr.sc.gov/
Contacts/outfitters: South Carolina Department of Health and Environmental Control, 2600 Bull St., Columbia, SC 29201, (803) 898-4300, www.scdhec.gov/environment/water

Put-in/Takeout Information

To takeout: From the intersection of SC 41 and SC 41 Business on the north side of Andrews, continue north on SC 41 for 0.8 mile to cross railroad tracks and immediately turn right on Reds Landing Road. Follow the road as it curves left, then dead-ends at a public boat ramp at 0.4 mile.

To put-in from takeout: Backtrack to the intersection of Reds Landing Road and SC 41. Continue north, crossing the Black River on a bridge. At 0.9 mile, turn left on SC 527 (Thurgood Marshall Highway) and follow it 4.8 miles to turn left on S45-688/Ervin Road in Bloomingvale. Follow Ervin Road to the Ervin Memorial Landing, on your right just before the road dead-ends.

Paddle Summary

This is a fun and diverse paddle due to the strangely alternating characteristics of the Black River. In places it flows wide, straight, and easy, then it suddenly narrows into sharp bends and shallows slaloming betwixt tree snags, the "Dr. Jekyll and Mr. Hyde" of South Carolina streams. These slender segments are canopied and impart a sense of wilderness swamp. The changes occur more frequently than you might imagine. The Black also bumps into terraced bluffs enclosing the floodplain swamp through which

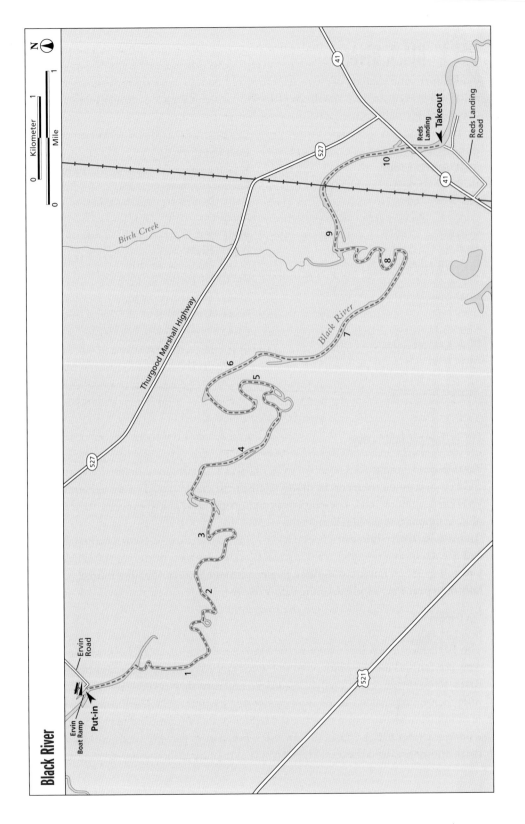

Black River

the river meanders. You will find a few houses on this higher ground. The paddle leaves fine Ervin boat ramp on a wide stretch, then you encounter the first of many sudden turns and changes of character. Often old sloughs break off the primary channel, but signs with arrows have been placed to help you with the correct route. These sloughs afford additional exploration possibilities. To ensure tracing the proper route, look for cut limbs and open, moving channels. These narrow, shallow, swift, and sandy sections retard motorboat traffic and leave much of this section to paddlers.

The first 5 miles are particularly twisting, making the paddling fun and sometimes challenging as you squeeze past tree snags. Then the river opens into wide, straight, and slower segments broken by concentrated shallow curves. The final stretch passes under a railroad bridge, then the US 41 Bridge. The paddle ends where the Black River begins to be tidally affected. The current of the river reflects its alternating characteristics, swift where narrow, and slow, nearly slack when wide and open, so expect to paddle some and perhaps fight a little wind in the lakelike locales.

River Overview

The aptly named Black River originates in Lee County, just south of Bishopville. Here, several swamp streams meet, and the Black River comes into its own east of Sumter. At this point, its floodplain widens, and the main waterway meanders through the Black River Swamp. Unfortunately, a part of this is channelized as the Black River passes under I-95. Below SC 40, where the river is no longer channelized, is the beginning of the 75-mile segment of state-designated scenic river. The waterway becomes paddleable with the addition of the Pocotaligo River and the interestingly named Pudding Swamp. It is at the town of Kingstree where the first landings and boat ramps are found. However, the water must be high to get through this part, and paddlers will find challenges in multiple channels, snags, and fallen trees. Nevertheless, this is a remote and wild part of the waterway. Our paddle is on the lower part of this stretch and ends where the waterway becomes tidal, near Andrews. Below Andrews, while still freshwater, the now-wider river is heavily used by motorboats, and it remains that way as it absorbs the downstream waters of historic Black Mingo Creek. The Black River passes through rice plantation country before it finally flows into the Great Pee Dee River near Georgetown.

The Paddle

The Ervin boat ramp has a large picnic shelter and parking area. The single ramp is very steep as it drops off a bluff. Enter the water just below the confluence of the Black River and a slough. Head easterly on a slow segment of river that stretches 120 feet wide. Cypress is prevalent in the swampy segments, while oaks rule the higher ground. At 0.5 mile, a slough keeps straight and was part of the old river, but now the flowing waterway curves sharply right on a narrow swift channel partially obstructed by snags. It does not seem the correct route, but you will encounter this repeatedly as you float

Morning sun illuminates Spanish moss overlooking the Black River.

down the river. This alternating characteristic of swift and narrow with slow and wide is what makes the Black River unique. The shallow segments reveal a sandy bottom that colors the water burgundy. The shallow sand segments will also scrape your boat at lower water levels. Expect to dance around snags. Thickly wooded overflow swamps border the moving channel. Briefly straighten out at 0.8 mile. Pass a house and huge cypress on river right at 1.2 miles. Resume multiple bends at 1.5 miles. Sandbars can be found on the insides of these bends. Watch for old channels that are either dead-end sloughs or high-water overflow channels. Either way, you will not go far on the wrong route, just suffer a little humiliation at the hands of your fellow paddlers. Signs will direct you on the correct route in many of these aquatic junctions.

Come along a long oak-topped bluff on river right at 2.7 miles. At 3.0 miles, open onto a lakelike, roundish section of river. Head right (east) here and resume the channel. The other possibilities are sloughs. At 3.5 miles, come to another slough on river left and keep right, passing a couple of houses on river left. The Black stays wide and straight for a while, then does its transformation act again at 4.6 miles. Here, it narrows and curves nearly back on itself before straightening out again at 5.6 miles. This ends the most circuitous segment of the Black.

Expect to paddle open, deeper water awhile rather than dancing through shallows and snags. Saddle alongside a bluff on river left at 6.4 miles, where a few dwellings stand. Pass under a power line at 6.5 miles. Keep southeasterly on a river that is now over 100 feet wide and lakelike. The long straightaway ends at 7.8 miles. The Black then turns north, narrows, and speeds. Watch for sandbars here. This is a fun stretch of paddling. At 8.9 miles, Birch Creek comes in on river left, but it looks more like another slough. The river opens and is slow the rest of the paddle. At 9.4 miles, pass under a railroad bridge as you make the final bend to the south. This section is wide and frequented by motorboats. Pass under the SC 41 Bridge at 10.2 miles, then get over to the right, reaching Reds Landing and the paddle's end at 10.4 miles.

THE KING'S TREES

The heart of the scenic river portion of the Black River is in Williamsburg County, the seat of which is Kingstree. The English originally christened Williamsburg County for King William of Orange; Kingstree was laid out in 1730. Tall, straight white pines grew in the area. These trees were ideal for making ship's masts. Therefore, the trees of the area were claimed by the King of England, giving rise to the name King's Tree. In 1886, long after the British had been sent back to Europe, city fathers officially renamed the town Kingstree, which is the moniker this town on the banks of the Black River goes by today.

30 Echaw Creek

Paddle in the shadow of massive old-growth cypress trees down a small stream, then open to big Santee River. Stop and visit a Civil War–era defense earthworks along the way.

County: Berkeley
Start: Pitch Landing
N33° 14.806' / W79° 34.661'
End: McConnell Landing
N33° 14.714' / W79° 31.258'
Distance: 4.6 miles
Float time: 3 hours, including a stop at Battery Warren
Difficulty rating: Easy to moderate
Rapids: None
River type: Tidally influenced wilderness creek, big coastal plain river,
Current: Moderate, some tidal influence
River gradient: None
River gauge: None

Season: Year-round
Land status: National forest, some private
Fees or permits: No fees of permits required
Nearest city/town: McClellanville
Maps: Francis Marion National Forest; USGS Quadrangle Maps: Honey Hill, Cedar Creek
Boats used: Motorboats on Santee River, kayaks and canoes on Echaw Creek
Organizations: Berkeley County Blueways, berkeleyblueways.com
Contacts/outfitters: Francis Marion National Forest, 2967 Steed Creek Rd., Huger, SC 29450, (843) 336-3248, www.fs.usda.gov/main/scnfs/

Put-in/Takeout Information

To takeout: From the intersection of US 17A and SC 45 in Jamestown, take SC 45 south for 8.5 miles to turn left on Chicken Creek Road. Follow Chicken Creek Road for 1.5 miles to make an acute left turn on gravel FR 204/Echaw Road; this left turn will come up as Chicken Creek Road is curving right. Turn left on FR 204/Echaw Road and follow it 4.5 miles to turn left on FR 204F. There will be a sign here for McConnell Landing. Follow FR 204F for 1.7 miles to dead-end at the landing.

To put-in from takeout: Backtrack on FR 204F to FR 204/Echaw Road. Turn right on Echaw Road and backtrack to turn right on Chicken Creek Road. Follow Chicken Creek Road out to SC 45. Turn right on SC 45 back toward Jamestown. At 2.2 miles on SC 45, just after passing a large whitewater tower and Shulerville Road, turn right onto gravel FR 151. Follow FR 151 north for 2.5 miles to FR 192. Turn right on FR 192 and follow it to dead-end at Pitch Landing at 0.8 mile.

Paddle Summary

Echaw Creek is one of those places best experienced in person. A tributary of the Santee River, this stream is home to massive cypress trees growing along the stream. The waterway starts quite small from primitive Pitch Landing, steeping in blackwater,

Echaw Creek

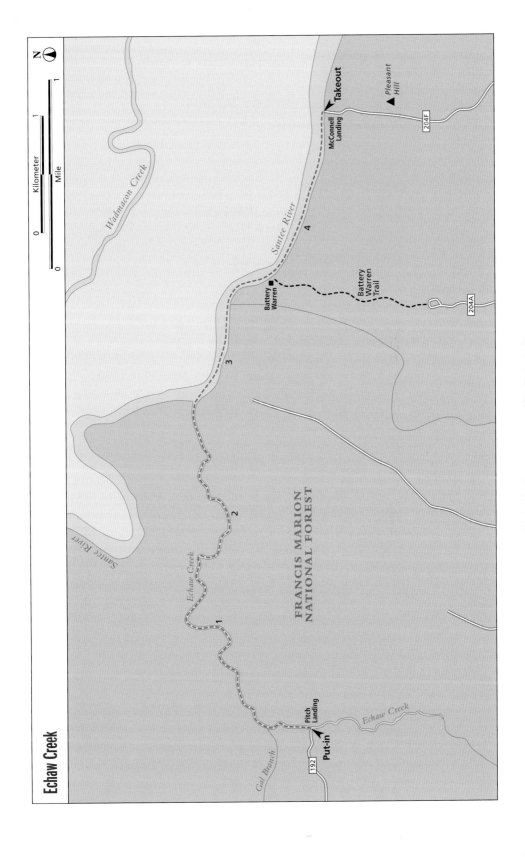

over which rises a daunting forest. Echaw Creek curves easterly as you crane your neck upward to the big cypresses. Bird life echoes through the forest, adding to the overall effect. The canopied waterway opens onto its mother stream, the wide Santee River. The big water experience contrasts completely with Echaw Creek. Here, you float down a watercourse hundreds of feet wide that delivers its own brand of remoteness. Curve downriver to make a riverside stop. From here, clamber up a hill to reach Battery Warren, a bluff-top Confederate defense post with its earthworks intact and stabilized. An interpretive trail runs south from the Battery Warren through hills to an auto-accessible trailhead. This makes for a fun and historic leg-stretcher that adds to the paddle. Once back in the boat, paddlers will soon reach their destination on the wide Santee, coming to McConnell Landing, also situated on a hill. There is a bit of a tidal effect. I recommend starting your paddle about 4 hours after high tide in Charleston Harbor to get a favorable downstream push.

River Overview

Echaw Creek flows from the swamps around Bark Island, deep in the Francis Marion National Forest. The small, short stream heads east, becomes somewhat of a creek near Shulerville, and takes on a few small tributaries by the time it passes under the SC 45 Bridge. The creek becomes paddleable about 0.5 mile above Pitch Landing, where this trip starts. It then passes rough Pitch Landing and heads northeast, picking up its biggest feeder stream, Gal Branch, just below Pitch Landing. It is but a couple more miles to its mother waters, the Santee River.

The Santee River drains the heart of South Carolina and mountain lands of North Carolina, including the Saluda, Broad, and Wateree Rivers. It is a major waterway, draining more of South Carolina than any other watershed, resulting in a huge waterway by the time it flows along the north boundary of the Francis Marion National Forest after emerging from Lake Marion. The Santee comes to be when the Wateree and Congaree Rivers meet. Thus begins the 143-mile journey to empty into the ocean in the appropriately remote Santee delta between Georgetown and McClellanville. During this final part, it divides into two major channels, the North Santee and the South Santee.

The Paddle

Pitch Landing, where this paddle begins on Echaw Creek, is also known as Price Landing, though the name Pitch Landing is on official USGS quad maps. The primitive gravel landing enveloped in forest sets the tone for this adventure. If you want to extend your paddle and see more of Echaw Creek, leave right from the landing. You can go about 0.5 mile before the creek closes in (that is not counted in the overall mileage of this paddle). No matter what, go upstream just a bit to view your first big cypress tree within sight of the landing. Afterward, head down the 30-foot-wide, ink-black creek bordered by cypress and gum trees. Overflow swamp stretches beyond

Echaw Creek is home to massive cypress trees like this one.

the water's edge. Gal Branch enters on your left after 0.25 mile. By 0.5 mile, the creek has widened, better enabling you to view the tops of cypresses rising above the main forest canopy. Huge trunks will be at the water—you can paddle directly up to the giants. Pass a bluff and a private landing at 1.0 mile on river right.

The old-growth cypresses occur randomly along the creek. Some look old enough that Francis Marion, South Carolina's hero of the Revolutionary War—the Swamp Fox himself—could have seen them. At 1.9 miles, pass another private dock on river right. Depending on the tides, the clear-green waters of the Santee will work up Echaw Creek, changing the stream from its normal dusky tint. The creek becomes canopied again before opening onto the Santee River at 2.7 miles. The sky will seem much brighter here, and the Santee seems impossibly big after floating Echaw.

Turn right downstream. Low but well-defined banks are richly wooded and wild. Stay on the right bank as the 250-foot-wide Santee curves right. At 3.6 miles on your right, look for a canal-like channel. Just past it are old pilings exposed at lower water levels. Pull in here and dock your boat. Walk downstream along the Santee through a wooded flat, then rise to a hill. Reach the earthworks of Battery Warren, complete with interpretive signage. The Confederate post never saw action but is considered one of the most intact defensive bulwarks in the state. Consider hiking the trail that leads out to FR 204A.

After returning to the Santee, cruise below Battery Warren. Ahead, you will see rock riprap. This is McConnell Landing. Reach your takeout and its steep boat ramp at 4.6 miles, ending the paddle.

FRANCIS MARION BASE CAMP: HONEY HILL CAMPGROUND

Honey Hill Campground, part of the Francis Marion National Forest, is situated just a few miles distant from Echaw Creek. Honey Hill is only 32 feet high, but a little height here in the Lowcountry can mean a lot. A gravel loop road circles the now-retired fire tower. Live oaks, hickory, sweetgum, and pines shade the free campground, open year-round. All the campsites are on the outside of the loop. The center of the loop has an information kiosk. A vault toilet is at the loop's beginning. The elevation of Honey Hill keeps it drier and less buggy than other area campgrounds.

In addition to paddling the streams of the Francis Marion, such as Echaw Creek, Wambaw Creek, Wadboo Creek, and Awendaw Creek, you can also hike and explore on foot. Little Wambaw Swamp Wilderness, at 5,000 acres, is very primitive. Explorers can follow old built-up tram roads amid swampland. The only catch is the tram bridges have eroded away, leaving wading a certainty. Wambaw Swamp Wilderness has even less dry ground in its 4,800 acres. It is said this swamp is the least visited locale in the whole state.

The Palmetto Trail, South Carolina's master path, begins its journey to the Upstate here in the Francis Marion. It starts near Buck Hall Campground and heads along Awendaw Creek toward the interior to Halfway Creek and beyond to Canal Recreation Area, near US 52 on Lake Moultrie, spanning a total of 49 miles. This trek is one of my favorites in the state. Consider doing parts of it along with your Echaw Creek paddle, making Honey Hill base camp for the many possibilities in Francis Marion National Forest. If you keep on SC 45 toward McClellanville beyond Chicken Creek Road, you will pass Honey Hill on your right.

31 Chicken Creek

This is a chance to experience three completely different yet remote waterways linked into one paddling adventure.

County: Berkeley
Start: McConnell Landing
　　N33° 14.714' / W79° 31.258'
End: Elmwood Landing
　　N33° 12.448' / W79° 28.117'
Distance: 9.3 miles
Float time: 5 hours
Difficulty rating: Moderate
Rapids: None
River type: Three types—big coastal plain river, junglesque tributary, tidally influenced wilderness creek
Current: Moderate, some tidal influence
River gradient: None
River gauge: None

Season: Year-round
Land status: National forest
Fees or permits: No fees or permits required
Nearest city/town: McClellanville
Maps: Francis Marion National Forest; USGS Quadrangle Maps: Honey Hill, South Santee
Boats used: Motorboats on Santee River, mostly kayaks and canoes elsewhere
Organizations: Berkeley County Blueways, berkeleyblueways.com
Contacts/outfitters: Francis Marion National Forest, 2967 Steed Creek Rd., Huger, SC 29450, (843) 336-3248, www.fs.usda.gov/main/scnfs/

Put-in/Takeout Information

To takeout: From the intersection of US 17 and US 17A in Georgetown, take US 17 north for 6.4 miles to turn left on Rutledge Road (look for signs to Hampton Plantation State Historic Site). At 3.3 miles, Rutledge Road turns to gravel and becomes FR 204. Continue straight for 0.6 mile farther and cross the bridge over Wambaw Creek. Elmwood Landing is on your right just after the bridge over Wambaw Creek. **To put-in from takeout:** Continue north from Elmwood Landing on FR 204 (Echaw Road). Follow the gravel national forest road for 3.5 miles to turn right on FR 204F. There will be a sign here for McConnell Landing. Follow FR 204F for 1.7 miles to dead-end at the landing.

Paddle Summary

The Francis Marion National Forest is your setting for this triple play. Start out on the big Santee River, where you will follow this wide, wooded waterway toward the coast. Make a big bend on this massive yet undeveloped segment of great river before joining Chicken Creek. This smaller waterway shortcuts more big bends in the Santee, striking its own course, curving past primeval shoreline that delivers a sense of being in the back of beyond. Emerge onto the South Santee River, once again on wide-open coastal plain waterway, before turning into the mouth of Wambaw

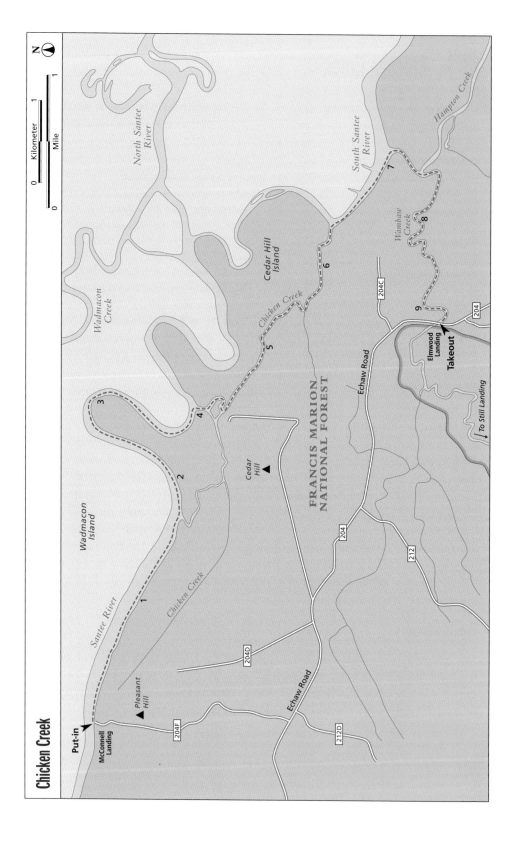

Creek. This wilderness blackwater stream is one of South Carolina's best examples of untouched Lowcountry. Wind up an ever-narrowing, cypress-lined creek to emerge at Elmwood Landing, completing this multi-waterway endeavor.

The entire paddle takes place in freshwater environments, but all the waterways are tidally affected. If you want to follow the tide, plan to start your trip at McConnell Landing about 3.5 hours after high tide at Charleston Harbor. However, even if you do have the tide in your favor along the Santee River and Chicken Creek, you will likely be going against the tide on Wambaw Creek. Expect to see plenty of birdlife and perhaps even other flora and fauna that inhabit the confines of the Francis Marion National Forest.

River Overview

The Santee River drains the heart of South Carolina and mountain lands of North Carolina, including the Saluda, Broad, and Wateree Rivers. It is a major waterway and arguably drains more of South Carolina than any other watershed, resulting in a huge waterway by the time it flows along the north boundary of the Francis Marion National Forest after emerging from Lake Marion. The Santee comes to be when the Wateree and Congaree Rivers meet. Thus begins the 143-mile journey to empty into the ocean in the appropriately remote Santee delta between Georgetown and McClellanville. On the way it divides into two major channels, the North Santee and the South Santee.

Chicken Creek is a tributary of the Santee River. It originates in the national forest just east of Pleasant Hill, near McConnell Landing, the put-in for this paddle. The stream drains swamps, heads easterly, then merges with smaller channels of the Santee. The lower part of Chicken Creek can be considered a channel of the Santee, since it links the Santee with the South Santee.

Wambaw Creek originates in Wambaw Swamp and courses northeast, then enters federally designated wilderness after reaching the SC 45 Bridge. Still Landing, downstream, is the first good access until the FR 204 Bridge, where this paddle ends. The stream meets the Santee River after 2 more miles. Along the way, a branch of Wambaw Creek known as Hampton Creek flows past Hampton Plantation State Historic Site.

The Paddle

McConnell Landing offers a hilly overlook of the Santee River. Camping is allowed here. Take your boat down the steep concrete ramp to the Santee, stretching more than 300 feet across. Huge Wadmacon Island stands across the shore. Though entirely freshwater here, tides do push this far inland. Head right, toward the coast. Choose one bank or another; I recommend the right bank—all natural forest—since that is the side where you will pick up Chicken Creek. The banks of the Santee are low but well-defined soil berms covered in junglesque forest that enhances the sense of

Paddling through Chicken Creek, just one of three diverse streams experienced on this paddle.

being in the boonies. Pine, cypress, sweetgum, river birch, and sycamore crowd the land, along with saw palmetto. I have seen bald eagles along this stretch of the Santee, among other birds. Look for deer and landlocked wildlife beyond the shoreline.

Fallen trees and snags litter the Santee near the shore. You can choose to weave among them or get farther out in the river. The undulation of the tide will also push floating logs and debris up and down the river. At 0.6 mile, pass a narrow, linear island covered in willows on river right. Just ahead, paddle under a big power line. At 1.7 miles on your right, look for a log-choked waterway that links to Chicken Creek. It is not regularly kept open, so use at your own peril. Instead, continue downriver, beginning a long bend of the Santee. Curve north as the river narrows a bit. The bend is so acute it forms a narrow neck of land. At 3.0 miles, the river is turning back south.

At 3.6 miles, begin a long curve to the left, southeasterly. Stay with the right-hand bank for sure now. At 4.0 miles, at the most southerly part of this latest curve, an 80-foot-wide channel leads south to Chicken Creek. There will be flow in this stream, in or out, tide depending. After entering, immediately look for another channel on your right—this is upper Chicken Creek. Stay left here and join Chicken Creek, heading southeasterly, then make a couple of dramatic bends, circling around a small unnamed island. Resume a southeasterly direction. Cedar Hill Island rises to your left. Tall, moss-draped, viney woods line low but still defined banks. Snags will be embedded in the stream bottom but will be easy to work around. I have seen alligators in here, which is fitting for such a primeval setting. A bluff rises on river right at 4.5 miles. This is part of Cedar Hill. At 5.5 miles, Chicken Creek makes a couple of quick bends as an unnamed tributary flows in on the right.

At 6.4 miles, Chicken Creek meets the South Santee River. You may be surprised that the main waterway is now smaller, but upstream the main Santee divided into two primary channels, and much of the flow went with the North Santee. Some banks are more low and brushy than before. Keep with the right-hand bank of the South Santee, which is beginning a big bend to the left. At 7.1 miles, come to the mouth of Wambaw Creek. Leave the South Santee and head south on Wambaw Creek. Its mouth is about 120 feet wide but quickly tapers. If you have had the tide in your favor this far, it will now be going against you.

At 7.4 miles, Hampton Creek leads left toward Hampton Plantation Historic Site. An aerial view here reveals old rice fields along Hampton Creek. Keep straight on Wambaw Creek, now narrowed to 60 feet wide. More bends lie ahead as cypress banks continue to taper. Depending on the tides, you may or may not have entered the black tannin-stained waters for which Wambaw Creek is known. At 9.3 miles, the FR 204 bridge comes into view. The takeout is on your right just before the bridge.

32 Wambaw Creek

Paddle an alluring blackwater stream entirely within the federally designated Wambaw Creek Wilderness, part of the Francis Marion National Forest.

County: Berkeley, Charleston
Start: Still Landing
   N33° 10.638' / W79° 29.795'
End: Elmwood Landing
   N33° 12.448' / W79° 28.117'
Distance: 6.6 miles
Float time: 4 hours
Difficulty rating: Moderate
Rapids: Class I
River type: Wooded wilderness swamp stream
Current: Moderate
River gradient: Less than 1 foot per mile
River gauge: None, no minimum runnable level
Season: Fall through early summer

Land status: National forest wilderness
Fees or permits: No fees or permits required
Nearest city/town: McClellanville
Maps: Francis Marion National Forest; Berkeley County Blueways; USGS Quadrangle Maps: South Santee
Boats used: Kayaks, canoes, a few johnboats
Organizations: Berkeley County Blueways, berkeleyblueways.com
Contacts/outfitters: Nature Adventure Outfitters, 483 W. Coleman Blvd., Mount Pleasant, SC 29464, (843) 568-3222, kayak charlestonsc.com

Put-in/Takeout Information

To takeout: From the intersection of US 17 and SC 45 in McClellanville, take SC 45 west, entering Francis Marion National Forest. After 4.0 miles, turn right on FR 211 (Mill Branch Road). Follow FR 211 for 3.2 miles, where you will pass the put-in, Still Landing, down FR 211B. Continue beyond FR 211B on FR 211 for 2.3 more miles to reach a T intersection (you will pass the turnoff for Elmwood Hunt Camp at 2.1 miles). Turn left at the T intersection onto FR 204 (Echaw Road). Follow it for 0.6 mile to reach the bridge over Wambaw Creek and a boat ramp on your right just after the bridge.

To put-in from takeout: Backtrack 0.6 mile to FR 211. Turn right on FR 211 and backtrack 2.3 miles to reach FR 211B. Turn right here and follow it 0.3 mile to Still Landing.

Paddle Summary

Wambaw Creek presents backwoods paddling at its finest. Eleven miles of this creek flow through the 1,640-acre Wambaw Creek Wilderness. The federally designated wild area is encased within the Francis Marion National Forest, making for a wild-on-wild setting. Still Landing, located on a piney bluff above Wambaw Creek, is your starting point. You will first paddle upstream, going against a light current. By the way, currents here are affected by tides to a degree, as well as recent rainfall. The banks

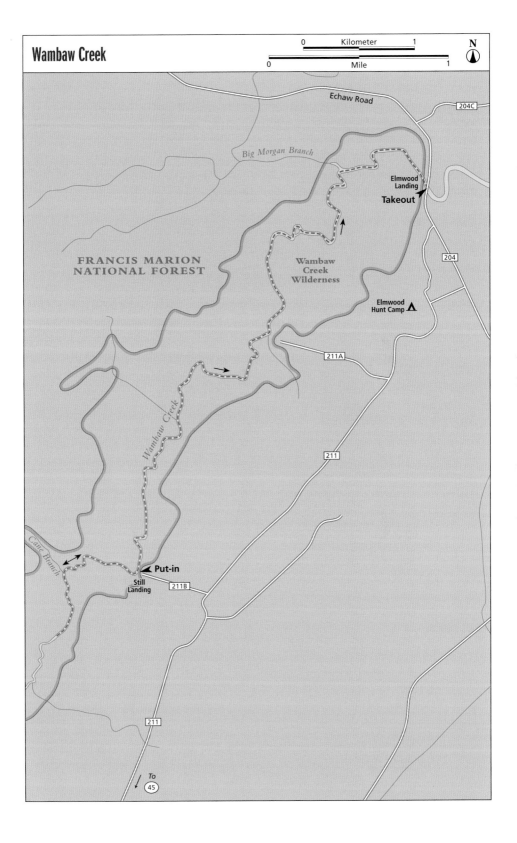

Wambaw Creek

0 Kilometer 1
0 Mile 1

N

Echaw Road

204C

Big Morgan Branch

Elmwood
Landing
Takeout

FRANCIS MARION
NATIONAL FOREST

Wambaw
Creek
Wilderness

Elmwood
Hunt Camp

204

211A

Wambaw Creek

211

Cane Branch

Put-in
Still
Landing   211B

211

To
45

quickly lower, and you paddle astride swamp woods, pocked with some impressive old-growth cypresses. After a mile, come to an especially large cypress, then turn around back to Still Landing.

The wooded swamp banks continue downstream of Still Landing, with nary a sign of civilization. Paddle near a piney bluff on your right, but mostly you will trace the blackwater stream on a winding course, cheered on by birdsong. Wambaw Creek widens a bit and becomes more tidally influenced, occasionally exposing mucky banks before reaching Echaw Road and the boat ramp, marking the end of the paddle and the end of the designated wilderness.

River Overview

It is perhaps only natural that Wambaw Creek would flow forth from Wambaw Swamp, in the heart of Francis Marion National Forest. Here, Wambaw Creek courses northeast, the same general direction it will follow from its origins to its mother stream, the Santee River. Along the way, Wambaw Creek gains more water in Coffee Creek Swamp, and then reaches the SC 45 Bridge. Here begins the wilderness portion of the stream. By the way, Wambaw Creek has to be floating high and fast to be floatable downstream from the SC 45 Bridge. Moreover, when Wambaw Creek is that high, it is also flowing out of its banks and into, alongside, and through swamps bordering it, creating navigation challenges for paddlers.

Mechaw Creek adds its flow to Wambaw Creek within the wilderness, as do Mill Branch and Cane Branch. Still Landing, where this paddle begins, is approximately in the middle of the long, narrow wilderness, and it is a nice sight for those who have attempted to make their way down from the SC 45 Bridge. Still Landing offers auto access and a piney place to stop, start, or simply relax and fish the creek for fighting redbreast bream. Wambaw Creek continues flowing through the heart of the wilderness and then silently flows under the FR 204 Bridge.

The stream stays in the national forest and flows out to meet the Santee River after 2 miles. Interestingly, a branch of Wambaw Creek, known as Hampton Creek, flows past Hampton Plantation State Historic Site. Here, rice fields once stretched across swampy flats among the Wambaw/Hampton/Santee confluences. The Hampton Plantation is open for tours.

The Paddle

For planning purposes, the tides reach Wambaw Creek about 3 hours later than times posted for the Charleston Harbor. Also, consider paddling here when the winds are howling—the creek is relatively narrow and treelined. A canopy blocks breezes and stretches over much of the creek, making it favorable on warm days as well.

Leave Still Landing and head left, upstream. The creek is around 40 to 50 feet wide. The bluff of Still Landing stands to your left. You are already in the designated

Wambaw Creek is bounded by a glory of trees in springtime.

wilderness, where cypress and tupelo rise high above the coffee-colored waters. Sweet bay, loblolly pine, and red maple find their places along the shore.

The banks lower, with overflow swamps stretching from the water. The biggest cypresses are not only found along the shoreline but also back from the water's edge. In warmer times, alligators will be sunning where rays of light penetrate the canopy. By 0.7 mile, Wambaw Creek has narrowed. You may have to work around an occasional log, but the first mile or two above Still Landing is usually passable without

A WAY OF LIFE GONE BY

If you paddle downstream from Elmwood Landing and bear right at the fork in Wambaw Creek, you can paddle to Hampton Plantation. This antebellum home once lorded over a vast rice plantation in the lowlands beyond, where rice fields grew into "white gold," bringing wealth to the Lowcountry. Here you can tour the grounds of the mansion at no charge, imagining a past ninescore distant when the home was alive with activity, and big Hampton Island, across the creek, was an agricultural beehive tended by black slaves. The island is still laced with old straight-line canals, easily visible on aerial maps.

Rice production at Hampton Plantation was some of the highest in the pre–Civil War United States. The home figured in Revolutionary history as well. The British, on their hunt for the Swamp Fox—Francis Marion—came to Hampton Plantation, but Marion laid low in the rice fields undetected (sometimes it seems Francis Marion was just about everywhere in the Lowcountry throughout the Revolutionary War). Hampton Plantation, a National Historic Landmark, was purchased by the state in 1971, and now visitors can explore a way of life gone by. Entrance to the plantation house requires a fee.

difficulties. At just short of a mile on the right, look for a giant cypress lining the shore. Its base is huge, and as you look up the trunk, its topmost part has been broken off—likely by a lightning strike. Ancient trees such as this one often are struck or crashed upon sometime during their long life. Some of the cypresses along Wambaw Creek are upward of 1,000 years old!

This is a good place to turn around; however, the confluence of Cane Branch and Wambaw Creek, another mile or so up, is also a good point to stop, as the stream becomes difficult above Cane Branch. A gentle backtrack returns you to Still Landing at 2.0 miles. If you forgot anything, now is a good time to retrieve it. Otherwise, continue downstream on Wambaw Creek, enjoying the push of the freshwater flow, aiming for the Santee River. It is 4.6 miles from Still Landing to Elmwood Landing. As you head downstream, occasional bluffs rise a bit on your right. Look left 1.3 miles downstream for an old rice plantation canal. The adjacent terrain is long overgrown. These old canals, barely discernible, are about the only evidence of man you will see here in the Wambaw Creek Wilderness. You will also see natural sloughs and small tributaries flowing into the stream.

At 1.5 miles from Still Landing, you will turn sharply right, southeasterly. Wambaw Creek travels southeast for 0.5 mile before resuming its northeasterly direction. As you come near FR 211A at 2.2 miles, the banks remain undeveloped. At 3.0 miles, Wambaw Creek splits around an island. The main channel is making a sharp bend to the right at this point.

Wambaw Creek is widening a bit. On a falling tide, when the mucky bank is exposed, look for fiddler crabs scurrying about. This is a sure sign of oceanic proximity. However, Wambaw Creek remains entirely freshwater. The bends of the waterway become more sweeping. Big Morgan Branch enters at 3.9 miles. Ahead, you will turn a corner, and the FR 204 Bridge comes into view. End the downstream part of the paddle at 4.6 miles, making for a 6.6-mile paddle if you also went upstream from Still Landing. The Elmwood Landing ramp is on your left.

33 Awendaw Creek Canoe Trail

This open tidal creek flows through a coastal estuary within the Francis Marion National Forest.

County: Charleston
Start: Awendaw Creek Canoe Launch
N33° 1.795' / W79° 36.179'
End: Buck Hall Recreation Area
N33° 2.285' / W79° 33.659'
Distance: 3.8 or 7.6 miles
Float time: 2.5 or 4.5 hours
Difficulty rating: Easy to moderate
Rapids: None
River type: Brackish tidal creek
Current: Tidal
River gradient: None
River gauge: None
Season: Year-round

Land status: National forest, national wildlife refuge
Fees or permits: Parking fee required at takeout
Nearest city/town: McClellanville
Maps: Francis Marion National Forest; USGS Quadrangle Maps: Awendaw
Boats used: Kayaks, canoes, motorboats on Intracoastal Waterway
Organizations: Palmetto Conservation, 722 King Street, Columbia, SC 29205, (803) 771-0870, palmettoconservation.org
Contacts/outfitters: Francis Marion National Forest, 2967 Steed Creek Rd., Huger, SC 29450, (843) 336-3248, www.fs.usda.gov/main/scnfs

Put-in/Takeout Information

To takeout: From the intersection of US 17 and US 17A in Georgetown, take US 17 south for 29 miles to Buck Hall Recreation Area on your left. Turn into the recreation area and follow the road to dead-end at the boat ramp. There is a parking fee.
To put-in from takeout: Backtrack from Buck Hall to US 17 and turn left (south) on US 17 for 2.2 miles to Rosa Green Road. Turn left on Rosa Green Road and follow it for 0.5 mile to turn left into the Awendaw Creek Canoe Launch and Palmetto Trail parking area.

Paddle Summary

This one of the most beautiful parcels within the scenic Francis Marion National Forest. Here you can take Awendaw Creek through cordgrass marshes bordered by a maritime woodland standing atop resplendent bluffs. The waterway makes a serpentine course southeasterly as it follows the daily fluctuations of the tide, for the mouth of this creek is less than 1 mile from the Atlantic Ocean. Awendaw Creek opens onto the Intracoastal Waterway. There, you will join boaters of all stripes, from anglers to sailors to paddlers like us. On one side you will have the national forest, and the other will be Cape Romain National Wildlife Refuge. The paddle concludes with a trip northeasterly on the Intracoastal Waterway where the boat ramp of Buck Hall Recreation Area awaits.

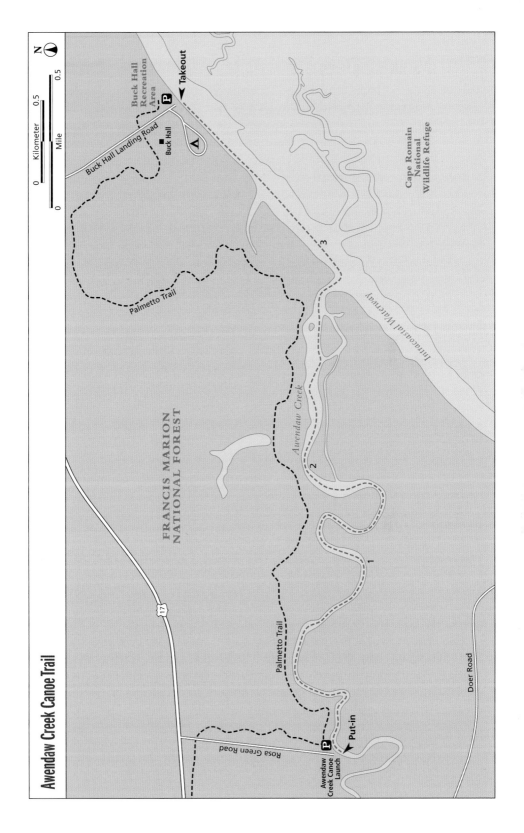

Awendaw Creek Canoe Trail

N

Kilometer
0   0.5   0.5
Mile

Buck Hall Landing Road

Buck Hall

Buck Hall
Recreation
Area

Takeout

Palmetto Trail

FRANCIS MARION
NATIONAL FOREST

Awendaw Creek

Intracoastal Waterway

Cape Romain
National
Wildlife Refuge

3

2

1

Palmetto Trail

17

Rosa Green Road

Awendaw
Creek Canoe
Launch

Put-in

Doer Road

One of the neat things about this trip is you can make it either a one-way or an out-and-back adventure. No matter your preference, factor in the tides. The tides here are about 2.5 hours behind that of Charleston Harbor. So if you want to do a one-way trip, start at the Awendaw Creek Canoe Launch about 3 hours after the high tide in Charleston, and the current will carry you out to the Intracoastal Waterway. You can also do a hiker or bicycle shuttle using the Palmetto Trail, which links the put-in and takeout. South Carolina's master hiking path has its southern terminus at Buck Hall Recreation Area. The Awendaw Passage of the Palmetto Trail roughly parallels this paddle. It is 3.8 miles one way via canoe or kayak between Awendaw Creek Canoe Launch and Buck Hall. If you walk the Palmetto Trail, it is 4.2 miles between the two places. Bicycles are allowed on this segment of the Palmetto Trail. Furthermore, you can even camp overnight at Buck Hall. It is a fine national forest overnight destination nestled among live oaks overlooking the Intracoastal Waterway. Therefore, I suggest you make a complete adventure of this paddle and include more than just floating Awendaw Creek.

River Overview

Awendaw Creek has its origins in the Francis Marion National Forest. Its headwaters drain parts of Little Wambaw Swamp and Wambaw Swamp. Cooter Creek and Steed Creek flow from these wetlands and along with Bell Creek, all come together to form Awendaw Creek. Here, the upper waters of Awendaw Creek briefly course through private land then reenter the national forest near the Awendaw Creek Canoe Launch. By this juncture, the stream is tidal and brackish. A wide cordgrass marsh forms a wide wetland bordered by bluffs. The creek wanders through this wetland until it opens to the Intracoastal Waterway, which here creates a wide channel heading southwest or northeast, depending upon your direction.

The Paddle

The parking area is on a bluff overlooking Awendaw Creek and the adjacent cord-grass wetland. The Palmetto Trail can be accessed from the parking area in addition to the canoe launch. The dock is an elaborate universally accessible wooden wonder. Make your way down the wooden walkway to reach a floating dock on Awendaw Creek. At this point, you will know the direction of the water flow.

Enter the brownish, brackish, 40-foot-wide tidal creek. A bluff rises on your left. Quickly, the meanders of Awendaw Creek take you away from the bluff. Cordgrass borders both sides of the stream. Small tidal channels enter the cordgrass and link to Awendaw Creek. At 0.2 mile, the stream makes a hard left. By 0.3 mile, you are back hard against the landward bluff, where live oaks, cedars, and pines rise. Turn back away from the bluff on your left, and by 0.9 mile you will be smack against the bluff on the right-hand side of the wetland. At 1.0 mile, pass under a power line.

Awendaw Creek cuts a placid path through cordgrass marsh bordered by wooded bluffs.

Awendaw Creek keeps bouncing off the bluffs that border the cordgrass flats. Return to the bluff on the left side of the creek at 1.2 miles. At this point, the Palmetto Trail is just above the shore on the bluff. Neat huh? By 1.5 miles, you are floating beneath the right-hand bluff again. This is a high bluff for the coast, extending about 20 feet up. Awendaw Creek curves along the bluff another 0.3 mile before turning away yet again. The stream continues to widen. More small channels form aquatic veins stretching into the cordgrass. As you near the Intracoastal Waterway, the cordgrass becomes more prevalent and the low shoreline opens the horizon. However, you are also more subject to wind.

At this point watch for exposed oyster bars when the tide is lower. The clusters of oyster shells are hard and sharp and can tear up a boat. Stay away. Weave among small cordgrass clusters to reach the Intracoastal Waterway at 2.9 miles. This seems a huge expanse compared to Awendaw Creek—and it is. Turn left here. The edges of the waterway are muddy shallows, in places too shallow even for self-propelled watercraft. Pass channel marker 57. Cape Romain National Wildlife Refuge is on your right, and the national forest on your left. Be alert for motorboats and their waves on the 300-foot-wide passage. Pass waterway marker 55 at 3.3 miles. Stay near the left shore, passing a small parcel of private property. Ahead, you will see the Buck Hall Campground. Continue a little farther, then reach the Buck Hall boat ramp on your left at 3.8 miles, ending the paddle.

AWENDAW PASSAGE OF THE PALMETTO TRAIL

Many consider the Awendaw Passage the most beautiful segment of the Palmetto Trail. It is the easternmost passage of the state-long master path of South Carolina, and you can use it for a hike or bike shuttle on this paddle. Heading from Buck Hall back to the put-in, the trail leaves on a boardwalk, which circles a palm tree, symbolizing the Palmetto Trail. The boardwalk reaches dry land just before crossing the entrance road to Buck Hall. Pass under a transmission line at 0.6 mile and another at 1.1 miles.

The trail winds through pines that devolve into thick oaks woods and then into maritime woods with cedar and palm. At 1.8 miles, the trail reaches a boardwalk with handrails and opens onto Awendaw Creek and the Intracoastal Waterway. Here, you can peer into the distance and see tidal marsh seemingly go on forever. The trail passes through wetter portions, crossing small boardwalks in the dampest spots as it keeps along the edge of the marsh. At 2.2 miles, wind beneath a dense palm copse. Palms remain common on Awendaw Creek, along with live oaks for the next segment, as it crosses a wide open boardwalk at 2.5 miles.

At 2.7 miles, meet a grassy roadbed coming in from the right. Stay left here to span a major tidal tributary on an elaborate bridge with iron rails. Extensive views of the marsh all the way to the Intracoastal Waterway spread before you.

The trail travels the margin where the saltwater marsh meets the forest, allowing you to look out on open tidal flats from the shade of live oak trees. The Palmetto Trail turns away from Awendaw Creek at 3.1 miles, passes over a boardwalk, then travels through oak woods before opening to cross a transmission line at 3.4 miles. Occasional contemplation benches are set along the bluffs.

Pass three last boardwalks before coming along the bluff a final time at 3.8 miles. The Palmetto Trail continues on the bluff, offering stellar marsh vantages before taking you back to the canoe launch at 4.2 miles.

34 Huger Creek/Quinby Creek

Paddle two scenically diverse, tidally influenced freshwater streams in the Lowcountry. This can be a one-way or two-way adventure.

County: Berkeley
Start: Huger Recreation Area
    N33° 7.875' / W79° 48.664'
End: Hamer Landing
    N33° 5.664' / W79° 48.480'
Distance: 3.9 or 7.8 miles
Float time: 2.0 or 4.0 hours
Difficulty rating: Easy
Rapids: None
River type: Freshwater tidally affected creeks
Current: Tidal
River gradient: None
River gauge: None

Season: Year-round
Land status: Private
Fees or permits: No fees or permits required
Nearest city/town: Huger
Maps: Francis Marion National Forest; USGS Quadrangle Maps: Bethera, Huger
Boats used: Kayaks, canoes, a few motorboats
Organizations: Berkeley County Blueways, berkeleyblueways.com
Contacts/outfitters: Francis Marion National Forest, 2967 Steed Creek Rd., Huger, SC 29450, (843) 336-3248, www.fs.usda.gov/main/scnfs/

Put-in/Takeout Information

To takeout: From the intersection of SC 41 and SC 402 in Huger (there is a tall cell-phone tower near this intersection), head south on SC 41 for 0.1 mile, then turn right on Cainhoy Road. Follow Cainhoy Road for 0.1 mile to the Ralph Hamer Landing on your right, just before the Quinby Bridge.

To put-in from takeout: Backtrack to the intersection of SC 402 and SC 41. This time, head west on SC 402 toward Moncks Corner. At 2.5 miles, a little after the bridge over Huger Creek, turn left into Huger Recreation Area; if you reach Rattlesnake Road you have gone too far. Stay straight in Huger Recreation Area as a loop goes right through the picnic area. Quickly reach a T intersection, then turn left to dead-end shortly at the boat ramp on Huger Creek.

Paddle Summary

This is a gorgeous trip on two different tidally affected freshwater streams. Leave from a landing that is part of the Francis Marion National Forest and includes a fine picnic area with a shelter (in addition to the boat ramp). There is also a small, accessible fishing deck at the landing. Here, Huger Creek is flowing out of the Francis Marion National Forest. You join this alluring blackwater stream southbound through rich waterside forest. It is not long before the forest gives way to open, lower banks interspersed with trees. This is plantation country, so you travel along old rice dikes as the creek widens. Pass Gough Creek. It offers a 0.5-mile exploratory out-and-back

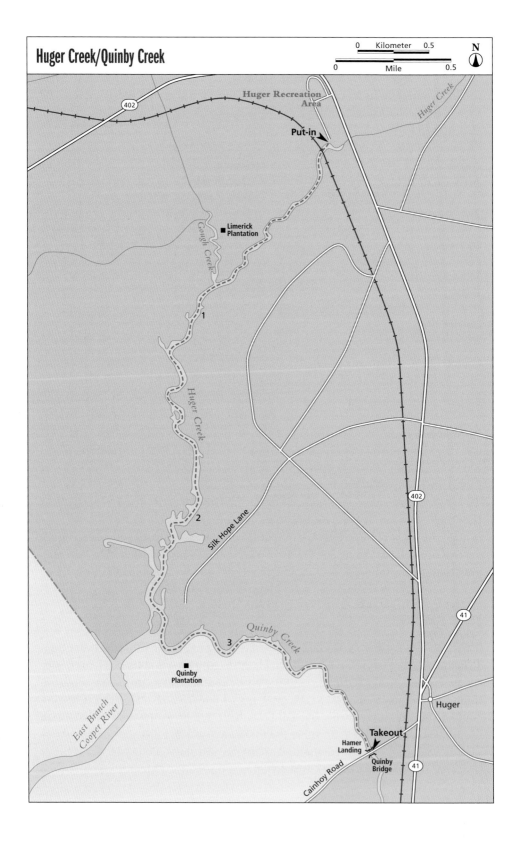

Huger Creek/Quinby Creek

0   Kilometer   0.5

0   Mile   0.5

N

402

Huger Recreation Area

Huger Creek

Put-in

Limerick Plantation

Gough Creek

Huger Creek

1

2

Silk Hope Lane

402

41

Quinby Creek

3

Quinby Plantation

East Branch Cooper River

Huger

Takeout

Hamer Landing

Quinby Bridge

Cainhoy Road

41

side trip. Aquatic vegetation adds beauty everywhere you look. Huger Creek meets Quinby Creek. Together they form the East Branch Cooper River, which is a fine paddling waterway itself, especially if you include a trip to the old Pompion Hill Chapel, a waterside brick house of worship built in 1764.

Our paddle heads left up Quinby Creek, itself tidally influenced. The old Quinby Plantation stands to your right as you head up Quinby Creek, winding on an ever-narrowing waterway. Streamside woods rise again before reaching Hamer Landing and Quinby Bridge, site of a Revolutionary War battle.

This paddle can be easily done as a one-way shuttle paddle or an out-and-back adventure, eliminating the need for a shuttle. Simply paddle to Hamer Landing at Quinby Bridge, take a break at the ramp and dock, then return to your starting point. The tides run about 3 hours behind Charleston Harbor, but since you are going down one creek and up another, you will be going against the flow at one time. I would not worry about trying to catch the perfect tide. The tides are not too strong here anyway. Just get in your boat and enjoy the trip, for it is a good one.

River Overview

Huger Creek is formed out of the swamps within the Francis Marion National Forest. Here, Turkey Creek and Nicholson Creek drain Jericho Swamp, Darlington Swamp, and other wetlands, all within the wooded confines of the forest. They come together shortly above Huger Recreation Area, where this paddle begins. Huger Creek is a black, treelined, clean stream when it passes by the put-in. From here, the creek quickly widens and passes several historic plantations, among them Limerick Plantation and Silk Hope Plantation. Here, its banks were altered with berms and gates to flood the rice fields in its valley. Huger Creek flows just a couple of miles before meeting Quinby Creek, together forming the East Branch Cooper River.

Quinby Creek also has its beginnings in the national forest and comes to be where Northampton Creek and Harleston Dam Creek merge. Quinby Creek flows westerly, passing under the historic Quinby Bridge, where this paddle ends. It continues winding westerly to meet Huger Creek. By the way, Quinby Creek is the official correct spelling, but it is alternately spelled as Quimby and Quemby.

The Paddle

Take note of the freshwater spring at the Huger boat ramp. Generations of locals have been getting their drinking water from there, despite its hint of sulfur. Although the picnic area and small concrete boat ramp are part of the Francis Marion National Forest, this paddle immediately leaves the national forest, heading right, southwesterly, down Huger Creek. You will shortly float under a railroad bridge. Forested banks of cypress, sweetgum, oak, wax myrtle, and pine line the 40-foot-wide creek. The current is slow to slack, depending on the tides.

The beautiful colors make fall a great time to be on Huger Creek.

At 0.5 mile, Huger Creek curves right. Aquatic vegetation begins lining the banks in places. At 0.9 mile, Gough Creek enters on river right. If you feel like exploring, head up this black tributary, northbound. Paddlers can make it about 0.5 mile before vegetation closes the creek. Limerick Plantation stands in the peninsula between Gough Creek and Huger Creek.

Brushy banks become more commonplace. The Kensington Plantation occupies the right bank beyond Gough Creek. You will see a dock of theirs on river right at

1.2 miles. A berm rises beyond here, on river right. Wetlands are on the other side of the berm, fronted with wood pilings. The widening Huger Creek becomes more subject to wind, especially with the low banks. It keeps a southwesterly direction. A channel comes in on river right at 2.2 miles. This is a remnant canal from rice days. Feel free to check it out. Otherwise keep heading south down Huger Creek. You will pass a house on river left, with a dock. Just beyond there, note more dikes and pilings from the rice days on river left.

At 2.6 miles, using the house just passed as your marker, look left for Quinby Creek. Downstream to your right, big East Branch Cooper River widely continues southwesterly for the coast. Quinby Creek, however, stretching about 40 feet across and bordered in low brush and aquatic vegetation, heads easterly.

Quinby Creek will be flowing opposite the current of Huger Creek. That is a clue to joining Quinby Creek. The effective paddling width of Quinby Creek quickly narrows to 30 feet or less. At 3.0 miles, pass an old wooden gate similar to that of rice days, when these gates were used to allow water in or out of fields. Quinby Creek continues to narrow. Cedars stand along the banks. At 3.9 miles, reach the low Quinby Bridge and Hamer Landing on river left. The level dock makes a good spot to relax if you are doing an out-and-back paddle.

BATTLE OF QUINBY BRIDGE

In summer of 1781, the British were losing South Carolina and losing the Revolutionary War. Yet they fought on. Nearby Moncks Corner was an important supply depot for the redcoats, yet they sensed the American noose tightening, so British lieutenant colonel James Coates retreated toward the British stronghold of Charleston the night of July 17. American forces pursued and found themselves right behind the English at Quinby Bridge, the takeout for this paddle. After crossing the span, the British began tearing up the bridge planking to slow the Americans, who were undeterred and jumped the missing planks on their horses or nimbly crossed the bridge on its support beams.

A short skirmish ensued before the British regrouped at nearby Shubrick Plantation, while the Americans conferred at Quinby Bridge. The brick plantation sat on a rise and was ideal for defense. The next afternoon General Thomas Sumter—against the advice of General Francis Marion and Lieutenant Colonel Henry Lee (father of Robert E. Lee)—ordered an assault on the well-fortified Shubrick Plantation. It was a disaster and an unnecessary loss of life for the Americans. After the battle, Sumter retreated across Quinby Creek, while Francis Marion, the Swamp Fox, resolved never to fight again with Thomas Sumter.

35 Wadboo Creek

Enjoy a narrow swamp stream, an open tidal waterway, and an exploration of old rice-field canals, all from one landing.

County: Berkeley
Start: Rembert C. Dennis Landing
    N33° 11.756' / W79° 57.185'
End: Rembert C. Dennis Landing
    N33° 11.756' / W79° 57.185'
Distance: 5-7 miles
Float time: 3-5 hours
Difficulty rating: Moderate
Rapids: Class I
River type: Swamp stream and tidal creek, rice field canals
Current: Moderate
River gradient: 1.0 foot per mile

River gauge: None, no minimum runnable level
Season: Fall through spring
Land status: Private
Fees or permits: No fees or permits required
Nearest city/town: Moncks Corner
Maps: Berkeley County Blueways; USGS Quadrangle Maps: Cordesville
Boats used: Kayaks, canoes
Organizations: Berkeley County Blueways, berkeleyblueways.com
Contacts/outfitters: South Carolina Paddlesports Industry Association, paddlesouthcarolina.org

Put-in/Takeout Information

To takeout: From the intersection of US 52 and US 17A in Moncks Corner, take US 52 West/US 17A North for 1.6 miles, crossing the tailrace canal connecting Lake Moultrie and the Cooper River, to reach SC 402. Turn right and join SC 402 south toward Cordesville. Stay with SC 402 for 1.9 miles to reach the Dennis C. Rembert Landing on your left.

To put-in from takeout: Put-in and takeout are the same.

Paddle Summary

A trip on Wadboo Creek explores very different waters all from one landing. Moreover, as an added bonus, no shuttle is required! From the large and sometimes busy Dennis C. Rembert Landing, you will first paddle up Wadboo Creek, passing an ecologically significant limestone bluff that harbors plant life rare in the Lowcountry. The stream narrows, and you enter Wadboo Swamp, a place where cypress and tupelo trees dominate the swampy shoreline. The stream narrows and splits, becoming barely wide enough for a boat. After a mile or so, you turn around and enjoy the push of the current back downstream to the landing.

At that point, follow Wadboo Creek downstream as it becomes increasingly tidal and wide. The shores turn grassy, and you reach the Cooper River. Briefly explore this wide waterway before turning back into channels and canals along Wadboo Creek. These channels are left over from the days when rice was cultivated in the

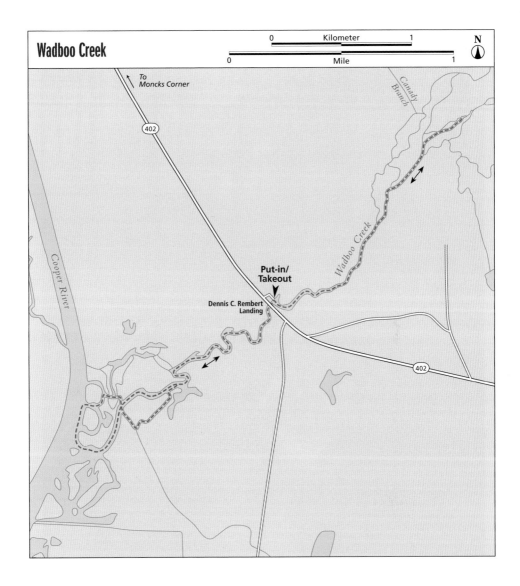

Kilometer

Mile

N

To
Moncks Corner

Canady Branch

Cooper River

Wadboo Creek

Put-in/
Takeout

Dennis C. Rembert
Landing

marshes along Wadboo Creek. On your return you can explore some of the narrow, linear, hand-dug canals used to irrigate rice fields over two centuries distant. Down here there is no specific route to follow. Simply explore the canals at your leisure.

River Overview

Wadboo Creek is born near the hamlet of Bonneau, French meaning "good water." The waters of Walker Swamp and Gravel Hill Swamp gather, flowing south through the Francis Marion National Forest. Wadboo Creek crosses South Carolina's master hiking path, the Palmetto Trail. A 300-yard portage on the Palmetto Trail is actually

Paddling up an old hand-dug, rice-field canal

used to reach upper Wadboo Creek, which can be paddled at high water levels by experienced swamp paddlers (paddlers will likely have to pull over obstructions). From there, Wadboo Creek flows in often-braided channels through pristine Wadboo Swamp for 5 miles to Dennis C. Rembert Landing. A marked paddling trail, with a signed campsite about halfway, helps keep paddlers on course. Still, expect challenges when traversing Wadboo Swamp. That is why your best bet is to start at the bottom of the swamp, paddle up the creek, and turn around at your leisure, rather than fight, end to end, though Wadboo Swamp.

Beyond Rembert Landing, Wadboo Creek widens, slows, and opens, flowing past the old rice fields. It then empties into the Cooper River, near the tailrace canal flowing from Lake Moultrie. Wadboo Creek formerly was the headwaters of the Cooper River.

The Paddle

Do not be intimidated by the large boat landing. Most motorboaters at the landing use Wadboo Creek to venture into the Cooper River and fish. Leave the boat ramp and head left (northbound) up Wadboo Creek, where few, if any, motorboats go. In winter and spring, when the water is up, you may feel a decent current; otherwise it should not be too challenging to paddle upstream. Be apprised the current may be affected by the tide as well as by whether Santee Cooper Power is generating at the Lake Moultrie Dam. In that case, the excess water flowing through the Tailrace Canal would back up Wadboo Creek and slow the current. Wadboo Creek starts about 50 feet in width but soon narrows. Quickly pass under a power line. Ospreys have been known to nest in the line support towers. After about 0.25 mile, you will come to the sheer limestone bluff on your right. Note how smooth the rock is, having been carved over time by Wadboo Creek. A small cave of sorts is exposed at lower water levels. Rare ferns such as blackstem spleenwort are found here. Trees found along the bluffs include hop hornbeam, white basswood, and black walnut. These bluffs are rare in the Lowcountry, making the plant communities on them special.

Ahead, the blackwater stream is bordered by cypress, tupelo, wax myrtle, and holly. Higher spots sport pine and palmetto. By now, the creek has narrowed to less than 30 feet. At 0.6 mile, on your left, look for a straight-line dug channel. It is an old rice-field canal, hardly recognizable now that it's surrounded by dense forest.

Wadboo Creek continues twisting, turning, and narrowing further. In places, small isles give paddlers choices for their routes. Your best bet is to look for the current and go up it. Some large and ancient cypresses stand tall along the shore. At 1.2 miles, the main flow curves sharply right. This is a good place to turn around. Canady Branch and Bull Head Run feed Wadboo Creek in this vicinity. However, the multiple stream braids make it difficult to discern a tributary from another braid of Wadboo Creek.

Your return trip will yield sights yet unseen. After passing the boat landing, your starting point at 2.4 miles, continue downstream on Wadboo Creek, passing under the SC 402 bridge. The waterway quickly widens as it aims for the Cooper River. Lily pads grow along still shorelines. Dead-end sloughs are still as well. The primary channel is easily seen. Keep an eye out for motorboaters heading for the Cooper River. Cattails and grasses prevail on the shoreline. You are more subject to wind here than upstream. Multiple channels break off the main stem and beckon exploration. For now, head on out to the Cooper River, 1.4 miles distant from the boat ramp. Houses are visible on the opposite shore.

Turn right up the Cooper River. Note the different color of the river, more greenish clear rather than the black swamp waters. Turn back into the drainage of Wadboo Creek and begin exploring. You will find curving natural channels and also the historic straight-line canals built when slaves first cleared the swamp of all trees by hand. Next, they dug ditches and built banks with hand tools. After that, they built wooden floodgates to control drainage and water flow to the rice fields. When this infrastructure was finished, they cultivated rice by hand using mules outfitted with special rawhide boots to keep them from sinking in the mud. Imagine the heat, the bugs, and potential for malaria.

South Carolina's rice production came into its own from 1839 to 1859 when the state produced 70 percent of the nation's rice. The falloff in 1859 was caused by the Civil War, and after the Civil War the plantations could not function as well without slave labor.

Now, we paddlers can float through these ditches and channels, considering how Wadboo Creek and others like it have changed, evolving from dark swamps to sun-scorched rice fields and back to destinations where we can enjoy nature's beauty, while still reflecting the hand of the past. One thing about exploring, you really cannot get lost here. The channels either dead end or connect to other channels. Furthermore, high, dry ground borders both sides of lower Wadboo Creek.

STRANGE NAME

Let's face it—Wadboo is a strange name. The Indian moniker for this creek was adopted by one of South Carolina's early settlers, James Colleton—yes, the same name from which Colleton County derives. But back to the name Wadboo. Lowcountry stream names ending with "boo" and "baw" mean water. James Colleton dubbed the 12,000-acre landholding and plantation Wadboo. His father, John Colleton, had been the recipient of the huge land grant from the king of England back in 1683. During the Revolutionary War, the Colleton clan remained loyal to England, and they suffered for it.

Toward the end of the war, when the British were still trying to hold onto the Carolinas, they attacked the Swamp Fox himself, ol' Francis Marion, as he and his troops were camped outside of Wadboo Plantation, on the far side of Wadboo Creek from today's Rembert Landing. South Carolina's hero beat back the British and made Wadboo Plantation his headquarters until the English evacuated Charleston, effectively ending the war in the Palmetto State. After the war, the Wadboo landholding was confiscated, broken up, and sold to what had become American citizens.

36 Duck Pond

This paddle explores big Lake Moultrie before entering intimate bays where rich vegetation creates a florally fascinating trip.

County: Berkeley
Start: Fred Day Landing
　N33° 17.710' / W80° 9.387'
End: Fred Day Landing
　N33° 17.710' / W80° 9.387'
Distance: 3.7 miles
Float time: 2.5 hours, including stops along sandy shore
Difficulty rating: Easy to moderate
Rapids: None
River type: Open lake and vegetated bays
Current: None
River gradient: None
River gauge: None

Season: Year-round
Land status: Santee Cooper lands
Fees or permits: No fees of permits required
Nearest city/town: Moncks Corner
Maps: Santee Cooper Lakes map; USGS Quadrangle Maps: Cross
Boats used: Motorboats on Lake Moultrie, kayaks and canoes in bays
Organizations: Berkeley County Blueways, berkeleyblueways.com
Contacts/outfitters: Santee Cooper Headquarters, 1 Riverwood Dr., Moncks Corner, SC 29461, (843) 761-8000, santeecooper.com

Put-in/Takeout Information

To takeout: From the intersection of US 17A and SC 6 in downtown Moncks Corner, take SC 6 west for 11.8 miles to reach a stop sign. Turn right here, staying with SC 6 west, which you will follow for 1 mile farther to turn right on Boat Landing Road. Follow Boat Landing Road to dead-end at the large Fred L. Day Landing.
To put-in from takeout: The takeout and put-in are the same.

Paddle Summary

This relatively short paddle is just one example of many paddling opportunities on both Lake Moultrie—where this paddle takes place—and nearby Lake Marion. This particular trip combines cruising the open shores of huge Lake Moultrie with an exploratory mission into some protected back bays, where tall cypresses and ample aquatic vegetation are the backdrop for bountiful wildlife such as alligators and shorebirds. Since you are making a loop, there is no need for a shuttle vehicle. You will encounter boats in the lake, but seeing them is less likely in the back bays—here, the Duck Pond. The trip leaves big Fred L. Day Landing, then enters a small sheltered cove. Reach the open waters of huge Lake Moultrie, where distant shores can barely be seen over the horizon. Cruise south along an alternately sandy and thickly vegetated shoreline. Cypresses grow out from the water's edge. You will leave the big water and enter a bay through sandy "gates." Here, the wind is stilled. Lily pads, duck moss,

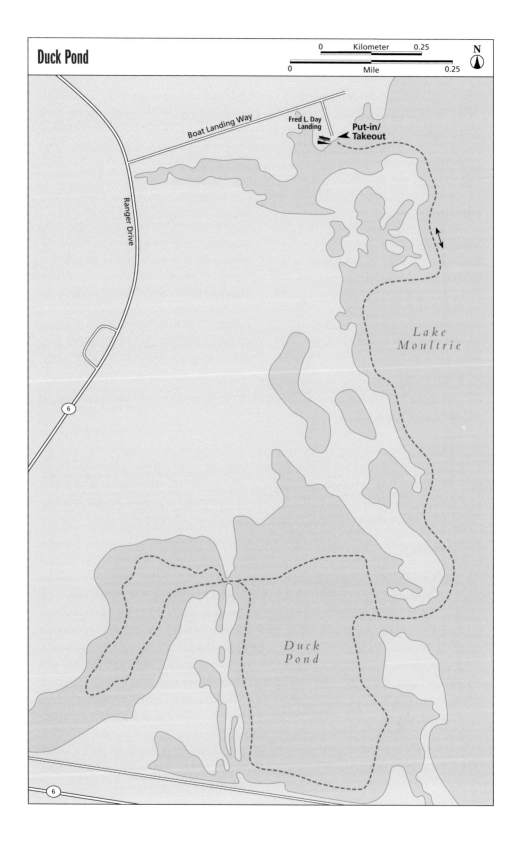

Duck Pond

0   Kilometer   0.25

0   Mile   0.25

N

Boat Landing Way

Fred L. Day
Landing

**Put-in/
Takeout**

Ranger Drive

*Lake
Moultrie*

6

*Duck
Pond*

6

and other waterweeds cover much of the surface. You sightsee in this bay only to find a second narrow "gate" that opens to yet another bay even more thickly overgrown. The vegetated bay seems almost like firm land. Enter a classic open swamp—duck moss, lily pads, and brushy grasses bordered by cypress. Make another loop back here, sometimes straining your paddle due to thick aquatic growth. However, there is enough open water to make it fun. Return to the bigger outer bay, explore it some more, then return along the main shoreline of Lake Moultrie, having learned there's a lot more to this lake than meets the eye!

River Overview

Lake Moultrie is one of the two primary impoundments of South Carolina's coastal plain, the other being Lake Marion. The two are linked by a diversion canal, which is where Lake Moultrie gets its water, siphoned off the Santee River drainage. Water flows out of Lake Moultrie via a different canal and into the Cooper River. Lake Moultrie and Lake Marion were created in the 1940s to provide low-cost electricity, water storage, and flood control, as well as recreation. At the time, it was the largest earth-moving project in recorded history. The two impoundments present a total of 450 miles of shoreline.

Lake Moultrie offers a wealth of boating opportunities for everyone from paddlers to yachters. Paddlers will find shoreline coves, such as this one, to explore, in addition to other sheltered areas.

The Paddle

Fred L. Day Landing has a huge parking lot and double boat ramp as well as a wooden observation deck overlooking an inlet linking to Lake Moultrie. You can paddle right (west) from the ramp, but the inlet quickly closes. Eventually, head left (east). Tall cypresses and lush vegetation border the clear but tea-tinted water. Willows and saw grass form shoreline thickets. Sand is commonplace along the shallows and where wave action pounds the shore.

The intimate cove opens into the balance of Lake Moultrie. The expanse of the lake will shock first-time visitors: You can barely see the far side of the lake over the horizon. It is huge. Woe to the paddlers if northeasterly winds are blowing. Picturesque moss-draped cypresses extend into the water and beg to be photographed. The water is relatively shallow. Turn right, southbound, with the shore to your right. You can hug the shore or meander among the cypresses that rise from the water. Small sandy spots make for easy landings. On the far southern shore, you can make out the long dike known as the West Seawall. It is part of what holds back the water here at Lake Moultrie.

At 0.8 mile, leave the main lake and turn right, easterly into Duck Pond, which comprises two bays. Enter a narrow inlet bordered by sandy beaches separated by 80 or so feet. A large bay opens before you. There are stretches of open water and parcels that are covered in lilies and aquatic vegetation. The wind will be noticeably less here if it has

Lily pads stretch across the Duck Pond.

been blowing on Lake Moultrie. Turn right and begin a counterclockwise circuit. The Duck Pond is often described as a mini Okefenokee Swamp, and there is truth in that. Between the cypresses, blooming lilies, and open sky, it does recall its Georgia brethren.

How much you want to explore depends upon your willingness to work through partly vegetated waters. It takes more effort to paddle your craft through water surface growth. The open stretches of water are obviously much easier. But I say go for it.

The overall distance is not hard, so the extra effort of pushing through the vegetation is easily doable.

As you circle around the north end of this bay, look for a second channel leading to the back bay. This gate is topped in sweetgum trees on one side and is but 15 feet wide. If you need to stop, hard, dry ground is on the right-hand side of the channel by the sweetgums. This second bay makes the first seem as wide open as Lake Moultrie itself. Saw grass and cypresses grow tall, and there are few immediately obvious paddle routes. A marked canoe trail would be dandy here—but you have to make your own way, perhaps pushing through thick duck moss and ranks of huge lily pads, but eventually you are going to see a fascinating flower or captivating wading bird. Bring your binoculars. Make your way as far southwest as you can, then circle back out. Pass through the channel, then open to the bigger part of Duck Pond. Turn south and paddle through some arm-relieving open water. Ahead, you will see the West Seawall flanking the far shore. After reaching the seawall, continue your circuit to emerge back onto the main body of Lake Moultrie. From here, backtrack to Fred Day Landing. Ample stopping spots along the shore make a picnic or swim stop worth considering.

OLD SANTEE CANAL PARK

Old Santee Canal Park combines natural and human history in a beautiful setting on the edge of Moncks Corner and is within easy striking distance of this paddle. Before the United States was even a country, the fathers of nearby Charleston sought a way for crops to be shipped from the Midlands down to Charleston, avoiding a dangerous trip down the coast from the mouth of the Santee River to Charleston. If the Santee and Cooper Rivers could be connected, then goods could be safely floated directly to Charleston, which was good for the farmers and good for the traders of South Carolina's shipping center.

With the blessing of one George Washington, the Santee Canal Company set about building the country's first "summit canal," a canal with locks that climbed and descended elevation along its length. The 22-mile canal was finished in 1800 after seven years, and began its fifty-year span of operation. Cotton and other goods were towed by mules and later with manpower using push poles. The nineteenth century moved on, and the canal became obsolete. Railroads shipped goods to Charleston and points beyond. The canal was abandoned, and later most of it was submerged under Lake Moultrie, ironically named for the South Carolina governor who got the canal moving forward. However, this section of the canal is still intact, and along with the historic Stony Landing House, the modern Tailrace Canal, and the waters of Biggin Creek, it makes for an interesting destination to visit. Today you can explore the canal area by foot trail plus paddle a segment of the old canal. For more information visit oldsanteecanalpark.org.

37 Edisto River

Paddle past swamps and bluffs on this fast-moving blackwater gem.

County: Dorchester, Colleton
Start: Colleton State Park Canoe Dock
N33° 3.868' / W80° 36.981'
End: Mars Old Field Ramp
N33° 3.276' / W80° 26.915'
Distance: 17.0 miles
Float time: 6.5 hours
Difficulty rating: Moderate
Rapids: Class I
River type: Swift blackwater river
Current: Fast
River gradient: 1.1 feet per mile
River Gauge: Edisto River near Givhans, SC, no minimum runnable level

Season: Year-round
Land status: Private, some state park land
Fees or permits: No fees or permits required
Nearest city/town: Canadys
Maps: Edisto River Canoe & Kayak Trail; USGS Quadrangle Maps: Canadys
Boats used: Canoes, kayaks, johnboats
Organizations: Friends of the Edisto, PO Box 5151, Columbia, SC 29250, (803) 256-4000, edistofriends.org
Contacts/outfitters: Carolina Heritage Outfitters, 1 Livery Ln., St. George, SC 29477, (843) 563-5051, canoesc.com

Put-in/Takeout Information

To takeout: From exit 68 on I-95 near Walterboro, take SC 61 east for 12.5 miles to Mars Old Field Lane (passing Colleton State Park along the way). Turn left on Mars Old Field Lane and follow it 1.1 miles to dead-end at the boat ramp.

To put-in from takeout: To reach the put-in, backtrack to SC 61 and drive west almost back to I-95 to turn right onto US 15 North and shortly enter Colleton State Park. Drive past the park office to the state park campground. Take the campground loop and look for the canoe launch trail leading downhill into the woods between campsites 19 and 20. Unload your boat and gear, then drive around the loop to the river access parking area, near the campground bathhouse. Do not park at the campsites unless you are staying at one. The access trail turns right after leaving the campground, then crosses a boardwalk to reach the canoe dock, shaded by cypress trees.

Paddle Summary

This section of the Edisto offers an excellent put-in and a good takeout, too. Nevertheless, the river between is the real star of the show. Being the longest free-flowing blackwater river in the United States is heady status for the Edisto, and this section of stream reflects its beauty, where wooded swamps and occasional higher shores border the surprisingly swift stream. Some paddlers may balk at the mileage for this day trip. However, the fast-flowing waters of the Edisto make a 17-mile day trip easily doable. And with camping at Colleton State Park, you can be ready to float the

Edisto River

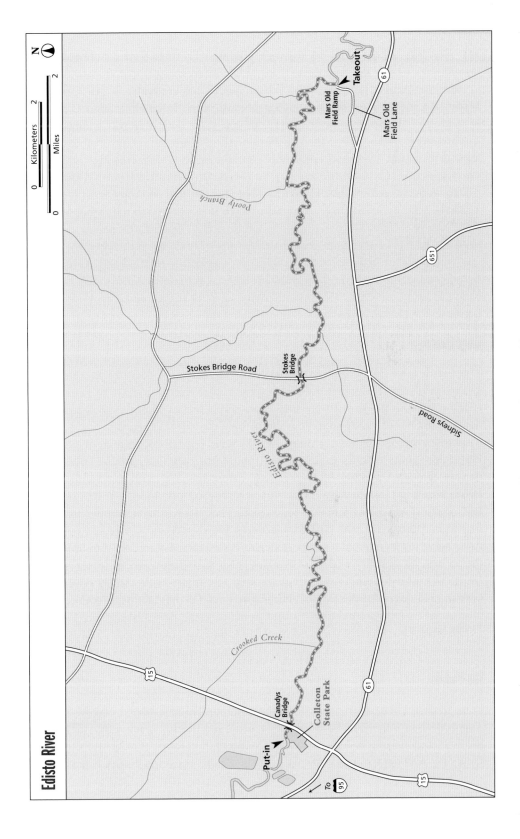

N

0   Kilometers   2

0   Miles   2

Takeout

Mars Old Field Ramp

Mars Old Field Lane

61

651

Poorly Branch

Stokes Bridge Road

Stokes Bridge

Sidneys Road

Edisto River

Crooked Creek

15

Canadys Bridge

Colleton State Park

Put-in

61

15

To 95

next morning, making an all-day trip on the Edisto a Palmetto State paddling day to remember.

Start your trip at the park canoe launch, quickly passing under SC 15, Canadys Bridge. Occasional houses occupy higher ground, especially the bluffs. After a couple of miles, river bends become frequent, and you snake your way past willows and overhanging trees. The Edisto then divides around an island and narrows before coming together again. The bends and beauty continue nearly to Stokes Bridge, which is over halfway.

Downstream, you will pass Cane Island but probably will not know it, with many a channel splitting off the main river stem, which is always easy to follow because of the giveaway current. The bends resume, and the Edisto widens a bit before coming to Mars Old Field Landing on your right. Be wary of strainers on this river; the current will take your boat directly into fallen trees, especially on the bends. Overflow swamps connect to the river throughout. At lower water levels, sandbars form on the bends, allowing for stopping spots; otherwise, look for higher piney banks. Private houses and ramps are sporadically clustered along the route.

River Overview

The Edisto is free flowing from its origins in the Midlands down to the Atlantic Ocean, and being the longest free-flowing blackwater river is its claim to fame. The river basin is also the largest watershed contained entirely within the boundaries of South Carolina. Its headwaters flow south from the hills of Edgefield and Saluda Counties, working southeast, picking up tributaries, respectively forming the South Fork Edisto and North Fork Edisto. Here, the North Fork flows around 100 miles, notably through the town of Orangeburg, before merging with the South Fork Edisto, which has also flowed a similar distance. The two forks meet near Branchville, and together form the swift flow of black liquid. The river widens, becoming floatable year-round, and creates the boundary between Dorchester and Colleton Counties. After being fed by the wild waters of famed Four Holes Swamp, the Edisto passes the ecologically significant bluffs of Givhans Ferry State Park where its southeasterly course was turned south by an earthquake long ago (some say the Ashley River follows the old course of the Edisto). The Edisto aims for the Atlantic, becoming the tidal giant that splits around Edisto Island, home of scenic Edisto Island State Park.

The state-sanctioned 57-mile Edisto River Canoe Trail starts at the US 21 Bridge up near Whetstone Crossroads and ends at Long Creek Landing near Cottageville.

The Paddle

Leave Colleton State Park canoe dock, pushing into the main stream near an island. The 100-or-so-foot-wide Edisto makes a bend and quickly reaches SC 15 and a public boat ramp on the left, as well as a local paddling livery, available for shuttles. Continue on under the span known as Canadys Bridge, bypassing houses. Paper birch

Sun rays penetrate morning swamp fog along the Edisto.

and willow trees, often growing partially in the water and overhanging the stream, find their place along the shore. In other areas, cypress and tupelo trees, with their buttressed bases, occupy the shore. On higher banks, laurel oaks, sporadic live oaks, and other hardwoods rise tall on shore. Drier places are often indicated by the presence of pine stands.

After 1.7 miles, leave the high bluffs on your right. The river narrows, and Crooked Creek comes in on your left, though it is hard to distinguish. The river maintains an easterly course. Low swampy banks occupy both sides of the Edisto. Start a period of river bends at 2.7 miles. The current often swiftens around these bends. Smart paddlers stay inside the bends and look ahead for fallen trees to work around. At higher water levels, the current will flow through the wooded wetlands inside the bends. At 3.7 miles, the Edisto splits around a large island. Take the right channel, floating past riverside cabins under a canopy of trees. The channel tapers to 30 or so feet. At 4.3 miles, the river comes together again.

Continue to pass occasional cabin clusters. Between 6.1 and 6.8 miles, the Edisto bends nearly back on itself. Watch for sandbars on these sharpest bends. Pass under Stokes Bridge Road and private landings at 9.4 miles. At 10.1 miles, the flowing channel shortcuts an old river bend. After passing some houses, the Edisto River flows through the swamp of the Cane Island area. These low banks keep the riverside scenery wild.

At 14.4 miles, the river makes a sharp bend to the right. Poorly Branch comes in here. The waterway keeps a relatively straight track, slowing a bit, before resuming its winding ways and then reaching the Mars Old Field boat ramp on your right. The concrete ramp rises to a grassy area. Mars Old Field has a host of spellings. I have seen it in print as Mauls Old Field, Maas Oldfield, and Mas Old Field. The state of South Carolina Department of Natural Resources spells it Mars Old Field.

TWO STATE PARKS ON THE EDISTO

In addition to Colleton State Park, where this paddle starts, there is another South Carolina state park along the banks of the Edisto River—Givhans Ferry State Park. Located 6 miles downstream of Mars Old Field boat ramp, the two state parks are separated by 23 miles of river. This distance makes for a very long day, but both parks make great base camps to enjoy numerous sections of the Edisto. Colleton State Park is smallish but does have a nice campground set just above the river. For paddlers, the park canoe dock makes a great starting point. Small motorboats share the launch. It is within walking distance of the campground. Speaking of walking, a short nature trail links the campground and park office, traveling along a cypress swamp. Campers are pleased to have water and electricity at each site, along with hot showers.

Givhans Ferry State Park has a more historical bent to it and is my preference. Originally the site of an eighteenth-century ferry operated by Phillip Givhan, the bluffs were developed into a state park by the Civilian Conservation Corps during the 1930s. The park office and other buildings were built then. These limestone bluffs are ecologically significant, hosting rare plants. The River Bluff Nature Trail offers a 1.5-mile excursion along the bluffs. The campground is located back from the Edisto but offers fully equipped sites suitable for tents or RVs. Paddlers can undertake the 6-mile float from Mars Old Field ramp down to Givhans Ferry State Park and view the bluffs from the river. For more information about these two riverside destinations visit southcarolinaparks.com.

38 Ashepoo River

Float this river as it transitions from slender swamp stream to broad tidal waterway through the scenic and ecologically important ACE Basin.

County: Colleton
Start: SC 303 Bridge near Green Pond
N32° 45.936' / W80° 37.433'
End: Joes Fish Camp off US 17
N32° 44.577' / W80° 33.382'
Distance: 6.1 miles
Float time: 3 hours
Difficulty rating: Easy
Rapids: None
River type: Tidally influenced coastal plain waterway
Current: Moderate
River gradient: 0.1 foot per mile
River gauge: None; none needed
Season: Year-round

Land status: Private, mostly large plantations
Fees or permits: Landing fee required at Joes Fish Camp
Nearest city/town: Green Pond
Maps: ACE Basin; USGS Quadrangle Maps: Neyles, Green Pond
Boats used: Kayaks, canoes, fishing boats
Organizations: The ACE Basin National Estuarine Research Reserve, PO Box 12559, Charleston SC 29422, (843) 953-9001, www.acebasin.net
Contacts/outfitters: South Carolina Department of Natural Resources, 585 Donnelley Dr., Green Pond, SC 29446, (843) 844-8957, dnr.sc.gov

Put-in/Takeout Information

To takeout: From the intersection of US 17A and SC 303 in Walterboro, take SC 303 south for 10.1 miles to Clover Hill Road (you will pass over the nondescript bridge on the Ashepoo, your put-in, 0.5 mile before reaching Clover Hill Road). Turn left on Clover Hill Road and follow it for 4.1 miles to US 17. Cross over US 17, then veer left to reach Joes Fish Camp, on the south side of the US 17 bridge. There is a self-serve fee box near the boat ramp.

To put-in from takeout: Leave Joes Fish Camp and cross US 17 to rejoin Clover Hill Road. Follow Clover Hill Road for 4.1 miles to SC 303. Turn right on SC 303 and follow it 0.5 mile to the bridge over the Ashepoo River. This is just a boat throw-in, no ramp. There is an old, decrepit closed wooden bridge running parallel to the SC 303 bridge over the Ashepoo River. Be careful as there is limited but viable shoulder parking on the south side of the bridge.

Paddle Summary

This is the *A* river in the ACE Basin, the 1.1 million–acre swath of coastal South Carolina encompassing one of the largest and most pristine intertidal ecosystems on the entire East Coast (the other two rivers of the ACE Basin are the Combahee and Edisto, also detailed in this guide). Upon leaving the landing-less SC 303 bridge, you

Ashepoo River

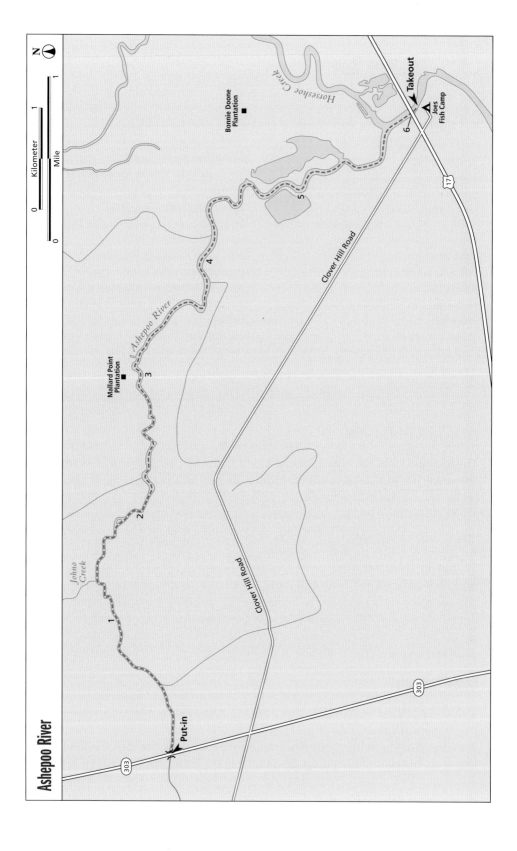

will pass a small housing enclave, then enter wild lands for which the ACE Basin is known. The Ashepoo flows swift and dark under rich and deep swamp woodland, exuding everywhere-you-look beauty. As it heads easterly toward the coast, the river widens and becomes more tidal, then enters former rice-field country, where the tall brooding swamp woodland gives way to lower marshy shores. Plantations border the waterway, keeping the shores undeveloped. Toward the end, the paddle nears historic Bonnie Doone Plantation. Lastly, the now-wide Ashepoo River meets Horseshoe Creek, another paddleable waterway, before passing under the US 17 bridge to reach Joes Fish Camp, a private, fee boat landing. Since the paddle is affected by tides, especially the lower half, it is recommended you start your trip about 5 hours behind high tide at Charleston Harbor.

River Overview

The Ashepoo River drainage is the smallest of the three primary waterways of the ACE Basin. The Ashepoo is located entirely within Colleton County. The Ashepoo River's most northerly upper drainages absorb low hills and then transform into lowland linear swamp streams, namely Jones Swamp Creek and Ireland Creek. The Ashepoo comes to be just west of Walterboro as a multi-channeled, difficult-to-navigate waterway known as the Great Swamp. The many fingers of the Ashepoo come together near Ritter, just before entering the ACE Basin boundary and the SC 303 bridge, where this paddle starts. From there, the waterway is much more navigable and keeps its southerly course, picking up big Horseshoe Creek. Tidal influence increases. Below, the US 17 bridge, where this paddle ends, the Ashepoo twists and bends but maintains its southerly course, emptying into the Atlantic Ocean at Saint Helena Sound just west of the mouth of the Edisto River, near Edisto Beach State Park.

The Paddle

The put-in on SC 303 is not obvious. And since the Ashepoo River is but a narrow tree-canopied waterway here, you just may drive over the bridge without even noticing the river. However, anglers bank fish along the shore near the SC 303 bridge, creating paths down to the water. The best kayak throw-in is on the southeast side of the bridge. Launch your boat and immediately enter a dark stream under a rich swamp forest of which moss-draped cypress and gum are a large part. Oaks find their place as well. Ferns and alligator flag thicken the lower reaches of vegetation and soften the meeting of water and land. A small housing enclave is on river right downstream. You will see several docks and small boathouses, but the residences are set well back from the river to avoid flooding. The waterway is but 30 feet wide here and has occasional fallen trees in it. However, local water enthusiasts keep channels cut in case trees block passage.

The upper part of the river exudes a junglesque aura, especially after you leave the housing enclave 0.5 mile from the SC 303 bridge. Narrow, log-choked waterways

The upper Ashepoo is a narrow blackwater creek.

and small channels flow into the river, including a fenced canal on river left at 0.9 mile. A steady but mild current runs past wood-duck nesting boxes placed in slower stretches of the stream. The Ashepoo widens to about 50 feet, and streamside brush appears with increasing frequency. At 1.2 miles, the river makes a sharp bend to the left then sharply right. Otherwise, it does not twist as much as most swamp streams. Johno Creek comes in on river left at 1.4 miles. It may have been channelized in days gone by, though judging by the current density of the forest that must have been a herculean feat.

Beyond Johno Creek, there is a conspicuous treehouse on river left, integrated into the forest and shoreline. At 1.8 miles, the Ashepoo divides around an island. The right channel is the larger one. The waterway comes back together at 1.9 miles. Pass under a transmission line at 2.1 miles. At 2.2 miles, as the river bends left, you will see a dock and large house on river right. The Ashepoo is transitioning to a tidal stream formerly bordered by rice fields. A line of trees continues directly alongside the river, but lower brush settles in back from the waterway. You will see a berm here on river right, perhaps a remnant of the rice field days. At 2.4 miles, look for an old floodgate on river right, once used to manage the flow of water into and out of the rice fields.

The Ashepoo keeps easterly without excessive curvature. Alligators become more common in this lower, slow tidal stretch. Other wildlife includes abundant waterfowl, herons, and songbirds. Mallard Point Plantation occupies the north bank here around 3.0 miles. The river widens considerably, and sloughs are common, though the main channel of the Ashepoo is obvious.

By 3.7 miles, the river is 150 feet wide and comes near a high pine bank, then resumes easterly. At 4.0 miles on river left, pass an elevated plantation building at the water's edge. At 4.7 miles, a large linear channel leads to Bonnie Doone Plantation, which is set back from the river. The estate originated in 1722 and was a royal land grant deeded to one William Hopton. The original house was yet another historic South Carolina structure burned by the Yankees during the Civil War. Rice was grown here on the once 15,000-acre plantation until 1911. The relic rice fields are still visible today along the Ashepoo and its tributary Horseshoe Creek and also Chessey Creek, the three of which virtually encircle Bonnie Doone. The current thirty-two-room house, with twelve bedrooms, was built in 1931 by New York stockbroker William H. Caspary. It is currently a Christian-owned retreat.

Beyond Bonnie Doone, the Ashepoo angles southeasterly. Pass a gated canal at 5.0 miles. The shoreline remains a mix of trees and brush, with an increasing amount of brush. Beginning at 5.6 miles, you encounter a cluster of riverside dwellings on the right. This indicates your nearness to US 17. Pass alongside these residences and weekend retreats. The US 17 bridge comes into view. Big Horseshoe Creek enters on river left. Pass Crosby Landing on river right just before the low US 17 bridge. Beyond the span, you will come to the ramp at Joes Fish Camp on river right, ending the paddle.

39 Cuckholds Creek

Paddle this ACE Basin tidal tributary astride a national wildlife refuge before reaching its mother stream, the Combahee River, which you will also experience.

County: Colleton, Beaufort
Start: Cuckholds Landing
　N32° 42.85' / W80° 41.67'
End: Steel Bridge Landing on US 17
　N32° 39.14' / W80° 41.03'
Distance: 8.7 miles
Float time: 4.5 hours
Difficulty rating: Moderate
Rapids: None
River type: Tidally influenced coastal plain tributary and waterway
Current: Moderate
River gradient: 0.1 foot per mile
River gauge: None; none needed
Season: Year-round

Land status: Wildlife refuge, large plantations
Fees or permits: No fees or permits required
Nearest city/town: Yemassee
Maps: ACE Basin; USGS Quadrangle Maps: White Hall
Boats used: Kayaks, fishing boats, canoes
Organizations: The ACE Basin National Estuarine Research Reserve, PO Box 12559, Charleston SC 29422, (843) 953-9001, www.acebasin.net
Contacts/outfitters: Ernest F. Hollings/ACE Basin National Wildlife Refuge, PO Box 848, Hollywood, SC 29449, (843) 889-3084, fws.gov/refuge/ACE_Basin

Put-in/Takeout Information

To takeout: From the intersection of US 17 and US 21 in Gardens Corner, north of Beaufort, take US 17 north for 5.7 miles to Steel Bridge Landing, on the west side of US 17 before the bridge crossing the Combahee River. The address for the landing is 993 Charleston Hwy.

To put-in from takeout: Leave Steel Bridge Landing and continue north on US 17. Follow US 17 for 3.6 miles to White Hall Road. Turn left on White Hall Road and follow it 4.4 miles to Combahee Road. Make a sharp left on Combahee Road and follow it 0.1 mile to angle left onto a gravel road, passing directly beside the Ebenezer AME Church before dead-ending at Combahee Landing at 0.2 mile. You have missed the last turn to the landing if you go over the bridge spanning Cuckholds Creek on Combahee Road.

Paddle Summary

This trip follows a tributary from its slender upper reaches along a wildlife refuge and onward as it widens into a large waterway bordered by former rice fields that are now transformed into waterfowl- and wildlife-rich wetlands. Then paddlers follow Cuckholds Creek to its end, where it meets the Combahee River, this wide and important vein of the ACE Basin. The Combahee funnels a lot of water through this preserved

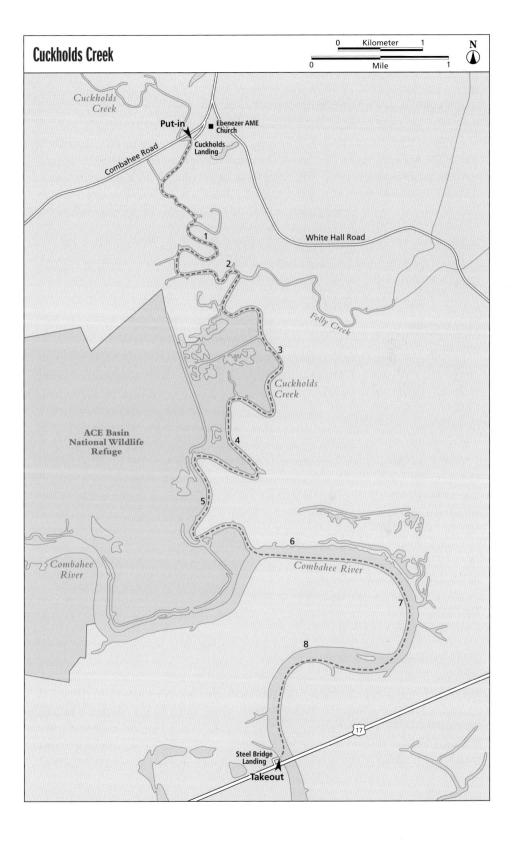

Cuckholds Creek

Cuckholds
Creek

Put-in

Ebenezer AME
Church

Cuckholds
Landing

Combahee Road

White Hall Road

1

2

Folly Creek

3

Cuckholds
Creek

ACE Basin
National Wildlife
Refuge

4

5

6

Combahee River

Combahee
River

7

8

17

Steel Bridge
Landing

Takeout

estuarine parcel of the Palmetto State. At this stage, the Combahee River is massive, adding to the paddling experience as you make a gigantic bend before reaching Steel Bridge Landing on US 17. Both ends of the paddle have fine developed landings. At Cuckholds Landing, Cuckholds Creek is but 20 feet wide and very different from the end of your paddle, where the Combahee River will be well in excess of 500 feet across. After leaving Cuckholds Landing, the stream will twist and turn, bordered by a mix of low brush and trees. The ever-widening waterway is punctured with old canals suitable for exploration, as is Folly Creek—a large tributary of Cuckholds Creek. After a while, lands of the ACE Basin National Wildlife Refuge will occupy the right bank. Even at that, the entire paddle will remain wild since much of the rest of the shore is occupied by large plantations. Be apprised that tidal influence is great on this paddle. It is best to start your trip around 4 to 5 hours behind high tide at Charleston Harbor. That being said, a strong paddler would have no problem defeating the tide. Bring your binoculars for viewing avian life. I personally have seen bald eagles here, among other interesting winged wonders.

River Overview

Cuckholds Creek is a relatively short stream. Its upper reaches are found in the middle part of Colleton County near the town of Hendersonville. Cuckholds Creek's headwaters drain the amusingly named Bluehouse Swamp as well as tributaries draining low hills just east of I-95. The waterways come together upstream of Cuckholds Landing, near the historic plantation known as White Hall. From there, Cuckholds Creek, the heart of this paddle, winds south to meet the Combahee River.

The Combahee River becomes the Combahee River near the town of Yemassee, upstream of this paddle, when the Salkehatchie and Little Salkehatchie converge. Therefore, the Combahee's upper reaches are the Salkehatchie River and its eleven tributaries covering 1,021 square miles in South Carolina, flowing south from Barnwell and Allendale Counties. The Salkehatchie flows southeasterly through the coastal plain to meet the Little Salkehatchie River and officially enters the ACE Basin, where Cuckholds Creek adds its contents to the Combahee River. From there, the Combahee River empties into the Atlantic Ocean near Saint Helena Sound.

The Paddle

This part of the Palmetto State is quite pleasant. The large plantations and copious public lands give the area a sense of solitude and serenity. Leave Cuckholds Landing and enter a dark, tannic, surprisingly swift stream. The shore is a mix of low brush and trees. Skeletal dead trees rise from the brush, lending an eerie look to the scene, especially as they are draped in Spanish moss, which sways in the afternoon breeze. These gray trunks also make excellent bird perches. Do not be surprised if you see alligators sunning where they can gain purchase on the shore, especially at low tide when they lie upon mud flats. Levees and canals are located just beyond the banks of

The moon sets at dawn over calm Cuckholds Creek.

the stream, relics from the old rice-field days. All this makes for a low horizon and gives the paddler expansive views of the skies above.

At 0.4 mile, a straight canal leaves northwesterly from Cuckholds Creek, the first of many exploration opportunities for those desiring to get off the beaten path. This is also the first area where nothing but reeds, saw grass, and rushes compose the shore. Tree copses will resume ahead and be present throughout the paddle. At 1.1 miles, the creek begins some major bends. Pass a wooden shed on river right at 1.5 miles. Meet Folly Creek at 2.1 miles. Stay right here. Cuckholds Creek will have a stronger current and is in excess of 100 feet wide. Staying with the tidal push will also help keep you on the correct track when encountering canals and sloughs. At 2.4 miles, see the first signs indicating the ACE Basin National Wildlife Refuge on your right. Here, the US Fish and Wildlife Service manages the old rice fields for wildlife, incorporating the historic levees and canals originally constructed to produce rice.

At 2.8 miles, pass a huge linear canal heading west–southwest into the refuge. An overhead view reveals a network of other canals spurring off this one that creates an enticing maze should a paddler want to get lost. If you explore off the main stream bring an electronic device downloaded with aerial imagery of the ACE Basin.

Cuckholds Creek continues south, passing other canals, including a large one on river left at 3.2 miles. You will also notice water control structures along the shore, used to let water in or out of basins bordering the stream, in order to produce the best conditions for flora and fauna of the adjacent area. At 4.3 miles, Cuckholds Creek gives up its southerly course for a sharp bend to the right, turning northwesterly. At 4.7 miles, pass a waterway on river right linking to the maze of channels in the national wildlife refuge. The now very wide Cuckholds Creek resumes its south-bound ways, aiming for the even wider Combahee River. Old wooden pilings give faint clues to past uses of the waterway and the land alongside it.

Reach big Combahee River at 5.8 miles. Head left, easterly. Beware of wind and tide on the river, which is in excess of 500 feet wide. If the tide is against you, take the inside of the wide, sweeping bend arcing right. As for wind, even though the banks are low brush, staying along the edge of the Combahee will provide a modicum of protection. This bend is huge. The low horizon offers glances at the traffic of US 17 in the distance. By 7.0 miles, you are heading south, but the curve continues until you are heading fully west, the opposite direction of when you entered the Combahee.

Pass a long slender island in the river at 7.4 miles. At 7.8 miles, you will see a canal heading south to US 17. At 8.0 miles, the Combahee makes its final turn before US 17. High trees mark the landing area. Ease over to the right-hand bank to meet the landing at 8.7 miles. Two ramps and a floating dock greet you at paddle's end. This ramp can be busy, so try to get off it as quickly as possible, keeping good relations between paddlers and motorboaters.

40 Combahee River

This unspoiled coastal plain waterway flows through the protected banks of plantation country.

County: Colleton, Beaufort
Start: Public Landing
  N32° 41.872' / W80° 48.730'
End: Sugar Hill Landing
  N32° 39.975' / W80° 45.288'
Distance: 8.2 miles
Float time: 4 hours
Difficulty rating: Easy
Rapids: None
River type: Tidally influenced coastal plain waterway
Current: Moderate
River gradient: 0.1 foot per mile
River Gauge: None; none needed
Season: Year-round

Land status: Wildlife refuge, large plantations
Fees or permits: No fees or permits required
Nearest city/town: Yemassee
Maps: ACE Basin; USGS Quadrangle Maps: Yemassee
Boats used: Kayaks, fishing boats, canoes
Organizations: The ACE Basin National Estuarine Research Reserve, PO Box 12559, Charleston SC 29422, (843) 953-9001, www.acebasin.net
Contacts/outfitters: Ernest F. Hollings/ACE Basin National Wildlife Refuge, PO Box 848, Hollywood, SC 29449, (843) 889-3084, fws.gov/refuge/ACE_Basin/

Put-in/Takeout Information

To takeout: From exit 38 on I-95 near Yemassee, take SC 68 east toward Yemassee for 1.3 miles, then veer right onto a connector for US 17A. Take the connector 0.1 mile then turn left onto 17A north toward Walterboro. Follow 17A north for 0.4 mile to a flashing light and Salkehatchie Road in Yemassee. Turn right and follow Salkehatchie Road for 0.2 mile to Railroad Avenue. Turn left on Railroad Avenue and follow it 0.3 mile to turn right on River Road, crossing railroad tracks. Follow River Road for 5.6 miles to Sugar Hill Landing Road. Turn left and quickly dead-end at Sugar Hill Landing.

To put-in from takeout: Return to the flashing light in Yemassee at the intersection of Salkehatchie Road and US 17A. Turn right and take US 17A north for 2.8 miles to Public Landing Road (en route you will pass over the Combahee River and the Combahee Landing off US 17A). Turn right on Public Landing Road and follow it to dead-end at the Combahee River at 1.1 miles.

Paddle Summary

Here is a chance to paddle one of the famed rivers in the ACE Basin, the wild jewel of coastal South Carolina, which derives its name from three important rivers—the Ashepoo, Combahee, and Edisto. Here, the tidally influenced Combahee flows through untamed banks protected as a wildlife refuge and large plantations that act as de facto refuges. Starting at Public Landing (yes, that is the landing's name), the waterway convolutedly courses through a swamp forest before opening into former rice fields. The swamps could be transformed to rice fields and led to the establishment of rice plantations, most of which come into being during the 1700s. As you work toward the coast, the Combahee widens and becomes more tidal. You will pass a few signs of these plantations, in the form of formal landings and docks. Pay attention to these landings as distance markers—though they are off-limits to the public. To access Sugar Hill Landing, you must take a tributary of the Combahee located just beyond one of these docks, then follow an ever-narrowing and winding tributary to the landing. In order to work the tides in your favor, try to put in about 5 hours after high tide in Charleston Harbor. If you want to add an extra 2 miles to your paddle, you can put in at the Combahee Landing on 17A near Yemassee.

River Overview

The Salkehatchie and Little Salkehatchie converge near the town of Yemassee to become the Combahee River, where this paddle begins. Therefore, the Combahee's upper reaches are the Salkehatchie River and its eleven tributaries covering 1,021 square miles in South Carolina, flowing south from Barnwell and Allendale Counties. The Salkehatchie River starts near the city of Barnwell, where Turkey Creek and Whippy Swamp come together. The Salkehatchie flows southeasterly through the coastal plain to meet the Little Salkehatchie River and officially enter the ACE Basin. From there, the Combahee River pours its contents into the Atlantic Ocean near Saint Helena Sound.

The Paddle

The upper reaches of the Combahee River near Public Landing are fresh and less tidally influenced. It seems more of a classic Carolina swamp stream at this point. The dark waters are stained an inky black from the leaching of tannins into the water from wetlands of the upper drainages. After leaving the boat ramp, paddlers are swept into long sweeping bends of the 60 foot wide river. Moss-draped oaks, sweetgum, maple, and other hardwoods occupy drier ground, while cypress, wax myrtle, and bay trees stand in lower ground, all forming a rampart of vegetation at the water's edge. Pines occupy the highest terrain. These upper banks are part of the ACE Basin National Wildlife Refuge, while downstream you will be passing alongside mammoth plantations consisting of thousands of acres each. Ahead, on the south bank, is Auldbrass; you will see its brick-and-wood landing on river right at 0.9 mile. Derived from the name "Old Brass," the plantation has been in operation since 1736. In addition to the landing, the latest main house and outbuildings were designed and built by famed architect Frank Lloyd Wright in the 1940s. Auldbrass is on the National Register of Historic Places. You drive by Auldbrass on the way to Sugar Hill Landing. Its fence

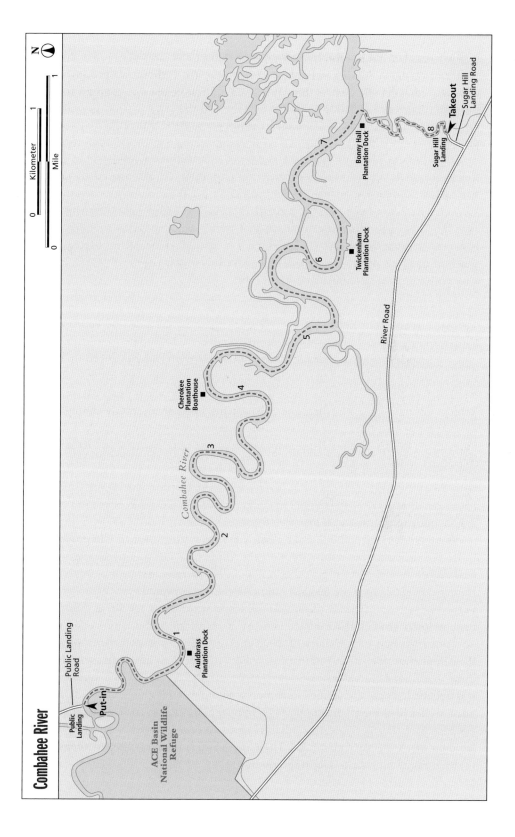

Combahee River

is distinctive. For the paddler these huge plantations mean a wealth of nature along the banks of the Combahee and a chance to glimpse the workings of these preserves, without which the ACE Basin would not be so clean and pristine, for you will notice the clean waters and shoreline on this paddle. You will also notice aquatic gates blocking some waterways and canals along the Combahee, as the plantation owners seek privacy.

Small sloughs break off from the waterway, especially near brushy shores. And slowly but surely, reeds and rushes increase in proportion. At 1.2 miles, the Combahee makes its longest straightaway and broadens a bit, then resumes its bendings at 1.7 miles. At 2.0 miles, watch for a ramshackle shack on river right. This is part of the Old Combahee Plantation, some lands of which are protected as a conservation easement through the Nature Conservancy. It is through arrangements like this that much of the ACE Basin is protected—the majority of its acreage is in private hands. This plantation was also initiated in the 1700s.

The Combahee continues to widen but retains its remote character. The river bends continue to widen as well. At 4.2 miles, pass an elaborate two-story boathouse on river left. This is part of the Cherokee Plantation, and you can make out its large brick house on the low horizon downriver. An elevated berm forms the left bank for a distance. Berms such as this were built along the riverbanks then floodgates were added to manage water flows for rice fields, which were once strewn along the river.

By this point, cattails, reeds, and brush form large swaths of shoreline. This lowers the horizon, creating big sky country. At 5.2 miles, a notably large channel enters on river right. At 5.7 miles, you will see another berm forming the riverbank on river left. At 5.8 miles, at the lower end of this berm, a canal leads left and shortcuts a huge bend. You can cut off 0.7 mile of your paddle by using this canal. Otherwise, stay with the main, and now very wide, waterway. Curve past the landing for Twickenham Plantation on river right at 6.2 miles. This three-centuries-old plantation covers 2,500 contiguous acres and is managed for nature, hunting, crops, and livestock.

Pass the other end of the shortcut canal at 6.5 miles. The Combahee begins bending to the right and aims southeasterly. Pay attention here. Get over to the right-hand bank. You will then pass three dead-end sloughs before reaching the boat landing for Bonny Hall Plantation. The original house for this pre-Revolutionary War estate was burned by William Sherman during his ruthless destruction of the South during the final period of the Civil War.

Turn right into the tributary of the Combahee River just after the Bonny Hall Plantation boat dock at 7.3 miles. This tributary will show tidal influence as well. Turn south and follow this brush-lined waterway. At 7.5 miles, the tributary makes a sharp bend, practically turning back north before resuming its southward course. Small feeder branches of this tributary will prove only temporarily confusing should you take them. Furthermore, you will pass three gated canals on the way to Sugar Hill Landing. The tributary narrows still. Then Sugar Hill Landing will appear seemingly unexpectedly. End your paddle at the landing at 8.2 miles.

Paddle Index

About the Author

Johnny Molloy is a writer and adventurer who has penned more than fifty outdoor hiking, camping, and paddling guides, as well as true outdoor-adventure stories. His nonfiction passion started after reading *In Cold Blood* by Truman Capote, which his father had left lying around. After that, he delved into all manner of nonfiction reading, from *Strange But True Football Stories* to books about the Mississippi River, Lewis and Clark, and the Civil War. He has since focused his reading on early American history and Christian studies.

His outdoor passion started on a backpacking trip in Great Smoky Mountains National Park while attending the University of Tennessee. That first foray unleashed a love of the outdoors that has led Molloy to spend most of his time hiking, backpacking, canoe camping, and tent camping for the past three decades. Friends enjoyed his outdoor adventure stories, and one even suggested he write a book. He pursued his friend's idea and soon parlayed his love of the outdoors into an occupation.

Molloy writes for various magazines, websites, and newspapers. He continues writing and traveling extensively throughout the United States, engaging in a variety of outdoor pursuits. His non-outdoor interests include serving God as a Gideon and University of Tennessee sports. For the latest on Johnny, visit johnnymolloy.com.

Other Books by Johnny Molloy

50 Hikes in Alabama
50 Hikes in the Ozarks
50 Hikes in the North Georgia Mountains
50 Hikes in South Carolina
50 Hikes on Tennessee's Cumberland Plateau
60 Hikes within 60 Miles: San Antonio & Austin (with Tom Taylor)
60 Hikes within 60 Miles: Nashville
A Canoeing & Kayaking Guide to the Streams of Florida
A Canoeing & Kayaking Guide to the Streams of Kentucky (with Bob Sehlinger)
A Paddler's Guide to Everglades National Park
Backcountry Fishing: A Guide for Hikers, Backpackers, and Paddlers
Beach & Coastal Camping in Florida
Beach & Coastal Camping in the Southeast
Best Easy Day Hikes: Cincinnati
Best East Day Hikes: Greensboro/Winston-Salem
Best Easy Day Hikes: Jacksonville
Best Easy Day Hikes: Madison, Wisconsin
Best Easy Day Hikes: New River Gorge
Best Easy Day Hikes: Richmond
Best Easy Day Hikes: Tallahassee
Best Easy Day Hikes: Tampa Bay
Best Hikes Near Cincinnati
Best Hikes Near Columbus
Best Hikes on the Appalachian Trail: South
The Best in Tent Camping: The Carolinas
The Best in Tent Camping: Colorado
The Best in Tent Camping: Georgia
The Best in Tent Camping: Kentucky
The Best in Tent Camping: Southern Appalachian & Smoky Mountains
The Best in Tent Camping: Tennessee
The Best in Tent Camping: West Virginia
The Best in Tent Camping: Wisconsin
Can't Miss Hikes in North Carolina's National Forests
Day & Overnight Hikes on Kentucky's Sheltowee Trace
Day & Overnight Hikes in West Virginia's Monongahela National Forest
Day Hiking Southwest Florida
Five Star Hikes: Chattanooga
Five Star Hikes: Knoxville
Five Star Hikes: Roanoke and the New River Valley

Five Star Hikes: Tri-Cities Tennessee and Virginia
From the Swamp to the Keys: A Paddle through Florida History
Hiking the Florida Trail: 1,100 Miles, 78 Days and Two Pairs of Boots
Hiking Mississippi
Hiking Through History: New England
Hiking Through History: Virginia
Mount Rogers National Recreation Area Guidebook
The Hiking Trails of Florida's National Forests, Parks, and Preserves
Land Between the Lakes Outdoor Recreation Handbook
Long Trails of the Southeast
Outward Bound Canoeing Handbook
Paddling Georgia
Paddling Tennessee
Top Trails: Great Smoky Mountains National Park
Top Trails: Shenandoah National Park
Trial By Trail: Backpacking in the Smoky Mountains
Waterfall Hiking Tennessee
Waterfalls of the Blue Ridge